S0-AHE-328

The Resegregation of Suburban Schools

The Resegregation of Suburban Schools

A Hidden Crisis in American Education

Edited by

ERICA FRANKENBERG

GARY ORFIELD

CABRINI COLLEGE LIBRARY
610 KING OF PRUSSIA ROAD
RADNOR, PA 19087

HARVARD EDUCATION PRESS
CAMBRIDGE, MASSACHUSETTS

LC
213.2
.R468
2012

8099386 89

Copyright © 2012 by the President and Fellows of Harvard College

All rights reserved. No part of this publication may be reproduced or transmitted in any form or by any means, electronic or mechanical, including photocopy, recording, or any information storage and retrieval systems, without permission in writing from the publisher.

Library of Congress Control Number 2012937484

Paperback ISBN 978-1-61250-481-0
Library Edition ISBN 978-1-61250-482-7

Published by Harvard Education Press,
an imprint of the Harvard Education Publishing Group

Harvard Education Press
8 Story Street
Cambridge, MA 02138

Cover Design: Sarah Henderson
Cover Photo: Cameron Davidson/Photographer's Choice RF/Getty Images
The typefaces used in this book are Adobe Garamond Pro, Futura, and Helvetica Neue.

Contents

1

Why Racial Change in the Suburbs Matters

ERICA FRANKENBERG AND GARY ORFIELD

This country is going through a demographic transformation that is already having major consequences for the world's first suburban society. Most Americans live in suburbs, and the focus of racial and economic transformation is now clearly in suburban areas. This book's major contribution is a consideration of how the change and resulting patterns of segregation affect schools. It broadens existing general understanding about the growing diversity in suburban areas by presenting a typology of patterns of demographic changes and case studies that discuss the implications of these changes for education. Our major conclusion, based on evidence from a multiyear study of suburban districts and communities, is that suburban school districts are feeling unsupported and unable to formulate a coherent response to the metropolitan demographic change of which their district is one relatively small part. There is much that suburban districts could do, but there's also much that other institutions could do to support them. Ignoring the implications of racial change will be destructive to many suburban communities, and doing nothing does not work in the face of resegregation threats. Suburban schools and communities can produce more effective outcomes but they require knowledge and thoughtful leadership.

Although the United States will soon become a nation where the schools have no racial majority there is deep and persisting inequality in the achievement of students by race, and very little progress over the past three decades in closing these gaps. As the proportion of students from groups that have been far behind in achievement and attainment rises, so do the stakes for the country. Statistics already show a remarkably high level of segregation for Latino and black students in the suburban rings around our large cities, and white populations are moving to the outermost rings much faster than the population is growing, leaving many communities and their schools behind.[1] There is no framework of law or support to help suburbs avoid the kind of rapid and destructive racial change that led to the decline of many city neighborhoods half a century ago. Some suburbs, in fact, are trying to retain white and/or middle-class residents with special schools and boundary changes that increase segregation and may well be illegal if they unfairly exclude black and Latino children.[2] As racial transformation of the suburbs continues, these demographic shifts affect the opportunities of low-income and minority (i.e., underrepresented minority) students in these communities, which may have limited political and institutional resources to serve them. Dated models drawn from biracial cities a half century ago don't tell us enough about how today's multiracial suburbs can enhance our understanding of race and educational opportunity.

Simply put, many suburbs in our large metropolitan areas are in the midst of rapid racial and socioeconomic change and have no policies addressing questions that often shape the future of communities.[3] Outdated stereotypes of a "suburban district" no longer fit the reality, and issues of racial change are central questions for the future of suburban communities. We failed to prevent very dramatic and damaging resegregation in our city school systems a generation ago and now face that issue in the suburbs. When resegregation occurs, there generally is a major decline in educational opportunity, and the future of suburban communities is imperiled on many dimensions. There are no federal or state policies constructively addressing these issues, leaving every suburb on its own. A starting point for development of public policy is understanding how, if at all, suburban communities are addressing this issue.

The United States today is a suburban nation that thinks of race as an urban issue, and often assumes that it has been largely solved. Discussion of segregation and desegregation are described as urban issues—even the word *urban* is often used as coded language to talk about areas that comprise mostly students of color or low-income students. Yet already over half of minority students in large metropolitan areas now attend suburban schools.[4] Similarly, there are more low-income people living in suburbs than in cities.[5]

Even though the demographic transformation has been going on for decades, few analytical frameworks are available to understand the complex social, political, and institutional context of suburban demographic change and factors predicting response to that change by suburban school systems. Although there were a few early suburban models of leadership on desegregation (Evanston, Illinois; Berkeley, California; Princeton, New Jersey; and New Rochelle, New York) there has been little research or policy that addresses how suburban school systems are responding to this increasing diversity. Unlike the cities, the diversity is a multiracial story, transformed by immigration reforms and declining white birth rates, particularly in metropolitan areas that are major immigration destinations.

School districts in any type of community are affected by changes in the housing market. Housing trends can profoundly change school district demographics and resources, and school policies and reputations can affect housing choices and neighborhoods. Many districts use assignment policies that send students to the nearest school, so housing choices are connected to school choices; these district policies reinforce the meaning of buying homes in certain neighborhoods. Yet there is extremely little discussion of interaction of these issues in either education or urban planning and housing research. Those in suburban communities are often more vulnerable to rapid change than city dwellers because individual suburbs usually contain only a small fraction of the metropolitan area's housing, and have fewer other resources and institutions.

This book is about the role schools and their leaders and faculty play in a social transformation, yet the issues reach far beyond traditional studies of educational policy, most of which for the last several decades have been about policies to create changes within schools. Educational policy in this period has overwhelmingly addressed standards and accountability, focusing on teachers and classrooms, not on social changes outside schools that transform schools and communities in very deep ways. Demographic shifts often receive little public attention, except among teachers who experience them daily and feel that they have scant support or resources to effectively meet the challenges. These changes and the lack of successful response have enormous aggregate consequences. To comprehend and address them will require interdisciplinary exploration of the dimensions of demographic change, the politics of race and urban policy, and examining in-school educational issues.

Many of the concerns once confined to urban schools are increasingly found in suburban districts, including: (1) increasing diversity among the school-age population in terms of racial/ethnic and socioeconomic composition; (2) inner-ring suburbs and satellite cities that are replicating patterns of racial and economic segregation found in some of our nation's central cities; (3) a teaching staff that may be inadequately trained to teach a diverse student population; (4) limited financial, human, and organizational resources to address these new challenges; (5) political institutions unprepared to accommodate increasing diversity; and (6) deteriorating or overcrowded infrastructure.[6] While the magnitude of these concerns may not be as great in some suburbs as in many central cities, if left unaddressed they are likely to create situations of separate and unequal schools. At the same time, the ongoing demographic change presents an opportunity for suburban communities that have been homogeneous to develop high-quality schooling for all students in racially and ethnically diverse schools and to create educational opportunities that have not been available in cities where demographic change occurred decades earlier.

Our argument is that educational leaders in the communities we've studied confront substantial constraints in dealing with the huge consequences this racial change portends. Contexts vary, policy values diverge, capacity to respond is uneven, and the interests and motivations of leaders are mixed. They face transformations rooted in the spread of residential segregation within communities where there is usually little or no coordination between municipal, educational, and civil rights officials. In these communities, educators often operate within a kind of "color-blind" ideology, believing that more of the standards-based reform that has dominated education policy for three decades will somehow address issues of racial change, issues that they generally prefer to ignore. Because individual suburbs comprise only small portions of the broader housing market, and because discriminatory real estate practices, including steering of both minority and white families, remain ubiquitous, educators seeking to respond to these issues would, in any case, face an uphill battle. If schools do not remain integrated, the white housing market is likely to quickly dry up.[7] Not only do very few communities have any kind of coherent integration strategy, but few even have policies for successful in-school integration that would facilitate a slower and less damaging racial transition. Nothing in the state and federal accountability systems addresses these issues. Worse, we find some communities are taking action to allow resegregation in some areas while creating exclusive new programs such as an International Baccalaureate program in a majority white area to try to cater to and hold on to the remaining white and Asian families. These policies produce deep inequalities, may even be illegal, and are very unlikely to succeed in the long run. Most of the suburbs we've studied are doing little to directly address this high-stakes dynamic. When they do, it is often in a halting, contradictory manner focused on changing classroom-level instruction instead of addressing larger structures that may be exacerbating the racial transformation. The resulting resegregation is already apparent in many inner-ring suburbs in diverse metropolitan areas.

This book is the first major publication from a Spencer Foundation–funded study of the effect of suburban change on the educational opportunity of poor and minority students.[8] The project, and this book, center around (1) describing the extent of suburban transition in major metropolitan areas, (2) how suburban communities conceptualize this change, and (3) how actors inside and outside the educational arena respond to it. The mixed-methods project explored these issues through a demographic analysis of the twenty-five largest U.S. metropolitan areas and the development of case studies in seven suburban districts across the country.[9] This chapter reviews the history of racial transition and describes the scale of suburban change that is occurring in our nation's largest metropolitan areas. It also describes the costs of ignoring the resegregation that is already happening in some parts of suburbia, as well as the possibilities the new diversity brings. Finally, we briefly summarize the project that is the foundation for this book and show that, while we currently find a lack of coherent vision or support for effectively responding to demographic change, there are possibilities to build on some of the constructive actions being undertaken in these suburban communities, which federal and state agencies should support.

HISTORY OF RACIAL TRANSITION

One of the major limitations to the spread of school desegregation into suburban areas, particularly outside the South, in the 1970s and beyond was the belief that private actions, not governmental policies, resulted in the segregated residential patterns and thus racially isolated schools. For example, in the *Milliken v. Bradley* decision, the U.S. Supreme Court ruled that suburban Detroit schools were not responsible for the segregation that existed in city schools. Yet, as scholars increasingly realize, segregated residential patterns—and their impacts on school composition—are not a "natural" phenomenon.

Instead, they are a result of decades of governmental policies, as well as a legacy of discriminatory practices such as racial steering and mortgage underwriting that combined to create and maintain racial segregation in central cities while simultaneously subsidizing white suburbanization in the post–World War II era.[10] Because of the interconnectedness of social policies, decisions about zoning, land use, and transportation, as well as housing, affect schools. Likewise, the way in which school district boundary lines are drawn affects school segregation and home seekers' perception of an area.[11] The fragmented nature of their jurisdictions can cause suburbs to compete for the most desirable residents and try to exclude less-affluent residents through zoning or transportation policies. Yet, despite the economic interdependence of the whole of a metropolitan area, many of the policies that directly affect patterns of demographic change are governed by municipalities. This first led to the racial transition in many central cities and is now reaching into inner-ring suburban communities as well.

Changing Population Patterns

We have lived too long in thrall to Robert Wood's concept of suburbia as a fairly unified type of community—an idea from the 1950s and 1960s that took hold as the vast expansion of metropolitan areas after World War II gave birth to the first predominantly suburban society. When Martin Luther King, Jr. talked about the white suburban noose during his great fair housing campaign in Chicago, issues of racial change applied largely to outlying neighborhoods in central cities. In 1968, President Lyndon Johnson's commission on the urban riots in Los Angeles, Newark, and elsewhere from 1965–1968 warned about the United States becoming "two societies, one black and one white," with black cities and white suburbs. This helped spur the passage of the Fair Housing Act, which was weakly enforced and sped the expansion of minority communities in the cities and across the city-suburban boundaries, bringing major racial change to many unprepared districts.

The monolithic suburban ideal was inaccurate since suburbs varied greatly by social class, and the post-war suburban expansion incorporated many small, older existing communities. Migration of blacks to the suburban rings began in earnest in some cities in the 1970s and would grow immensely in the coming decades. The sweeping racial change in U.S. cities in the 1950s to the 1970s was accompanied by major civil rights battles, including *Brown v. Board of Education*, federal war on poverty, urban riots, and presidential commissions to study issues of race. The result was the creation of fair housing laws, urban school desegregation, magnet school programs, and many other initiatives, chiefly designed to integrate black students into majority white schools. This biracial dynamic that no longer holds for our nation's central cities *or* its suburbs; demographics have been transformed through the huge growth of Latino communities, which had been virtually invisible outside the Southwest and a few metropolitan areas in other states until the 1980s, as well as the expansion of Asian populations—who often immigrated directly to the suburbs. Latinos are now the largest group of minority students and account for most of the growth in suburbia and in many regions, including New England and major parts of the South. In metropolitan Boston, for example, three-fourths of Latinos go to school outside the city, often in resegregating suburban districts.[12]

Lack of Helpful Policy or Legal Civil Rights Framework as Suburbanization Accelerates

After the unprecedented surge of public policy addressing issues of discrimination, segregation, inequality, and poverty in the 1960s and early 1970s, a major political transition took place following the 1968 election. The successful Republican "Southern strategy" mobilized southern whites and produced dramatic reversals of civil rights and poverty policies and a transformation of the courts and the law. Since the early 1970s, there have been no major new civil rights or urban policy initiatives.

The reversals limited the impact of the new federal law against housing discrimination.[13] Under President Nixon, to comply in part with the 1968 Fair Housing Act, HUD secretary George Romney had devised a suburban housing desegregation demonstration program, which he believed would also reduce racial segregation in cities and suburbs and address minority unemployment rates.[14] Yet this initiative was blocked by the president and set the precedent for the failure of subsequent administrations to enforce the Fair Housing Act. In the last forty years, except for brief challenges from HUD secretaries during the Carter and Clinton administrations, Nixon's policy inaction was largely maintained—no doubt due, in part, to politicians' fear of pushback from white suburban voters who have become an increasingly important segment of voters and donors in elections. As a result, we have systematically turned a blind eye to the pervasive, underlying inequities in our metropolitan areas for almost half a century.

There has been deep division over race-conscious policies to address discrimination and sharp reversals by a Supreme Court that was transformed by conservative appointments more than two decades ago. Court decisions made it virtually impossible to seek explicit regional solutions to segregation problems through the courts just as substantial minority suburbanization began in the 1970s; authorized dissolving existing desegregation plans in the 1991 *Oklahoma City v. Dowell* decision; and, in the 1995 *Missouri v. Jenkins* decision, held that a desegregation plan could not include funding an effort to attract students from other school districts to preserve or expand integration.[15] More recently, a 2007 ruling—decided shortly after two Bush appointees were confirmed—took away most of the tools long used in voluntary desegregation plans, such as some types of race-conscious, controlled-choice plans that balanced family choices about schools with district goals about diversity.[16] During this period, states that had once had strong integration laws and policies that were applied to suburban districts, including Massachusetts, California, Illinois, Minnesota, and Pennsylvania, reversed or severely weakened these policies. Moreover, there was no significant enforcement of federal and state fair housing laws, and segregation steadily spread into larger sectors of suburbia.[17]

In 1981, as demographic change accelerated, the Reagan administration eliminated the voluntary program of assistance to school districts wishing to work on issues of successful race relations and desegregation.[18] In addition, the civil rights initiatives, funding and technical support for successful integration, and serious enforcement of civil rights law ended in most areas by the early 1980s.[19] Magnet schools, which were invented to foster voluntary desegregation, were increasingly detached from integration goals, and charter schools, which had no such goals and many of which are racially isolated, received active state and federal funding since the early 1990s.[20] The net result is that the leaders of suburban school districts have few policy or legal tools and little or no funding to address the issues of racial change.

Aside from the Obama health reform, social policy efforts aimed at equalizing opportunity have had very little success while political battles to sharply reduce taxes and limit public resources and programs have triumphed.[21] Public services have been cut or contracted out to the private sector. The only Democratic presidents elected since 1964 have come from the centrist wing of the party, which has strongly downplayed civil rights issues and emphasized the needs of the middle class. Today there is no coherent national policy guidance to help diverse suburbs achieve lasting integration and very little aid available for efforts they might wish to launch on their own. If a strong and effective response to suburban demographic change is to be developed, this must change.

The Instability of Racial Diversity in Neighborhoods and Schools: Why Explicit Policies Are Needed

The process of resegregation is difficult to stabilize once begun, particularly given the lack of meaningful fair housing enforcement and regional school desegregation. This has especially significant effects for suburban school districts that are often fragmented and vulnerable to demographic change. There is growing awareness that resegregation is now remaking some suburban communities as well while leaving others virtually untouched.[22] As neighborhoods experience white, middle-class flight, they lose cultural and business institutions, and these changes may decimate a once-flourishing community. Such communities often experience a rise in the number of single-parent households, renter-occupied housing stock, and growing unemployment that separates them from the mainstream economy. What's more, as scholars note, these communities begin to develop concentrated poverty and new social norms and expectations that run counter to those in more stable, middle-class environments—increasing the likelihood of social problems such as dropping out of school, inability to attain a job, and higher crime.[23]

These factors, in turn, can depress home values and loss of remaining middle-class residents as well as businesses, other public institutions. This pattern serves to deepen the stereotypes about neighborhood change and the influx of minority families. Middle-class Latino and black families who moved out from central cities expecting something very different can see segregation and poverty following them. As a result, many will move again, joining the outward exodus and leaving the community to neither of the middle-class groups who wanted to live there but to a growing concentration of poor nonwhite families. Local governments, confronted with the need for more public services and a dwindling tax base, are often faced with unenviable policy options as well and may find it difficult to provide necessary services. In other words, these communities are trapped in a downward spiral that limits their opportunity and inability to attract those who might stem such a pattern. Eventually, after resegregation occurs, some people will say, "Why didn't we do something?"

Although residents of all races usually express a preference for integration in public opinion surveys, white residents tend to favor a modest level of integration and fear rapid change while families of color prefer a significant presence of their own group and are not concerned if it reaches half or more.[24] As a result, white residents and home seekers may see what nonwhite families perceive to be a well-integrated area as a community facing imminent resegregation. Since real estate markets are built on perceptions and expectations about the future, such fears can rapidly become self-fulfilling prophecies unless they are effectively countered. If people believe the community is going to be stable and more desirable, and if that belief is reinforced by important institutions, it is more likely to happen.[25] Local educational leaders, by not recognizing the powerful momentum toward resegregation built into the housing market and the beliefs and fears of whites as well as the desires and hopes of nonwhite families able to reach the suburbs, are missing the opportunity to foster that positive cycle.

Despite the lack of policy initiative supporting the creation and maintenance of stable communities and schools, research indicates growing numbers of stably diverse neighborhoods and the presence of thousands of stably diverse schools in suburbia.[26] Research has also found that stably diverse neighborhoods have more socioeconomically advantaged populations than similarly diverse but transitioning neighborhoods.[27] Likewise, analysis of the nation's schools has shown that stably diverse schools are similar to more homogeneous white schools in their ability to stem the transition of teachers from more diverse schools.[28] These schools and neighborhoods that are valued by many could be strengthened and other diverse areas stabilized if meaningful regional policies designed to support such areas were put in place.

Schools, particularly elementary schools, are often where the first manifestation of social and economic change is evident, with changes in enrollment patterns an early warning of impending flight by the middle class. Since perceived school quality is essential in attracting and maintaining middle-class residents, districts are likely to adopt strategies and policies aimed at maintaining the stability and equilibrium of the system.[29] The capacity of districts to confront issues of demographic and social change is likely to vary depending on a combination of political, institutional, and policy influences. For example, housing and transportation policies contribute to how metropolitan areas develop, shape the quality of schools, and influence the choices available to families who are deciding where to live.[30]

Today, residential areas reflect racial segregation beyond what can be explained by economics alone.[31] Inaction in the face of housing segregation in metropolitan areas, coupled with the structure of school district boundary lines and Supreme Court decisions that ended many school desegregation plans resulted in persistently high levels of residential and educational segregation across metropolitan areas.[32]

THE SCOPE OF RACIAL TRANSFORMATION IN CONTEMPORARY SUBURBAN CONTEXTS

Although suburbia has long been part of our nation's geography, it lacks clear definition—as have governmental policies encouraging segregated settlement of suburbia.[33] The decennial Census, for example, does not identify geographies as "suburban," instead identifying principal cities in metropolitan areas. Perhaps the Census definition "not in the central city" is more useful than "suburb," which is a relic from decades ago. Patterns of migration and segregation differ by region, due to factors such as population growth and the way in which jurisdictional boundaries are drawn (or redrawn). Some suburban communities may have limited resources to serve growing numbers of low-income and minority students.[34]

Suburbs have become more differentiated economically, and while some are locked into rapid resegregation, others are maintaining affluence, leading to vast differences across suburban boundary lines.[35] Likewise, since 2000, far more people have moved to majority-minority suburban communities than to exurban communities in the nation's largest metropolitan areas.[36] Inner-ring suburbs are losing population and becoming increasingly poor. Some developing suburbs are experiencing rapid population growth; others, often those with more restrictive housing markets, are growing more slowly. The fast-growing areas often have lower tax capacity and per-pupil spending than their more affluent neighbors, making it more difficult to address the social and academic challenges they face.[37]

As one analysis has concluded "Just as in cities, the growth of racial and ethnic groups fueled the bulk of the population growth in suburbs in the 1990s."[38] By 2000, for example, a majority of Latinos lived in the suburbs and the Latino population there had increased 71 percent in the 1990s alone. Yet in more than one-quarter of suburban communities—especially in the Midwest—there was a decline in population during this time.[39] By 2008, nearly half of those receiving housing choice vouchers (HCVs, formerly known as Section 8 certificates) lived in the suburbs; and since 2000, black HCV recipients have suburbanized at the highest rate, although they are still a smaller presence in suburbia than white recipients.[40] More than

6 million people moved to inner-ring suburbs from 2000 to 2010, and the suburban-city demographic disparity is continuing to narrow.[41]

Demographers have sought to understand how this multigroup out-migration has affected metropolitan segregation. One study of metropolitan patterns decomposed segregation into geographical components and determined that "[White/nonwhite] dissimilarities between suburban communities rather than neighborhoods are accounting for larger shares of metropolitan segregation."[42] There was evidence of white/nonwhite integration within principal cities of these areas, while city-suburban segregation accounted for a majority of overall metropolitan area segregation. This and other research shows that neighborhood segregation is declining in importance relative to segregation across political boundaries.[43]

Additional factors relating to sharper suburban declines in the percentage of whites were existing suburban diversity and overall growth. There were larger declines in the shares of white suburban residents in metropolitan areas that already had more racial diversity in suburbia in 1990; for example, Atlanta's suburban population experienced the largest decline in white percentage of residents during the 1990s, and was 77 percent white in 1990. Another factor of racial change appears to be that areas in which the population has grown—perhaps a reflection of a booming economy or other factors that make the area more "liveable"—are also places in which there are lower shares of white residents since growing areas tend to attract more immigrants. Conversely, suburban areas where population growth was low, or even declined, during the 1990s have not attracted nonwhite residents and remained, in 2000, overwhelmingly white.

Growth and Diversification of Suburban Enrollment

These population shifts are, of course, affecting the suburban school enrollment, which is booming in the largest twenty-five metropolitan areas. It grew from 8.6 million students in 1990 to 12.0 million students in 2006, accounting for approximately one-fourth of all U.S. public school students. Enrollment numbers vary widely—from more than 1 million students in the largest three metropolitan areas to under 100,000 students in Tampa. These differences are partially due to the structure of school districts in each area. Florida, for example, has countywide school districts and thus what would be considered a suburban district elsewhere is contained within a district that also includes the central city. In other metropolitan areas, dozens or hundreds of small districts exist in suburbia.

Suburban school enrollments have grown in every metropolitan area since 1990–91, although the rate of growth and their size vary. The percentage of students in these schools has risen in each metropolitan area since 1990. Overall, by 2006, 59 percent of students in the largest twenty-five areas attended suburban schools, and in all but five, a majority of students attended schools in the suburbs, not central cities. Rust Belt metropolitan areas had particularly high shares of students in suburban schools. Suburbanization of students was lower in the Sun Belt, but growing at a faster rate, suggesting these patterns may change. In nine areas, the suburban enrollment increased by at least half since 1990–91.

In terms of racial composition, the 12 million suburban students closely resembled the entire U.S. public school enrollment in 2006–07. In the suburbs of the largest metropolitan areas, 58.5 percent of students were white, 20.5 percent Latino, and 6.4 percent Asian. Black students were slightly underrepresented in the largest suburban areas, accounting for 14 percent of students.

White students are not disproportionately located in the suburbs of the largest metropolitan areas. When aggregating the entire suburban enrollment of the metropolitan areas, the percentages of white students are declining in each of the largest twenty-five largest metropolitan areas, while Latinos have grown substantially in suburban schools (see table 1.1). While the percentage of white students enrolled in city schools of the largest metropolitan areas is disproportionately low (only 7.9 percent), the share of all white and Latino public school students in their suburban schools is similar—25.3 percent and 24.4 percent, respectively.[44] Among the four largest racial groups, the suburbs educate a disproportionately lower share of blacks.

As their white student populations decline, suburban districts are eager to attract students to offset any drops in enrollment and funding. There has been an increase of more than 850,000 Latinos in suburban schools of our nation's twenty-five largest metropolitan areas in just the seven-years from 1999–2000 to 2006–07. Combined, black and Asian student enrollments have increased by more than 500,000 during this time while the number of white suburban students has *declined* by more than 170,000.

The extent and variety of suburban transformation is also evident in the racial composition of students in schools in each of the twenty-five largest metropolitan areas in 2006–07. Most suburban enrollments in these areas retained a white majority, but the suburban enrollment in seven of them had a majority nonwhite enrollment. All seven areas were located in the most

TABLE 1.1

Enrollment of students in city and suburban schools in the 25 largest metropolitan areas, by race, 2006–07

| | 25 LARGEST METROPOLITAN AREAS | | | | ALL U.S. STUDENTS |
| | CITIES | | SUBURBS | | |
	Enrollment	% of all U.S. students	Enrollment	% of all U.S. students	Enrollment
Native American	43,789	7.44%	58,927	10.01%	588,953
Asian/Pacific Islander	676,222	29.66%	751,408	32.96%	2,279,868
Black	2,242,591	27.10%	1,675,738	20.25%	8,275,666
Latino	3,106,054	31.25%	2,420,594	24.36%	9,938,381
White	2,168,440	7.93%	6,907,373	25.26%	27,347,536

Source: NCES Common Core of Data, 2006–07.

diverse regions of our country: four in states with a history of de jure segregation regions and three in the West (all in California). One (Los Angeles) had a majority of suburban students who were Latino. What's more, due to the high percentages of suburban students, overall metropolitan diversification patterns are in most instances more similar to suburban racial composition than to that of city schools.

A key component of suburban diversity is that in many metropolitan areas, including the three largest (New York, Los Angeles, and Chicago), at least three racial groups each comprised at least 10 percent of the suburban enrollment. Most such multiracial suburban areas are composed of white, black, and Latino students, and many are located in the South. Patterns are different in the West, where three of the largest metropolitan areas in California have a different combination of racial groups in suburbia: significant percentages of white, Latino, and Asian students. The suburbs in industrial metropolitan areas are the least likely to be experiencing racial diversity, much less the multiracial diversity seen elsewhere. Six of the largest twenty-five areas, mostly located in the former Rust Belt, have predominantly white-black suburban enrollments. Additionally, two slow-growth Rust Belt metropolitan areas—Pittsburgh and Cincinnati—had overwhelmingly white suburban enrollments.

While the suburbs are becoming diverse in almost every metropolitan area, they retain a disproportionately higher percentage of white students than do cities.[45] In fifteen of the twenty-five studied, the percentage of white students in the suburbs is at least twice that of white city students. Virtually all suburban areas have a lower percentage of black and Latino students than their corresponding city. In some places, the discrepancies between black and white enrollments are great, most notably in the midwestern and, to a lesser extent, northeastern metropolitan areas. In many of these cities, blacks comprise at least 60 percent of students; in the suburban areas, however, blacks comprise less than 20 percent of enrollment.

Almost all of the studied areas have lower Latino percentages in suburban schools than in city schools. The differences in percentage are not as extreme, due in part to the fact that the percentages of Latino students in the city districts in these metropolitan areas is not as high; in areas with high Latino urban enrollment, the suburban schools also reflect higher Latino shares. Reports have documented the extensive integration, at the aggregate level, for Asian students.[46] This integration extends across city/suburban lines.

Growing Latino Presence and Shrinking White Share in Suburbia

Though differences remain between city and suburban enrollment, these disparities have become smaller over time, particularly over the last decade. Changes in white and Latino student populations illustrate this trend best; since 2000, the percentage of suburban whites has declined more sharply than in the city (although there were fewer whites in central city schools), while during this same time period, Latinos have surpassed blacks as the second largest group in suburban schools.

In just seven years, from 1999–2000 to 2006–07, the percentage of white students in the largest suburbs' schools declined nine percentage points, to 57.5 percent. This decline was reflected in *each* of the twenty-five metropolitan areas studied here, although the rate of decline varied.[47] In nineteen of the twenty-five, the percentage decline in white students in the suburbs since 1999 was *greater* than that of white students in city schools. This decline was highest in Dallas (15 percent), which also had among the largest percentage increases in Latino suburban students during this period. Metropolitan areas where white suburban decline was smaller than in urban schools generally had extremely high percentages of white students, suggesting that many of these areas have not yet experienced the diversification happening elsewhere.

The increase of Latino students is seen in the suburbs of virtually every large metropolitan area, where the Latino suburban enrollment has more than doubled since 1990—in some, many times over. Overall, growth in the Latino student population since 1999 accounts for 70 percent of the increase in suburban student enrollments. In nine metropolitan areas, the Latino suburban enrollment has doubled in just seven years (1999–2006). Many of the areas experiencing rapid Latino enrollment growth were places such as Dallas that during the 1990s saw rapid growth of the entire metropolitan area population. The increase in Latino students was larger in the suburbs than in the cities in most metropolitan areas. As a result, by 2006–07, in fifteen of these areas, the number of Latino suburban students was greater than that of Latino city students.

The patterns of black student enrollment in the suburbs were much more mixed. In one-third of the largest metropolitan areas, black students accounted for the largest growth in suburban students from 1999 to 2006. While Atlanta, a traditional center of black migration, was one of these eight metropolitan areas, most others were located in the Midwest and may reflect within-metropolitan area migration because these areas also experienced a decline in the number of black city students during the same time period. In Detroit, perhaps the most segregated metropolitan area for black students, the percentage of black student suburban growth since 1999 outpaced that of Latinos and Asians.[48] The percentage of black students declined in three of the metropolitan areas studied.

Not Just Racial Change: Growing Poverty in Suburbia

During the 1990s, a time of economic prosperity, the share of low-income residents in a majority of both city and suburban areas of our largest metropolitan areas declined; yet because of increasing suburbanization, the number of poor suburban residents grew.[49] Since 2000, U.S. poverty rates have increased, and although poverty is much less concentrated in suburbia than in cities, it has grown sharply in areas commonly thought of as affluent. Student enrollment patterns in the free and reduced-price lunch program also reflect the way poverty is growing faster in the suburbs and the city-suburban poverty gap is closing.[50] This trend is projected to continue despite the fact that suburbs are often unprepared to offer the same social services traditionally available to the poor in cities.[51]

The majority of the growth in low-income students since 1999 has happened in suburbia. From 1999 to 2006—before the great recession—there was an increase of more than 2 million students from low-income families in schools in the largest metropolitan areas, and more than 60 percent of these students—1.2 million students—are in suburban schools. In twenty of the metropolitan areas studied, the number of poor students in suburban schools increased more than that in city schools.[52]

The number of poor suburban students increased in all of the metropolitan areas we studied. While there is a substantial difference between the number of poor students in city and suburban schools for all of them, the gap is wider in some areas than in others. In general, the poverty rates in cities and suburbs are most similar in parts of the South that tend to have larger, countywide districts. The largest gaps in the percentages of low-income students across city-suburban lines are the large metropolitan areas in the Northeast and Midwest, where city students' poverty was quite high and where many metropolitan areas have percentages of student poverty that are 30 percentage points (or more) lower in suburban schools than in their central cities. Further, due to the correlation between race and class, metropolitan areas with lower shares of suburban white students also tend to have higher shares of free and reduced price lunch students in suburban schools.

How Racial Change Has Transformed the Suburban Enrollment

Taken together, these trends raise an important question: How useful is the concept of suburbia now, at least in our nation's largest metropolitan areas? While differences remain, in the aggregate, between city and suburban enrollment, the suburban population dwarfs that of the cities in virtually every large metropolitan area. Major parts of suburban rings face what were long seen as "inner city" social and economic problems. The population shift to suburbia may portend important policy consequences as cities contain just a fraction of the residents and public school students.

Of equal significance is that if these trends of rapid racial change continue, the distinction between city and suburb may become further blurred. Indeed, the demographics of the suburbs now closely reflect the composition of the entire nation. Thus understanding the change that is happening in the suburbs—a change that is creating a multiracial diversity more complex than the racial change of prior generations—is critically important to understanding change happening in our country.

THE OPPORTUNITIES RELATED TO GROWING DIVERSITY AND THE CONSEQUENCES OF DOING NOTHING ABOUT RESEGREGATION

The importance of responding to current patterns of racial change and the potential of growing segregation is only intensified by decades of social science evidence indicating that integrated education provides better learning experiences and preparation for postgraduation experiences than does segregation. While most high-profile desegregation cases have focused on urban districts, the importance of integrated schooling is no less significant for suburban students or their communities. As some observers noted, while integrated suburbs represent "a great hope for a cohesive future, they also face some of America's most serious challenges to their prosperity and stability . . . most communities that were integrated in the not-too-distant past are now largely nonwhite."[53]

The *Brown* decision in 1954 represents one of the first times in which the federal government recognized the harmfulness to students of segregated schools. Declaring that segregated schools provided inherently unequal educational opportunity, the decision was based in part on social science research documenting the ways in which attending all-black schools had harmed the "hearts and minds" of children. More recently, in 2007 the Supreme Court affirmed the compelling governmental interest in reducing racial isolation in schools, and the Obama administration has supported this aim, offering guidance to districts about permissible strategies to accomplish such goals but offering little tangible aid.[54]

Beginning with the 1966 Coleman report, researchers have recognized that both the individual background characteristics of students' families and the composition of the school's student body impact student achievement.[55] Researchers have found, for example, significant improvements in educational outcomes, improved job opportunities, and college attendance when urban poor and minority students attended integrated middle-class schools in the suburbs.[56] Contemporary research finds that segregated schools often have fewer of the key resources that are important for students' learning: a high-quality, experienced, and stable faculty and a challenging curriculum.[57] At the same time, researchers also have examined the effects of changing demographics on the educational policy agenda or the allocation of state resources, noting that a shift in state power from the cities to the suburbs has resulted in a policy shift away from concerns about equity to concerns with educational outcomes.[58] These studies suggest that greater economic and racial diversity in metropolitan areas will likely impact institutional and political support for particular educational policies.

Another rationale for the importance of diverse schools is newer research detailing the benefit of integrated schools for students of all racial/ethnic backgrounds. Experience in integrated settings, particularly for younger children, helps students to develop cross-racial friendships, challenges stereotypes, and reduces prejudice. Some studies have suggested that having students from diverse backgrounds in a classroom can also aid the development of critical thinking skills. Students in diverse schools report higher levels of comfort across racial lines, a skill that is critically important for their adult lives living and working in our multiracial nation. Importantly, these benefits accrue as a result of intergroup contact, particularly when structured appropriately, that cannot happen in even the most elite, homogenous settings (white or nonwhite).[59] Thus, suburban districts that have not yet experienced racial/ethnic change or diversifying suburban districts that retain white enclaves may not provide an educational experience that fully prepares their students for life in a diverse society.

Informed by these findings, it is important to understand the extent to which demographic change in suburbia is affecting the integration of schools, in order to assess the opportunities for students and the potential long-term effects on suburban communities' stability. Social science suggests that both segregated white and nonwhite schools should be concerned about the lack of student diversity in their schools.

THE CONTRIBUTION OF THIS BOOK

The objective of this book is to challenge educational leaders to respond effectively to the trend of resegregation in the suburbs and to look at the experience of communities across the country. Most districts are trying to ignore the issue while pretending that focusing on state standards will somehow solve what are serious and complex racial and class issues. Sometimes leaders are quietly trying to implement policies to hold existing white, Asian, and middle-class families, letting segregation spread or even concentrating black and Latino children in one part of the district. As resegregation happens, high-quality, experienced teachers tend to move, as do many middle-class parents. Doing nothing is surrendering to segregation and its many powerful consequences. This book gives communities and education leaders a background and a language to frame the issues, and also shows that there are a number of things educators *can* do when presented with an opportunity for a community that is more open and just, more diverse—and more stable.

Methodology

We identified seven metropolitan areas—Atlanta, Boston, Chicago, Los Angeles, Minneapolis, San Antonio, and a Florida metropolitan area—and one suburban district within each, to study. A first criterion for inclusion was an *increasing share of minority and low-income students.* Such districts are likely to face similar circumstances—greater diversity among the school-age population; a teaching staff demographically different from and inadequately trained to teach a diverse student population; limited instructional processes appropriate for a diverse student population; increasing concerns about patterns of race and school achievement; and anxiety among parents, particularly white, who may exit the system.[60]

To choose from among these many suburban districts, we looked for variation on two factors: rate of demographic change and type of district jurisdiction (e.g., municipal or countywide districts). The latter variable is likely to be a proxy for other political and institutional differences, such as in school governance, district size, and local governance structure.[61] These characteristics may either facilitate or constrain the policy options available to school districts. A broad and varied housing market, for example, may give countywide districts a wider range of policy options than smaller suburbs since policy is less likely to be subservient to neighborhood politics. Exit to other school systems may be a more realistic option in municipalities that are located in close proximity to other suburbs than in countywide districts.

Our second criterion was to stratify on rate of *racial transition*, a variable that measures the stability or lack of stability (transition) in a district's racial composition over time. Of our demographic variables, racial transition was likely to be the most politically salient, particularly in communities with little history of diversity. In addition, since race and income levels are correlated, changes in racial composition often bring changes in socioeconomic composition, although this is not always the case.[62] How change is perceived—either as a challenge or an opportunity—may in turn impact the policy response and the urgency to address the change. We include districts where racial transition is stable because these districts may tell important stories about how to maintain integration over a longer period of time and how to do it successfully. In districts experiencing more rapid change, increasing diversity may be a relatively new phenomenon and thus elicit different policy responses, including denial.

Finally, we also sought sites where we thought *diversity was a current issue for communities and where three or more racial/ethnic groups were present.* The group of metropolitan areas and districts provides an opportunity to analyze geographical diversity, rate of transition, and differences in the number and identity of racial groups that are increasingly present in suburban schools. While these can not represent *all* suburban communities, they represent the direction that suburbia is headed. Obviously, given the enormous diversity of the nation, we found many similarities coming from studies independently carried out by a racially and disciplinarily diverse research team in very disparate districts, parallels that lend great strength to the central argument of this book.

Gaining access to a district to study a sensitive issue not discussed in public was difficult. In most cases, we had to promise anonymity to most respondents and their districts. Obviously this limits the possibility of readers and local community members to check the responses or judge the performance of local institutions. We took great pains to record, transcribe, and carefully analyze interviews and to analyze local data; we believe that this is the only way the study could have been done.

We identified three groups of respondents within each community that we would seek to interview (see table 1.2). *Formal actors* are individuals who are in a position to influence important actors in local decision making across a wide range of policy issues; these may include leaders in government, business leaders, and teacher union representatives. *Informal actors* are representatives of community-based organizations, including educational advocacy groups, minority organizations, neighborhood organizations, parent organizations, and the media. *Educational actors* are those persons who are knowledgeable about the implementation of school system policies and programs. This includes both people with policy-making authority and school-based staff charged with implementing the policies. Through expert sampling we identified the significant actors in a community. We expected that the mix of actors and groups would vary by community. As a result, in addition to identifying the types of actors we wanted to interview across all seven sites, we allowed for "wild cards" to permit interviews unique to a site's particular issues. For example, the mayor may be an active participant in some

TABLE 1.2

Interviews conducted by site and role of participant

Role	All sites	Atlanta	Boston	Chicago	Los Angeles	Minneapolis	San Antonio	Florida
School district								
District employee	56	8	3	13	11	6	8	7
School board	13	2	1	4	0	1	3	2
School employee	0							
Administrator	44	6	3	4	10	5	13	3
Teacher	44	4	9	0	7	5	13	6
Other personnel	21	3	0	1	1	1	9	6
External actor	0							
Business	8	0	2	0	2	2	1	1
Real estate	3	1	1	0	0	0	0	1
City/county government	15	2	0	6	2	2	3	0
Informal actor								
Parent/parent group	7	0	2	0	1	1	1	2
Community activist	4	0	2	0	0	0	1	1
Nonprofit group	9	1	4	2	0	2	0	0
Total	224	27	27	30	34	25	52	29

communities but not in others. Minority groups may be a dominant influence on the policy process in some communities, while business interests predominate in others. Seeking out these respondents was informed by our conceptual framework, which delineates political factors (i.e., actors both inside and outside the school system that influence educational policy) and institutional factors (i.e., formal organizations with decision-making authority and informal organizations with an interest in the outcomes of suburban diversification) as shaping school policy.[63]

Our interview procedure was to ask individuals in each group the same set of questions appropriate to their role within the community as well as some questions that overlapped between groups about major community issues. Interviews were semistructured, to allow for inquiry into important issues. In addition to our interviews, we collected key documents such as policies, data, and statements from the districts and school boards, government agencies; business, community, and parent organizations; teacher unions; advocacy groups; and schools. Within our case study districts, we collected, to the extent possible, school enrollment and faculty data by race/ethnicity and student achievement results. Finally, while each case study was conducted independently by research teams in a particular site, we facilitated cross-site discussion in addition to regularly providing data and checking in with each research team member individually.

Plan of the Book

The bulk of the book consists of seven chapters each drawing from in-depth case studies in a suburban community. Each is accompanied by data contextualizing the current and ongoing demographic change in the metro, suburban rings, and district studied. Many chapters present findings that are illustrative of much of the diversity of experiences facing suburban communities and districts around the country. The exceptions to this are those suburban districts that have already resegregated or in which diversity has not yet affected the demographic composition of schools and communities.

Chapter 2, by Erica Frankenberg, frames and contextualizes the case studies that follow. It describes the current extent of demographic change in suburbia in our nation's metropolitan areas. It also argues that the concept of "suburban" no longer accurately describes non-city parts of metropolitan areas, and instead suggests a typology of suburban school districts.

The case studies that follow show that none of the communities we examined has a fully developed strategy for responding to this change. It is easy and rewarding for the educational leaders in a huge suburban district in Texas to talk about their tough academic standards and to struggle for success on the state testing program (chapter 3). Yet, as Jennifer Jellison Holme, Anjalé Welton, and Sarah Diem find, the issues of successfully educating and incorporating into suburban life families with origins in Latin America and the urban barrios are not at the center of the agenda.

In Orange County, California, a center of white suburban conservatism a generation ago, the county now has a nonwhite majority (chapter 4, by Lorrie Frasure-Yokley). Individual districts in this vast suburban region are seeking their own solutions, often confronting differences between its more affluent areas and a stream of newcomers with very different backgrounds and needs.

In New England, Susan Eaton describes an older suburb trying to fit current population changes into the older immigrant story, but there are differences that must be addressed (chapter 5). The district hopes that doing well on standardized tests will somehow resolve racial issues but leaders take no action to integrate schools or to share the best schooling opportunities with the growing populations of minority students. In the Minneapolis area, Baris Gumus-Dawes, Myron Orfield, and Thomas Luce examine a major racially changing suburban community where the educational leaders saw a need for action but the community is deeply divided (chapter 6).

In Florida, Kathryn Wiley, Barbara Shircliffe, and Jennifer Morley studied a large metropolitan district where the court ended a decades-long program of far-reaching desegregation (chapter 7). The district, with no explicit strategy to address this, is quietly letting the district resegregate, but looks at the situation with regret—remembering integration, hoping it will continue, but not willing to seriously pursue it.

In the Atlanta area, Elizabeth DeBray and Ain Grooms examine a rapidly growing outer suburban district with many middle-class black residents not worried about race issues and a school district that ignores these issues—despite a big racial gap in school outcomes and growing poverty (chapter 8). In Oak Park, Illinois, a community that has by many measures been residentially integrated for generations, there is a tendency to take the housing success for granted and not to engage the kind of energy created in the days when the suburb was seriously threatened by decline. Here, Gary Orfield finds that serious issues of inequality in the schools erupt every few years with demands for equity and new solutions but no easy answers (chapter 9).

The book concludes by considering the current state of policy and leadership in suburban communities and districts. In this summing up, Gary Orfield offers suggestions of best practices drawn from suburban communities and assesses the possibilities for leadership. Suburban communities are facing changes that will define their future and reshape their society but their educators, who first see the changes in terms of very tangible alterations of their school populations, usually rely instead on the rhetoric of test scores and accountability and achievement gap plans and workshops. School officials often fear that local residents will resist change and do not want to do anything that could put their career and their local relationships at risk. Often schools and districts have largely white staffs with little understanding of the newcomers. None of these districts has been required to act by a court or a federal or state agency and none has received much external support. It is, of course, very difficult to take long-term action on very sensitive and potentially explosive issues when none of the major institutions of educational leadership are requiring or supporting it.

There are positive things suburban districts, and the nation, can do. This book describes the current state of things, which may appear bleak. But through the case studies and more generally from the literature, it also explores what can be and why it is so important to develop a more coherent vision of and support for the possibilities that racial change brings to suburbia. We have met suburban leaders from across the country who think deeply about their everyday experiences, and are anxious to understand what the possibilities are. We hope this book is a resource for these leaders to understand the broad demographic changes under way, the importance of comprehensive articulation of the opportunities of diversity, and how to effectively respond, collaboratively, to suburbia's transformation. The stakes are too high to fail: the future of our nation depends on these communities' successfully answering this call to educate the coming multiracial and multilingual generations of citizens.

2

Understanding Suburban School District Transformation

A Typology of Suburban Districts

ERICA FRANKENBERG

Racial change is happening in suburbia. Yet although it is commonly thought of as a monolith and defined broadly as the part of a metropolitan area that is *not* a central city, suburbia is no longer so easy to define. And suburban racial change, like the development of suburbs themselves, is happening in very different ways and at very different speeds. The scale of the change varies by metropolitan area; for example, suburban areas and their central city counterparts are much more homogeneous in the Rust Belt and in metros with little population growth. The identity of the racial change also varies by region, although as a general trend, Latino populations in suburbia are exploding. Simply put, we need a new way of thinking about suburbs and suburban school districts. The aim of this chapter is to understand the different ways in which suburban districts are changing, propose a typology of suburban districts, and describe what types of districts this book will examine.

Suburban areas within the same metropolitan area also differ: those located near the central city may have already gone through a period of rapid racial transition and now mirror city demographics; some may be experiencing racial and economic diversity for the first time; and others still, such as those on the fringes, may be largely untouched by the demographic wave affecting the rest of the area. Suburban school districts no longer fit the notion of homogeneous, affluent havens. As the growing diversification of suburbia occurs, how are student enrollment patterns changing in major metropolitan areas?[1] Are suburbs places of integration or are patterns of segregation spreading across city-suburban lines? The answers to these questions have implications for both the opportunities and challenges suburban districts face in providing high-quality educational opportunities for all students.

Analyses of suburban communities have suggested several ways of categorizing suburban communities as a way to understand this new diversity. While much policy and discussion still delineates a city-suburban binary, *suburb* actually encompasses substantial diversity in terms of population characteristics, economic base, and housing stock. These distinctions lead to considerable differences in the prospects of suburban communities, and Myron Orfield has argued that rather than a single "suburban" category, there exists instead a typology of suburban communities that have dramatically different tax bases and populations that require varying levels of government services.[2] A similar categorization scheme using demographic and voting data has divided the entire country by both congressional districts and counties into a dozen categories, of which the largest is the "monied 'burbs."[3] Now, when the housing market crisis and lowered immigration rate have dramatically slowed mobility, is an opportune time to evaluate what types of suburban communities and districts exist, what the opportunities each type has to respond to racial and economic change, and what challenges the particular categories of suburban districts may need to consider to prevent widespread resegregation.

This chapter explores differences between suburban districts to illuminate the scale of suburban demographic change, diversity of district types, and how patterns of segregation are connected to district configuration. It does so by examining the suburban school districts in the largest twenty-five U.S. metropolitan areas (which includes districts in twenty-five states and the District of Columbia[4]), which enroll one-quarter of all students. To measure student enrollment trends in these districts, this chapter relies on the NCES Common Core of Data (CCD). The CCD's Public School Universe provides the opportunity to analyze student enrollments, by race/ethnicity and poverty, across districts and years. In particular, it uses school-level and district-level data from 1990–91, 1999–2000, and 2006–07. Suburban districts are defined as those serving areas within a metropolitan area that are not the principal or central city. The research sample represents different regions of the country and thus different patterns of suburban diversification. In several places, data were not available for earlier years.[5] The last year of data, 2006–07, preceded the economic crisis that may have affected poverty trends and altered patterns of racial diversity, since the impact of subprime mortgages was disproportionately on minority families.

Several dimensions of segregation are analyzed here for student enrollment by race/ethnicity: (1) the index of dissimilarity, to measure the evenness of the population's distribution; and (2) the percentage of students in intensely segregated schools, to measure concentration.[6] These indexes allow us to measure how different groups are distributed across the metropolitan area and within and among districts. In addition, the distribution and concentration of poverty across districts is examined using the index of dissimilarity and the percentage of low-income students in schools, respectively.

This chapter focuses on how suburban change is affecting particular types of suburban communities and districts. The first section describes a district-level analysis of how students are sorted by district lines. Second, the chapter describes a typology of suburban districts and analyzes school-level composition and segregation trends. It concludes with a consideration of how this typology relates to the seven case studies that comprise chapters 3 through 9. It is important to note that while this typology identifies six clusters of suburban districts, this study is most concerned with diverse districts, not those that have already transitioned or ones in which little racial change has occurred to date.

DISTRICT-LEVEL ANALYSIS

As described in chapter 1, metropolitan areas exhibit wide differences in terms of scale and speed of demographic suburban change, and it seems reasonable to expect that there would also be variety within each area's suburbs. Because of the importance of the school district as a unit to determine policy—and ultimately to determine response to demographic change—this section analyzes how the vast suburban racial and economic changes affect the thousands of districts in the twenty-five largest metropolitan areas. In particular, we seek to understand whether the jurisdictional nature of suburban districts accounts for the way the changes vary.[7]

The Changing, Varied Nature of Suburban School Districts

One of the most important reasons that racial change in suburbia may have vastly different consequences for districts than the racial transition of central cities decades ago is the fragmentation that exists in most of the suburbs of these areas. While central cities are almost always designated as one district, dozens or hundreds of separate suburban jurisdictions can exist within the metropolitan area as a whole. Combined, there are more than eight times as many public school districts in the suburbs in 2006–07 as in the central city regions of the largest metropolitan areas. The number of suburban districts has remained relatively stable and in fact declined slightly since 1999. The number of suburban districts is lowest in Florida, where there are county-wide school districts across the state. New York City, the largest metropolitan area, has more than five hundred suburban school districts. Seven other MSAs have at least one hundred noncharter public school districts.

As is the case in non-educational governments (e.g., municipalities, as compared to school districts), the suburban districts in the midwestern and especially northeastern metropolitan areas have, on average, the smallest enrollment and represent the most extreme fragmentation of the suburbs in 2006–07. In three midwestern metropolitan areas, suburban district enrollment averages fewer than three thousand students. These district sizes are obviously considerably smaller than the urban districts they surround. In contrast, the South and Border regions, where countywide districts are more common, have metropolitan areas where the average suburban district has tens of thousands of students. These patterns may have major implications for segregation if the populations are homogeneous within districts, since student assignment almost always occurs within district boundaries. Further, because individual districts likely contains only a small share of the enrollment, they may be especially vulnerable to even small demographic shifts.

The decline in the percentage of white students has affected both city and suburban districts, and in the most recent years, has affected them in the aggregate very similarly. The overall decline for the district percentage of white students in all suburban districts from 1990 to 2006 was 12.5 percentage points on average. More recently, from 1999 to 2006, the average suburban district saw a decline in white students of 7.3 percent, while the decline in the average city district during this time was 8.4 percent. Thus, changing student composition is affecting suburban districts to nearly the same extent as urban districts in the nation's largest metropolitan areas.

Examining means describes one aspect of the general tendency of racial change but does less to help us understand what types of changes specific districts are experiencing. Overall, almost one in five (19.5 percent) suburban districts are experiencing *rapid* racial change, which is defined as racial transition at least three times that of the entire enrollment (an annual decline of white students of at least 1.8 percentage points over a seven-year period). This share was slightly lower than in urban districts (21.1 percent), and accounted for more than 3.5 million suburban students in our largest metropolitan areas (nearly 30 percent of all suburban students in these areas). Majorities of suburban students in five of these areas, including three in the South and one in the Border region, are in rapidly transitioning districts. Another one-seventh of suburban districts are experiencing *moderate* racial change, which is decline in the percentage of white students at twice the overall rate.

City districts were more susceptible to extremes in racial change, while district-level change in suburbs was not as large. A greater percentage of suburban districts are categorized as undergoing *slow* change, meaning the decline in white enrollment was between 0 and 8.4 percentage points from 1999 to 2006.[8] A majority of suburban school districts were experiencing slow change, compared with only 38 percent of urban districts. A higher percentage of city districts (22.6 percent) had an increasing percentage of white students than did suburban districts (9.4 percent), which is not surprising since many urban districts have small shares of white students.[9]

Some metropolitan areas have an especially large share of districts undergoing rather dramatic transformation. Six had at least one-third of suburban districts experiencing rapid racial change. Atlanta was one such metropolitan area, and it had almost another one-fifth of districts with an increasing percentage of white students, indicating that its suburban districts were experiencing diverging patterns. Atlanta is distinctive among metropolitan areas with big suburban systems because it is such a focus of Latino migration. In three of the areas studied, no districts were experiencing rapid white decline. That each of these had districts organized on a countywide basis suggests that larger district size helps to moderate racial transition. In Boston and Pittsburgh, which had high percentages of white students, less than a tenth of suburban students were in rapidly changing districts.

Recall that there was rising poverty from 1999 to 2006 among suburban students in virtually every metropolitan area. On average, across all of the largest metropolitan areas, suburban districts had a smaller increase in the percentage of low-income students since 1999—less than 4 percentage points, as compared with nearly 7 percentage points in urban districts—which was surprising, given that the majority of the increase in poor students is occurring in the suburbs. This pattern was also true in most of the twenty-five metropolitan areas we studied. This is likely due to the rising enrollment of students in suburbia during this time; thus despite the larger number of new low-income students, the *percentage* of low-income students, on average, is lower than in central city districts.

In most metropolitan areas, the magnitude of district-level change in the percentage of low-income students in suburban districts is less than that of change in the percentage of white students. Yet, in one-sixth of suburban districts, the percentage of low-income students rose by at least ten percentage points from 1999 to 2006. And, in more than one-quarter of suburban districts, the percentage of low-income students declined since 1999.[10]

District-Level Segregation

What do these differential rates of racial and economic change mean for segregation at the district level within suburbia? Simply put, we find extensive segregation of black students from white and Asian students in many metropolitan areas. This analysis considers dissimilarity between suburban districts within each metropolitan area, and examines dissimilarity between each pairing of the four racial/ethnic groups: Asians, blacks, Latinos, and whites (see table 2.1).[11] In addition, we extend the use of dissimilarity to examine the evenness of the distribution of poor and non-poor students across suburban districts.[12]

White-black dissimilarity levels between suburban districts remain high; many of the highest are in the Midwest and New York City, all areas with dozens or hundreds of suburban districts. Notably, none of the suburban

TABLE 2.1

Dissimilarity levels of suburban districts of 24 of the largest metropolitan areas

	DISTRICT-LEVEL DISSIMILARITY INDEX, 2006–07		
	Below 30	30–60	Above 60
White-black	3	15	6
White-Latino	3	19	2
White-Asian	4	20	0
Black-Latino	8	15	1
Black-Asian	5	11	8
Latino-Asian	3	20	1
Poor-nonpoor	7	17	0

Source: NCES Common Core of Data, 2006–07.

Note: Miami not included.

areas with the highest district-level dissimilarity for white and black students was in the South or Border regions—regions where the most active desegregation efforts took place a generation ago. Some places with the highest dissimilarity indices experienced declines since 1990, but most were modest.

There were fewer suburban areas with high district-level dissimilarity for Latino and white students—only New York and Boston, where the Latino population is primarily Puerto Rican and Dominican—but a slightly higher number of metropolitan areas where suburban district dissimilarity was increasing. When comparing these figures with segregation levels in 1999–2000, Latino-white dissimilarity was on the rise in suburban districts in most of the metropolitan areas in the South and Border regions. Latino-black segregation is far less extreme than other racial pairings, and is on the decline between suburban districts. In one-third of the suburban rings of the largest areas studied, black-Latino district dissimilarity was relatively low. Most of these suburbs are in the West, where Latinos far outnumber blacks and where black students often attend majority Latino schools—or in the South and Border regions, which are experiencing sweeping Latino migration.

The segregation of Asians from whites and from Latinos is similar in magnitude, and much less severe than that of Asian segregation from blacks. Asians are the least segregated of the four racial/ethnic groups studied. White-Asian segregation is the only type of district-level dissimilarity in which the suburbs of no metropolitan area rate "high" (greater than 60). Likewise, Latino-Asian dissimilarity in suburban districts is moderate or low in almost every metropolitan area. The story for Asian-black segregation is much different, however, where segregation was high, particularly in the Midwest. Conversely, there are more suburban regions with low black-Asian segregation, mostly in the West, where black students account for a relatively low share of the enrollment.

In sum, we find tremendous variation across suburban school districts in terms of the racial and economic change affecting major metropolitan areas. The destiny of districts' transition varies by region of the country, but also differs within metropolitan areas as well. One troubling finding is that those regions with more suburban fragmentation have districts experiencing rapid transition and high racial and economic segregation, which may indicate that only portions of suburbia are open to black, Latino, and/or low-income families. While it is likely that the segregation levels reported here would be higher if urban districts were included as well, these findings indicate that stratification is spreading beyond city boundaries to encompass a larger geographic spread.

TOWARD A TYPOLOGY OF SUBURBAN DISTRICTS

One of the reasons we may see this population sorting across suburban school district boundary lines is the diversity that exists between districts. Orfield's analysis of a suburban typology considered the characteristics of a jurisdiction's total population.[13] Given the dramatic changes many suburban districts are experiencing, this analysis seeks to uncover whether similar groups of suburban districts may be emerging.

Ability to Recruit New Students: Comparing Growing and Shrinking Districts

While overall suburban enrollment is booming, this trend, like that of demographic change, is not evenly shared across all suburban districts, which indicates that sorting is occurring. Twenty-one of the twenty-five largest metropolitan areas had suburban districts that were both increasing and decreasing in enrollment since 1999, although enrollments in the vast majority of districts (79 percent) were increasing. If districts are losing enrollment, it suggests that they are unable to recruit new students at a rate replacing those exiting the system.[14] Do the characteristics of these suburban districts differ significantly from those with increasing enrollments? Across all suburban districts, the answer is yes: there were significant differences in student composition, on average, by racial and poverty status. Yet, these varied by race and metropolitan area.

Not surprisingly, in most metropolitan areas (eighteen of the twenty-five studied) the percentage of white students was higher, on average, in increasing-enrollment districts than those whose enrollment had declined, often by large amounts (e.g., 20 percent). In three of the metropolitan areas, the percentage of white students is *lower* in districts with an increasing enrollment, all on the West Coast, where Asian students also were in increasing districts to a higher extent. The pattern was similarly uniform for black students, albeit the reverse of changes in white student enrollments. In the vast majority of metropolitan areas (except those with few black suburban students), the percentage of black students in suburban districts with increasing enrollment was much lower, on average, than in districts with declining enrollments. In some areas, the percentage of black students in declining enrollment districts was two to three times higher than the share of black students in increasing districts, on average. To some extent, this represents a geographic extension within suburbia of the pattern central cities faced when locked into declining enrollment and higher shares of black and

Latino students compared with booming, largely white suburban districts a generation ago.

Taken together, these patterns suggest not a universal type of suburban district but instead several distinct types of suburban districts. Most suburban districts are growing and have had increasing student enrollments since 1999. The most consistent trend is that the average percentage of low-income students was lower in growing districts within each MSA than in declining districts. Districts in high-cost, high-tax parts of suburbia that attract affluent residents are likely to have increasing enrollments.[15] More likely than not, districts gaining students had higher percentages of white students and lower percentages of black students than nearby districts that had declining enrollment. What's more, these differences remained consistent with differences in district characteristics in 1999, the beginning of the period examined. Districts that declined over the seven years from 1999–2000 to 2006–07 were already different at the beginning of the period in terms of the racial composition of students, and were particularly sensitive to larger percentages of black students. There was considerably greater ambiguity as to the sorting pattern of Latino, Asian, and English language learner (ELL) students within increasing- and decreasing-enrollment districts, which may reflect the considerable diversity that exists in each of these groups and regional variation. It could also reflect the fact that these recent migrants, like white internal migrants, are attracted to economically growing metropolitan areas; recall that growing sections of suburbia were likely to be experiencing increases in Latino residents. Understanding how these growing subgroups of the student enrollment are sorted within growing and shrinking districts will impact the demographic future of suburban districts.

Suburban District Clusters: Emerging Student Patterns in Suburbia

Following Myron Orfield's analysis of suburban communities, this chapter used cluster analysis to group the 2,364 suburban districts into six distinct clusters.[16] Using the K-means clustering procedure to cluster large numbers of observations (in this case, suburban school districts) into distinct groups, this analysis created clusters using racial and economic characteristics of the district enrollment, size of enrollment, and racial change that had been converted to percentages relative to the entire metropolitan area's enrollment for a given indicator. These relative demographic measures were then used in the cluster procedure.

The cluster analysis reveals considerable variety among suburban districts and distinct student patterns (summarized in table 2.2). Minority students are underrepresented in several types of suburban clusters. Stable mixed-income districts, for example, have low percentages of black, Latino, and Asian students on average. Not surprisingly, the decline in the percentage of white students from 1999 to 2006 in these districts was much lower than the decline in surrounding suburban districts in their metropolitan area. Exclusive enclaves are another type of suburban cluster in which Latino and particularly black students are likely to comprise a lower share of students than in the entire metro's suburban enrollment; exclusive enclaves also have a disproportionately lower share of low-income (free and reduced-price lunch) students. While satellite cities have an overrepresentation of Latino and black students, Asian students are underrepresented in comparison to their share of the metropolitan area's suburban students.

TABLE 2.2

Description of suburban district clusters, 2006–07

Cluster	Number of districts in cluster	Description
Exclusive enclaves	703	High shares of white students, low poverty, minimal racial change
Countywide districts	13	Very large districts, racially diverse with moderate percentages of black and Latino students
Stable, mixed income	1,102	Very little racial change, few minority students, mixed socioeconomic status, many located far from central city
Inner-ring transitioning	75	Extremely rapid racial change, small size, moderate percentages of minority students and low-income students, few whites, located close to central city
Satellite cities	305	Moderate racial change, low-income students with high percentages of black and Latino students, larger size
Developing immigration meccas	142	Slower racial change, larger size, moderate percentages of Asian, Latino, and low-income students

Source: NCES Common Core of Data, 2006–07.

These data suggest that old stereotypes of a "suburban district" may no longer fit the reality in our largest metropolitan areas, and that developing policies that only reflect a city-suburban divide is no longer the reality. Some of the inner-ring transitioning districts may, in fact, be more similar to urban districts than to exclusive enclaves. Given the continuing suburbanization amid racial and economic change, this cluster analysis illustrates the differentiation between suburban districts and the diversity of suburban district types.

Racial Change and School Concentration

With the varying types of suburban districts in mind, this section explores the characteristics of schools in each cluster. It does so by examining racial change and economic and racial concentration at the school level (see tables 2.3 and 2.4 for a description of school characteristics in the clusters).

In these findings, a *stable, mixed-income district* contained approximately one in three of the suburban schools in the largest twenty-five metropolitan areas, and may in many respects bear little resemblance to other schools in the metropolitan areas. These schools might, for example, have only recently been included in metropolitan area definitions, since many are located far from central cities. Districts classified as stable, mixed income have less than four schools per district on average, another indication of their relatively rural nature. There was minimal racial change (averaging less than half a percentage point for the seven-year period) and a high percentage of students in segregated white schools. Yet, perhaps because the stable, mixed-income districts in the South might include some rural black communities, more than 18 percent of students also attended 90–100 percent minority schools. Nearly one in nine schools in stable, mixed-income districts had more than 75 percent of students from low-income households; just under half of the schools in 2006–07 were classified as low-poverty, or had less than one-quarter of students from poor or near-poor households.

Exclusive enclaves had relatively low racial change during the same period and were also distinguishable from districts in other clusters by the high degree of low-poverty schools. Very low shares of students (less than 7 percent in 2006–07) were in 90–100 percent minority schools, and these enclaves had among the highest shares of students in segregated white schools (10.77 percent), although there was a substantial decline in the percentage of students in segregated white schools as well by 2006–07. Nearly two out of

TABLE 2.3

Characteristics of suburban schools in largest twenty-five metropolitan areas, 1999–2000 and 2006–07, by suburban cluster

	Number of schools 2006–07	School-level white percentage change 1999–2006	PERCENTAGE OF STUDENTS IN 90–100% MINORITY SCHOOLS		PERCENTAGE OF STUDENTS IN 90–100% WHITE SCHOOLS	
			1999–2000	2006–07	1999–2000	2006–07
Satellite cities	1,381	−14.38	2.45%	13.66%	7.01%	0.78%
Exclusive enclaves	3,478	−8.46	3.27%	6.69%	27.61%	10.77%
Countywide	518	−11.86	17.66%	23.66%	15.33%	5.14%
Stable, mixed income	4,068	−3.27	15.34%	18.41%	45.42%	35.74%
Developing immigration meccas	2,480	−12.79	5.52%	12.92%	17.03%	8.25%
Inner-ring transitioning	312	−19.30	1.43%	6.11%	8.33%	0.00%
Total	12,237	−8.61	8.04%	13.27%	27.22%	15.70%

Source: NCES Common Core of Data, Public School Universe, 1999–2000; 2006–07.

TABLE 2.4

School-level poverty concentration in the suburbs of the 25 largest metropolitan areas, 1999–2000 and 2006–07, by suburban district cluster

Suburban district cluster	Low poverty		Extreme poverty	
	1999–2000	2006–07	1999–2000	2006–07
Satellite cities	37.6%	27.4%	7.1%	13.5%
Exclusive enclaves	70.5%	64.1%	4.1%	5.3%
Countywide	56.4%	40.0%	8.2%	17.7%
Stable, mixed income	55.5%	48.3%	11.2%	11.9%
Developing immigration meccas	51.1%	42.6%	8.1%	15.4%
Inner-ring transitioning	58.8%	40.1%	3.2%	2.9%
Total	57.2%	48.7%	7.7%	10.9%

Source: NCES Common Core of Data, Public School Universe, 1999–2000; 2006–07.

Note: low-poverty schools had less then 25% of free/reduced price lunch students; extreme-poverty schools had more than 75% free/reduced price lunch students.

three schools in this cluster had less than one-quarter of students from low-income households, and only 5 percent of schools had extreme concentrations of poverty.

Schools in *inner-ring transitioning* districts experienced the most dramatic racial change of all clusters, with an average annual rate of white decline of nearly three percentage points during the period examined. This rapid change resulted in no schools with more than 90 percent white students by 2006–07 and, somewhat surprisingly, a relatively low percentage of segregated minority schools as well. There was a sharp decline in the percentage of low-poverty schools, to 40 percent in 2006–07, among the lowest of all the clusters. There was a modest decline in the percentage of extreme poverty schools during the same time period, however, at a time when the overall percentage of such schools increased. Taken together, these trends suggest that while dramatic transitions were occurring, as of 2006–07 at least, they had not created significant concentrations of low-income or minority students.

Satellite city districts' schools also experienced substantial racial change during the period examined, with a slightly more than two percentage point decline in white student enrollment per year. As was the case with inner-ring transitioning schools, there was a sizeable drop in the percentage of segregated white schools but, unlike inner-ring transitioning, there was a subsequent jump in the percentage of students in 90–100 percent minority schools (13.66 percent in 2006–07). Since 1999–2000, there was a small fraction of low-poverty schools in the satellite city cluster, while the percentage of extreme-poverty schools nearly doubled between 1999–2000 and 2006–07. The districts had 4.5 schools, on average.

Countywide school districts consisted of approximately forty schools, on average, but these schools too displayed fairly substantial racial change from 1999 to 2006. This cluster had the highest share of segregated minority schools, nearly one in four by 2006–07, and a decline in the percentage of segregated white schools to only 5 percent. As was the case with inner-ring transitioning, the share of low-poverty schools declined from 1999 to 2006, but these districts also had a sharp increase in the percentage of extreme poverty schools and had the highest percentage of such schools of any cluster.

Developing immigrant meccas had substantial numbers of schools per districts (more than seventeen on average) and substantial racial change at the school level. There was a marked increase in the percentage of students in segregated minority schools by 2006–07, although it was still lower than in many of the other clusters. There was also a significant percentage of students in segregated white schools (8.25 percent). The percentage of extreme-poverty schools increased to among the highest of all the clusters, and a somewhat lower percentage of schools were classified as low poverty in 2006.

TYPES OF SUBURBAN DISTRICTS EXAMINED IN THIS BOOK

This book contains case studies from four of the six types of suburban clusters and is illustrative of many (but not all) of the different types of districts existing in our large metropolitan areas. We deliberately avoided studying inner-ring transitioning districts, believing that those districts were likely so far along in the continuum of racial transition as to have very different sets of possibilities than the rest of suburbia. Likewise, none of the seven districts were classified in the exclusive enclave category, although, as I will discuss below, Oak Park is somewhat of an anomaly and may well be similar to such districts.

Two districts—Beach County (chapter 7) and metropolitan Atlanta (chapter 8)—were countywide, and reflect the variety within this category. Both are geographically expansive districts, and Beach County (in a Florida metropolitan area) includes one of the central cities in its metro while Sewell (in metropolitan Atlanta) remains at a considerable distance from the central city. Beach County is one of the largest districts in the country, and both have sizeable shares of white students as well as black and growing Latino populations. This type of suburban district has experienced an increase at the school level of extreme poverty, and both Beach County and Sewell have pockets of high poverty in some schools.

Waltham (chapter 5), in suburban Boston, is an example of a satellite city district. Somewhat larger in size than other satellite city districts described above, it has a growing share of Latino students and is the county seat. Yet, while less advantaged than its nearest neighbors, it does not have the share of poor and minority students found in the central city district, Boston Public Schools. It has experienced moderate racial change in a metropolitan area with a lower decline of white students overall. Waltham also exemplifies satellite districts by having a higher share of low-income students than the average across all suburban districts in this MSA.

Perhaps due to our interest in examining multiracial districts, three of the case studies are classified in the developing immigration mecca category: the Southern ISD, Azalea, and Osseo districts (chapters 3, 4, and 6, respectively 6). Southern and Azalea, in suburban San Antonio and Los Angeles, respectively, have large shares of Latino students, and Azalea also has a substantial share of Asian students. Osseo, in suburban Minneapolis, has a lower share of minority students (about one-fifth of students are Latino and Asian) but nearly 10 percent of students are ELLs. Each of these districts is medium to large. Southern and Azalea have lower shares of low-income students than the overall suburban percentage in the metropolitan areas of which they are a part, while Osseo has a higher share, perhaps reflecting the fact that many of its immigrant students are from more disadvantaged groups; for example, Southeast Asians. Each of these districts comprises two distinct geographical areas: a largely white, affluent section and a section with enclaves containing a higher concentration of poor and minority students.

In this typology, Oak Park (chapter 9) was classified as a stable, mixed-income district, although it does not share all the characteristics of districts in this group, illustrating the anomalous nature of having a stable, mixed-income district so close in to the central city. Oak Park's elementary and high school districts are both somewhat whiter and more affluent than the entire suburban Chicago area, and are particularly disproportionately advantaged in comparison with their near neighbors. Like other districts in this group, there has been minimal decline in the percentage of white students since 2000, particularly at the elementary school level. Oak Park's two districts have maintained relatively integrated schools; this, together with the community's residential integration, makes Oak Park somewhat different from the other districts in this category, which exhibit high levels of white and minority segregation.

DISCUSSION AND IMPLICATIONS OF SUBURBAN RACIAL TRANSFORMATION

In most metropolitan areas, suburban students outnumber city students, often by considerable and increasing margins. Differences still persist across city-suburban lines in the share of poor students. Racial diversity in suburbia does not necessarily mean integration; similar to urban patterns, the trend is often toward resegregation, and this research indicates that such patterns are emerging. Such trends have major implications for the educational opportunity for students in our nation's largest metropolitan areas.

Just as the student enrollment has grown more diverse since the time that segregation was thought of as between whites and blacks to multiracial segregation between whites and nonwhites and among nonwhite students as well, so too have our metropolitan area districts grown more complex. Instead of considering districts as either city or suburb, it may be more appropriate demographically to think about—and develop policies cognizant of—city districts and an array of types of suburban districts. Even the suburban districts we studied that had high shares of white students had differing characteristics: some had little poverty and were exclusive while others located at a further distance from the central city had more mixed-income students. Immigration and racial transition closer to the city also affects the different types of districts found within the nation's largest metropolitan areas.

District-level segregation between suburban districts is high between certain racial pairs, and a disturbing trend is that as the number of Latino students in suburbia has grown, so too has their segregation from white students. While Latinos are present to a larger extent in growing districts—which also have a higher percentage of white students, suggesting a certain degree of white-Latino integration—whites are more likely to leave districts where the Latino population exists at even a small percent.[17] Yet the patterns of racial change and segregation vary for Latinos across the largest metropolitan areas, and these differences may be related to regional variation or national origin of Latino students.

Economic segregation at the district level was lower across the largest metropolitan areas, but more likely to be higher in metropolitan areas with more district fragmentation. District-level racial concentration revealed that, particularly in the Midwest, high percentages—the majority of suburban districts in some metropolitan areas—were unaffected by the changing racial patterns. On the other hand, in some of the areas studied, a tenth or more of suburban districts had very few white students, replicating patterns commonly thought of as urban. Many metropolitan areas had districts with 90–100 percent white as well as districts with 90–100 percent nonwhite enrollments. These district-level racial patterns will have a major impact on the extent of racial integration that is possible at the school level in these districts. Taken together, these segregation analyses illustrate the ways in which fragmentation can result in disparate racial and economic district enrollments within the suburban rings of metropolitan areas alone. As stated above, such segregation would likely be higher if urban districts were included.

Finally, this analysis has suggested one way of understanding the new suburban diversity by outlining a typology of suburban school districts. There are distinct clusters by district characteristics and notable patterns of school-level characteristics and segregation in these six types of suburban districts as well. Such a typology could help refine our understanding of distinct types of suburban districts, and as a result, more successfully design policy to fit these changing suburban districts. If these trends continue, patterns of separation and inequality found in many large urban districts will replicate on a larger geographical scale.

The remainder of this book examines these vital issues through in-depth case studies of seven suburban districts illustrative of several of the types of suburban districts. By identifying how metropolitan area schools are changing, where the growth of the nonwhite and low-income populations are concentrated, and how rapidly change is taking place, this book contributes to understanding the implications of demographic transformation on the schools. How suburban communities respond to increasing diversity in the schools has implications for the educational opportunities available to low-income and minority students and for the educational outcomes these students are likely to achieve.

3

Pursuing "Separate but Equal" in Suburban San Antonio

A Case Study of Southern Independent School District

JENNIFER JELLISON HOLME, ANJALÉ WELTON, AND SARAH DIEM

Southern Independent School District (ISD) is a large, racially diverse suburban district located in the San Antonio metropolitan area, one of the largest and fastest-growing metropolitan areas in Texas.[1] In the 2008–09 academic year, Southern ISD ranked as one of the largest districts in the state of Texas and among the hundred largest districts in the United States.[2]

The district has experienced explosive growth over the past decade. Between 2000 and 2010, overall student enrollment grew by 33 percent, with most of the gains among low-income and nonwhite students. During this period, Latino student enrollment grew by 31 percent, and the enrollment of students who are considered by the state to be "economically disadvantaged" grew by 58 percent. The enrollment of white students declined by 3 percent over this same period (see table 3.1 and exhibit 3.1).

In this chapter, we describe Southern ISD's history and the demographic changes that have occurred, and then examine how the district responded to the growing diversity. We illustrate how Southern adopted what could be characterized as a "separate but equal" response to demographic change: while the district devoted resources to an impressive array of instructional interventions designed to address the learning needs of students considered academically "at-risk," it took a laissez-faire approach toward the growing

TABLE 3.1

Southern ISD demographics, 2000–2010

	% OF ENROLLMENT			
Demographic group	1999–2000	2009–2010	Percentage change	Enrollment change
White	50.1%	36.8%	–13.3%	–2.8%
African American	9.5%	9.4%	–0.1%	30.7%
Latino	37.7%	49.4%	–11.7%	73.7%
Asian	2.4%	4.1%	1.7%	125.3%
Limited English Proficient	3.4%	8.3%	4.9%	225.7%
Economically disadvantaged	36.0%	42.8%	6.8%	57.8%

Source: Texas Education Agency, Academic Excellence Indicator System, 2011.

problem of segregation, even enacting some policies (particularly school choice policies and school boundary changes) that exacerbated levels of segregation between schools.[3] The district did engage in efforts to address cultural difference, but they were focused almost exclusively on administrators and did not consistently reach the campus level. As a result, the district's predominantly white teaching force was left with little consistent training about how to respond effectively to the rapidly shifting student demographics. While district leaders did attempt to ensure that the increasingly separate schools were equal with respect to resources and facilities, the district's ability to sustain the costs associated with such an approach remains in question as the state budget situation deteriorates.

For this case study, we drew on interviews with fifty-two individuals in a range of roles and positions: eleven district-level actors (administrators and school board members), six external actors (community members, city council members, and parent leaders), and nine school principals across a range of district schools (in terms of both diversity and school level). Because the case study was concerned with both district- and school-level responses, we selected three "focus" schools for more in-depth study, located in the area that was undergoing the most change at the time of data collection. We interviewed twenty-six educators (including principals and vice principals, teachers, and counselors) across these three focus schools.

EXHIBIT 3.1

Southern Independent School District

Percentage change of San Antonio suburban ring and Southern Independent School District

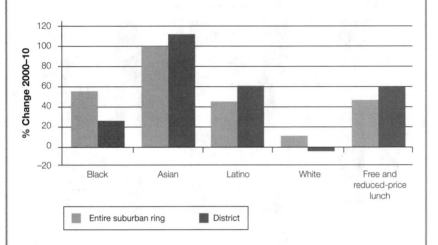

Racial and poverty composition of San Antonio metropolitan statistical area, Southern Independent School District, and district first grade, 2009–10

	% Black	% Asian	% Latino	% White	% English language learners	% Free and reduced- price lunch	Total enrollment
Total MSA	8.0	2.1	63.7	25.9	8.2	46.2	407,120
Principal cities	7.6	1.86	73.8	16.5	11.3	39.7	170,493
Suburbs	8.2	2.3	56.5	32.7	5.9	51.0	236,632
District	9.4	4.1	49.4	36.8	6.5	42.7	65,498
First grade	8.7	4.3	52.1	34.5	—	—	4,964

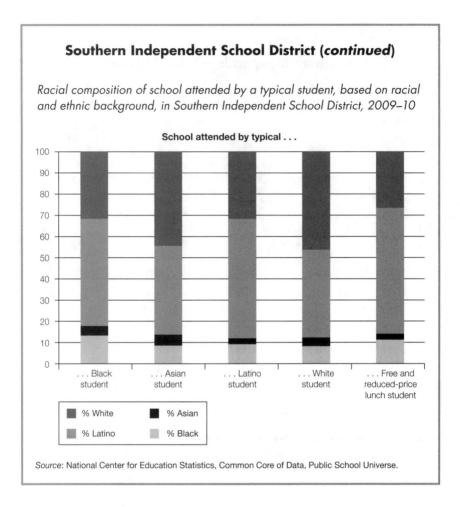

Southern Independent School District (continued)

Racial composition of school attended by a typical student, based on racial and ethnic background, in Southern Independent School District, 2009–10

School attended by typical . . .

| | . . . Black student | . . . Asian student | . . . Latino student | . . . White student | . . . Free and reduced-price lunch student |

Legend:
- % White
- % Asian
- % Latino
- % Black

Source: National Center for Education Statistics, Common Core of Data, Public School Universe.

DEMOGRAPHIC CHANGE IN SOUTHERN ISD

Southern ISD was formed in the mid-twentieth century as a rural school district outside the city of San Antonio. In the 1960s and 1970s, as the San Antonio metropolitan area grew, the city's population growth began to spill over into what was becoming suburban Southern ISD. The bulk of the growth during this period occurred between the boundary of the central city school district (San Antonio ISD) to the north, and Southern ISD's major east-west freeway, Loop 110 to the south.

In the 1980s and 1990s, as the MSA population expanded further, Southern ISD's growth exploded, fueled by both push factors (growing poverty in the central city district, San Antonio ISD) and pull factors (newer suburban housing).[4] During this period, the district population expanded further south, and the city's premier high schools were those that were "south of the Loop." Reflecting the affluence in this area at the time, the football game between Southern ISD's elite high school within this area, McKinley High School, and another area, elite school was dubbed "the Gucci Bowl."

Between 2000 and 2010, the San Antonio MSA expanded from 1.7 to 2.1 million people.[5] Accordingly, Southern ISD's population pushed further south, past a new social class and racial line: Loop 810. Today the district's most affluent families have moved south of Loop 810, and this is where newer housing and schools are currently being constructed.

Today, the district is composed of roughly three sections or "zones," illustrated in figure 3.1 (and described in table 3.2), using high schools as a means of defining each zone. The northern portion of the district, Zone 1, is closest to the central city and is what could be considered an "at-risk segregated suburb" with large numbers of low-income Latinos and African Americans migrating south.[6] Many of these families are fleeing the deteriorating central city schools.

The middle section of the district, Zone 2, located further south between Loops 110 and 810, is composed of "at-risk older suburbs."[7] Zone 2 is currently experiencing the most rapid demographic change in its schools; however, neighborhoods in this zone are changing less rapidly because many

FIGURE 3.1

Suburban typologies within Southern ISD

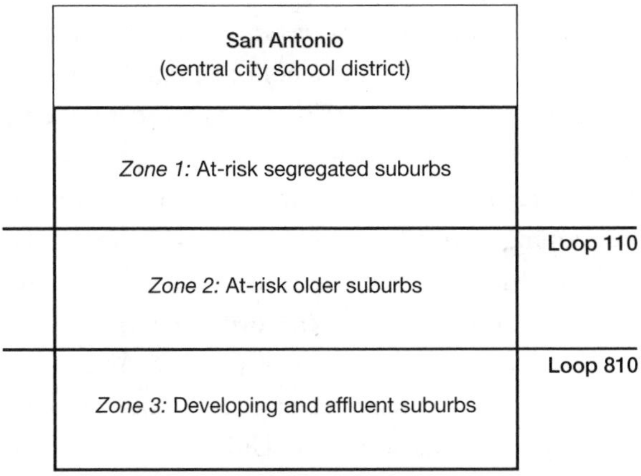

San Antonio
(central city school district)

Zone 1: At-risk segregated suburbs

Loop 110

Zone 2: At-risk older suburbs

Loop 810

Zone 3: Developing and affluent suburbs

TABLE 3.2

Southern ISD: Shifting demographic zones, 2009–2010

	White	Latino	African American	Economically disadvantaged	Limited English Proficient
Zone 1					
Wilson HS	19.9%	51.0%	24.3%	61.7%	4.5%
Jackson HS	13.9%	78.8%	5.8%	63.2%	7.0%
Average	17.2%	63.4%	13.8%	62.3%	5.7%
Zone 2					
Coolidge HS	43.1%	42.3%	10.7%	34.7%	2.8%
Warren HS	38.9%	46.5%	11.1%	37.9%	1.6%
McKinley HS	52.7%	39.3%	5.1%	23.4%	1.8%
Average	44.7%	42.9%	9.0%	32.2%	2.0%
Zone 3					
Ford HS	56.6%	30.2%	5.0%	10.2%	1.6%
Carter HS	54.2%	32.7%	6.3%	10.2%	1.6%
Average	55.5%	31.4%	5.6%	10.2%	1.6%

Source: Texas Education Agency, Academic Excellence Indicator System, 2011.

neighborhoods consist of aging residents who no longer have children in schools. The newcomers to schools in Zone 2 live primarily in the many apartment buildings that sprang up within this zone in the 1980s and 1990s. Many white parents here, according to top-level administrators in the district, have elected to send their children to several of the nearby private schools rather than the more racially diverse neighborhood schools. A teacher in our focus high school in this zone, Coolidge High School, told us: "As everyone moves further south, Coolidge is seen as more inner city even though it hasn't moved; but the city has moved."[8]

The far south part of the district, Zone 3, consists of what could be considered as "developing and affluent suburbs," with an upper-middle-class population and the district's most "elite" schools. While these schools have become significantly more racially diverse over the past decade, they are still majority white and have very low levels of poverty. As table 3.2 illustrates, segregation in these schools is relatively higher by income than race, reflecting larger demographic trends across the United States that show the growing isolation of low income from the affluent families.[9]

These demographic shifts across the three zones have resulted in significant changes in overall district enrollment (refer back to table 3.1 and exhibit 3.1). Over the course of ten years (between 1999–2000 and 2009–10), the white proportion of the population has declined by 13 percentage points, the proportion of Latino students has grown by 12 percentage points, and the number of Limited English Proficient students has doubled. As one of the district's administrators noted of these changes: "If you look at the growth of the experience throughout that twenty-plus year period, essentially all of the growth has been minority. The total number of Anglo students is almost unchanged over twenty-five years."[10]

UNDERSTANDING SOUTHERN ISD'S RESPONSE
TO DEMOGRAPHIC CHANGE

In the following discussion, we examine how Southern ISD has responded to these rapid demographic changes. We show that while the district adopted an impressive array of instructional interventions for its growing population of low-income students, it has left the high levels of segregation within the district unaddressed. We conclude by describing the district's efforts to create equity between its increasingly separate schools.

Instructional Supports and a Focus on Accountability

Southern ISD has in many ways responded proactively to its increasingly diverse student population. The district has a strong commitment to decentralized decision making and local capacity building, and it has marshaled its strong local tax base, as well as state and federal funds, to hire support staff and provide professional development training. These supports for schools, as we will illustrate, were adopted in large part as a response to the growing pressures of the state and federal accountability systems.

One of the core capacity-building initiatives within the district has been the provision of instructional specialists who provide support and mentoring to teachers. As one central office administrator notes, these specialists are "out on the campuses every day and they are working with teachers. They are working with students. They are role modeling. They are doing staff development after hours. They are in my opinion the meat and potatoes of what we're doing to impact instruction."[11] While most elementary and middle schools share specialists, all Title 1 elementary schools have specialists who are housed at that campus and who serve on the campus leadership team.

These specialists take some responsibilities off principals and teachers. The principal of Mission Elementary notes: "They've provided us with not just opportunities to get more text or activities and include those into our lessons, in our planning, they also are helping us with disaggregating data so that we can look at the data a lot more carefully . . . They'll provide us with spreadsheets and help us figure out who needs the most support . . . whereas in the past we would rely on the district, and sometimes we couldn't get somebody out as quickly."[12] At the high school level, the district used a special allotment of funding from the state for high schools to hire "academic deans" who are in charge of the core administrative areas and who provide types of support similar to that provided by the instructional specialists on primary campuses. Overall, each of the principals was positive about the support they received from the central office. As one principal noted, "The district is fabulous about, 'What do you need, how can we get it for you?'"[13]

While the district has given a great deal of autonomy to local campuses in terms of curriculum and instruction, at the time we were collecting data the central office had held a large training for all the teachers and administrators on "differentiated instruction"—a key term that we heard many interviewees use, including external actors. Differentiated instruction involves offering instruction in multiple learning modalities to serve the multiple student learning needs at each campus.[14] Principals and teachers viewed it as a way to address the needs of the increasingly diverse population. As the principal of Mission Elementary noted: "As our classrooms are getting more and more diverse, you can't teach one way and hold kids to that same standard . . . [So you look at differentiated instruction] so you can meet the needs of all those kids . . . As we're working more and more into inclusion, we don't section kids out and group them like we used to in the olden days, and so if you're not a master in [differentiated instruction], you're way behind the curve already."[15] A principal at a middle school agreed that differentiated instruction is being pushed heavily by the district because of the changing population. He also added that its purpose should be to meet the different needs of each student, regardless of the student's background: "I think the biggest movement we have is differentiated instruction. [It's really] very timely and very appropriate to what's going on . . . But it really is effective in terms of looking at our kids because differentiated instruction talks about what do [you do] with those kids' needs in that classroom and how do you meet a whole range of abilities and levels . . . Not everybody can sit still, look straight forward with their feet on the floor, and listen for an hour. It just doesn't happen."[16]

The district has also provided teachers with professional development to meet the needs of its second language learners, requiring all teachers to receive training in Sheltered Instruction Observation Protocol (SIOP). As a district administrator describes SIOP:

> [It's] a framework for teachers to use in scaffolding their instruction with the ELL students. It allows them to tap into the student's background knowledge, as opposed to teaching everybody the same when they walk in. It allows them to post not only the content objective for the day but . . . post a language objective for the day. So it has really opened up the eyes of the teachers to what some of these students are going through. And we've had an initiative now for two years that ends this coming August where we have trained every . . . professional employee in the district in SIOP for a three-day training, and then [for] any new people coming in we give them two years to get the training done.[17]

Another goal of the SIOP training is to build capacity among all teachers at the campus level so that ELL specialists and content-specific specialists can work together in the language development of ELL students. Schools have also been strategic in hiring and placing English as a Second Language (ESL) teachers: one of our case-study schools, Alamo Elementary, had hired one ESL-certified teacher at every grade level.

These strong professional development efforts and instructional supports were motivated by both the changing demographics in the district and the pressure of the state and federal accountability systems, which hold the district responsible for meeting the needs of the growing nonwhite and low-income student populations. As one of the more respected school districts in the metropolitan area, Southern ISD is expected by both the community and parents to perform consistently well—that it will have high numbers of schools reaching "recognized" or "exemplary" status—which places a great deal of pressure on the entire district. Changing demographics have served to increase this pressure.

To meet state and federal accountability targets, district and campus leaders have emphasized the need to focus on specific subpopulations within each campus (referred to as "sub-pops") to be sure that each subgroup that counts for accountability purposes gets adequate instructional attention. However, such a conceptualization can lead educators to frame diversity as a challenge to be addressed. One high school principal, for example, reflected on the importance of attending to the needs of all students within a subpopulation in the accountability rankings. He recalled a time when he and his assistant principal were reviewing the school's scores and realized that: "Oh, my God, we were two African American students in math [away] from being low performing. And what would the news [media] say? '[Our] high school, the only low-performing school in San Antonio, Texas,' right?" [I asked my assistant principal] "Well . . . how many kids were we from being recognized [in the accountability rankings]? Twenty-two kids.' And it's the African American population. If you have such a small number that are testing—just enough for them to count—*it can either kill you or make you* [emphasis added]."

This principal and his assistant principal responded by seeking out and identifying each individual student that had not met the threshold for passing: "One of the things we did, which has been real key, is we ask . . . who are those two kids, give me their names, who are their teachers, what are they in? [And] those twenty-two kids—what are their names, what are they taking, what's their background? [Let's] get really strategic."[18]

We also saw this intensive individual-level approach at several high-poverty schools in the district. In one elementary school, for example, we were shown a system of color-coded cards that represented every child in the school and contained information about whether or not each student had met a particular testing benchmark that counted for accountability rankings (math, English Language Arts, or science) or how far away that student was from reaching the benchmark. As the principal of another middle school told us, the accountability system made them pay close attention to every "subpopulation" that counts for accountability (ELL, low income, etc.). She reflected that they can't ignore any of the subpopulations: "There aren't any sub-pops that are free rein; everybody counts, everything matters, every student matters."[19]

The district holds schools accountable for their subpopulations through "data coaching" meetings between campus leaders and the district's top administrators. In these meetings, local administrators break down their data and indicate progress for each group that counts for accountability purposes. These efforts are not solely in the interest of addressing the achievement gap between students of color and their peers, but also by the need to receive the recognition of "exemplary" status and thus avoid surveillance of the district.[20] The principal of a predominantly nonwhite, low-income middle school reflected on the challenge faced by a school with such demographics: "Compared to my colleagues in other schools, we've just got our work cut out . . . It is stressful. I wear it pretty heavily . . . we're tackling it, we're facing it, we're trying to figure it out, but I don't have the magic formula. I wish I did."[21] This school and other high-poverty nonwhite schools may have a more difficult time meeting accountability mandates as the proportion of low-income students increases. The level of segregation in those campuses is worsening, in part as a result of school district policies.

Unaddressed Segregation within the District

As Southern ISD has grown more diverse, many of its schools have become increasingly segregated. As table 3.3 illustrates, the proportion of schools with 70–100 percent nonwhite enrollment (African American, Latino, and the district's small proportion of Asian students) has increased over the past ten years, from fourteen schools in 1999–2000 (22 percent of schools) to twenty-nine schools in 2009–10 (45 percent of schools.) At the same time, the proportion of schools that are largely white has declined significantly: from twelve schools in 1999–2000 to one school in 2009–10.

Poverty concentration has also grown within the district (see table 3.4), although not quite as dramatically: the number of schools with 70–100 percent of students receiving free and reduced-price lunch grew by just three schools between 1999–2000 and 2009–10 (from 25 percent to 30 percent of schools.) The number of low-poverty schools, however (less than 30 percent of students in poverty) declined more significantly in that period, from twenty-five (39 percent of schools) to eighteen schools (28 percent of schools).

TABLE 3.3

Racial concentration in Southern ISD schools

% nonwhite students (African American, Latino, and Asian)	1999–2000		2009–10	
	Number of schools	%	Number of schools	%
90–100	1	2%	7	11%
70–90	13	20%	22	34%
50–70	18	28%	19	30%
30–50	20	31%	15	23%
0–30	12	19%	1	2%
Total	64	100%	64	100%

Source: Texas Education Agency, Academic Excellence Indicator System, 2011.

TABLE 3.4

Poverty concentration in Southern ISD schools

% low–income students (FRL*)	1999–2000		2009–10	
	Number of schools	%	Number of schools	%
90–100%	0	0	3	5%
70–90	16	25%	16	25%
50–70	7	11%	13	20%
30–50	16	25%	14	22%
0–30	25	39%	18	28%
Total	64	100%	64	100%

Source: Texas Education Agency, Academic Excellence Indicator System, 2011
*Free and reduced-price lunch.

The growing racial isolation and high levels of poverty concentration within the district's schools, however, has been largely unaddressed by central office leaders. This is in part because the declining proportion of whites and high levels of poverty make it difficult to create racial and social-class diversity within many schools in the district, and in part because tackling such issues is perceived to be politically risky.

The political volatility surrounding segregation is most clearly evident in debates about school attendance boundaries. These boundaries initially became the subject of debate when, as the district grew outward in Zone 3 (see table 3.2), a new high school was constructed in that area of the district to accommodate growth. When the new high school opened, the district had to redraw attendance boundaries in the middle part of the district (Zone 2) that had been undergoing the most rapid demographic change. In the original boundary proposal, the east-west Loop 810 served as the boundary that separated the neighborhoods in Zone 2 from schools in Zone 3. The more affluent parents within Zone 2, however, put pressure on the school district and board to zone them into the more affluent Zone 3 and into the new higher-income high school. As a school board member noted, there are steep political costs for going against the wishes of those parents:

> I think that if you had it to do all over, if you started a school district and all your schools were on the ground that are there today, you would never draw the lines the way they have been drawn . . . If you looked at a map of

our school districts, the lines are really catawampus, they're crazy, but you can't touch those boundaries . . . and survive politically . . . Those are hard-fought battles and they pit neighborhoods and have and have-nots [against each other]; whether it is really that way or not, that's the way they perceive it, and so those are pretty intense battles.[22]

Another district administrator noted: "We recognize that when we're talking about changing attendance boundaries, we're messing with people's two most important assets—we're messing with their house and with their kids. It's going to be an emotional topic."[23] We also heard of zoning irregularities at the elementary level; several campus-level administrators told us about an instance in which a more affluent school was kept under-enrolled while the immediately adjacent high-poverty school was so overcrowded it was using portable facilities.

While the boundary decisions have aggravated segregation by race and social class, the district has also adopted several school choice policies that have had a similar effect, according to the people we interviewed. One such policy, "School of Choice," allows students to opt out of their home school into schools with available space. Parents are required to provide their own transportation under this policy. Data we received from the district show that participation rates are reflective of overall district enrollment by race and social class. However, we heard from a number of interviewees at different campuses (administrators, teachers, and parents) that while participation rates may reflect district composition at the aggregate, this choice policy has led to further segregation by race and class between schools, particularly schools undergoing rapid demographic shifts. For example, the Parent Teacher Association president of Mission Elementary (a school that has changed from 52 percent white to 29 percent white in just ten years) told us that as the school grew in diversity, many white and middle-class parents either moved out of the area to the newer homes in neighborhoods with more affluent schools or took advantage of open choice to transfer their children to a different school. She observed that much of this flight was in response to the Title 1 designation the school received recently:

> *Respondent:* Most of those people that have changed schools or [who are] wanting to change schools were not here long enough to really feel that this [Title 1 designation] is a good thing . . . I think just the wording of it—Title I—scared them [so] that they needed to move out of that area.

Interviewer: So they literally bought a home in a different area?

Respondent: Or they have done School of Choice. I know they pretty much can't sell their homes right now but I know that some of them have . . . changed [schools] with School of Choice. And . . . all of them said it's not anything to do with a bad experience as far as [teachers] or anything but demographics.[24]

According to our interviewees, middle-class families have used the School of Choice policy to flee high schools with growing diversity as well. The principal of McKinley High—a Zone 2 high school that is undergoing some demographic change but that is still predominantly white—observed that he receives transfer requests from the upper-middle-class families who live in the boundaries of Jackson High, the racially segregated high school in Zone 1: "Our neighboring school to the north is Jackson High School, predominantly Hispanic, and there are zones within Jackson High School's boundary that are upper-middle-class. Those families will tend to School Choice to us. Do we have some families that School Choice to the [more affluent high school in Zone 3] further south? Sure. We would probably have more if it weren't for the poor traffic problems in the far south."[25]

According to our interviewees, the School of Choice policy stratifies not only by race and class but also by achievement. The principal of the above-mentioned high-poverty, segregated Jackson High noted that many of his highest-performing students of color "choice out" of his school for a school that is perceived to be higher performing or are engaged in other school activities. He notes:

We lose a lot of good kids to McKinley High School, a lot; probably about over two hundred in the four grade levels. As a matter of fact, of their fourteen national Hispanic scholars, I think four of them should have been coming to Jackson High. [On the] boy's basketball team, they have a starting kid that should be going to Jackson High. The girls' basketball team has three girls that should be going to Jackson High. It's significant. Their band at McKinley High School probably has about twenty-five kids that should be going to Jackson High School.[26]

In addition to the choice policies, the district has established magnet schools as a way to manage declining enrollment in schools toward the northern area of the district. None of these magnets were specifically designed around the issue of race; they were created with the expressed goal of increasing enrollment in schools that were losing students. As one administrator noted, "One of the ways that we have attempted to keep enrollment at some of the more inner or northern campuses is by instituting magnet programs that draw kids from other schools."[27]

Because racial diversity is not a goal of the magnet programs, they have no racial balance guidelines and receive no federal magnet school funding. The schools are open to all students in the district, and admission is through either lottery or an application process, depending on the goal of the school. Students must, however, provide their own transportation. According to the campus principals we interviewed, magnet schools tend to recruit more middle-class and white students and thus have a less diverse and more advantaged population than the "regular schools" in which they are housed.

The district's first foray into magnet schools involved the establishment of a program that was separate and obtained its own state identifier code, which essentially separated the magnet students for reporting and accountability purposes. The district administration soon realized this "mistake" in terms of accountability rankings because the separate code meant that the magnet kids could not improve the overall school accountability rankings by lifting up the scores of the nonmagnet students. The administration therefore resolved that any future magnets be established as a "school within a school" program rather than a separate school (or "code"), even though most of the magnet programs are effectively separate.

The district-level people interviewed framed the magnets as an effective way to increase campus-level diversity and as a means to entice people to schools that they would never have attended through zoning or mandatory assignment. As one district-level administrator observed: "Had [we] tried to zone those families to the north, it never would have happened; but by giving them elective programs of choice they've come [to the north] freely and enthusiastically . . . [t]he whole idea of choice, small learning communities, has been a very effective way of diversifying schools and giving . . . our population a choice between a big comprehensive school and a smaller school."[28]

While central office administrators admit that the magnets are less diverse (more white) than the regular schools, it is difficult to say just how diverse these schools are because their data is merged with the regular schools when the data is reported to the state.

Responding to Cultural Difference: Uneven Training and Limited Reach

While central office officials left the growing racial isolation within the district largely unaddressed, district leaders did attempt to make educators within the (separate) schools more culturally responsive by instituting diversity training at the district level.[29] The issue of teachers' cultural awareness is particularly salient in this district, which has a teaching staff that is 73 percent white (see table 3.5), compared with an overall district student population that is just 37 percent white. While the district has made an effort to hire teachers who are more reflective of the student population, one administrator told us that that it was difficult to recruit teachers of color to the district because of the outdated perception of the district as predominantly white. The administrator notes: "We have a better demographic spread among our administrators than we do our teachers . . . Our recruiting has been very strong in terms of trying to get people of color to come to our school system and to realize it is a minority-majority school district."[30]

While the district did provide diversity training for its central office leaders and campus principals, the district's decentralized decision-making structure meant that local campus leaders were left in charge of implementing appropriate training for their own campuses. The primary training the district provided to the principals was a professional development program, Difficult Dialogues, that is designed to help campuses engage in constructive dialogue about difficult issues such as race, social class, and gender. The district also brought a nationally respected scholar to the district to talk to central office leaders about race and the achievement gap.

TABLE 3.5

Teacher ethnicity in Southern ISD

| | 1998–99 | | 2003–04 | | 2008–09 | | PERCENTAGE CHANGE | |
	District	State	District	State	District	State	District	State
Black	1.6%	8.3%	2.2%	8.9%	2.9%	9.7%	81.3%	16.9%
Latino	12.9%	16.3%	18.5%	19.5%	23.3%	22.1%	80.6%	35.6%
White	84.7%	74.6%	78.4%	70.3%	72.7%	66.7%	14.2%	10.6%
Asian	0.5%	0.6%	0.6%	1.0%	0.9%	1.3%	80.0%	116.0%

Source: Texas Education Agency, Academic Excellence Indicator System, 2010.

As one administrator told us, conversations about race are occurring at the central office level: "We talk about teaching diverse students, we talk about cultural proficiency. We've been to professional development workshops, conferences. So the leadership team has done a good job of trying to absorb information and knowledge and what's out there. So from that we . . . did several book studies based about race. We've called it our 'courageous conversations' about race."[31]

Yet because the district gives a great deal of autonomy to local administrators, this type of diversity training was not implemented consistently at local campuses. While several teachers we interviewed mentioned participating in "book studies" related to diversity at some point in their time in the district, many reported that such studies were not necessarily being conducted at their current school and/or with their current principal. One longtime teacher at Mission Elementary, for example, told us that he had done a book study with that school's previous principal, who had left more than seven years before our interview: "With the previous principal . . . we've done book studies that help us understand cultural diversities and struggles that single-parent families go through, and try to get us to understand that it's not that people don't want their kids to succeed; it's that they are in a bind and they don't have the time because they're working many jobs, because they just don't know how. So it's just awareness of how the cultural differences are between people that have and people that don't have."[32]

According to another teacher at one of the high schools, the only training she received (which was itself not helpful) was in college: "[In this district] there isn't any, in the basics. Even in my undergrad stuff it was like—well, the African American children won't look you in the eye; the Latino children, they go through these little physical cueing things—but at least it was better than nothing . . . There were a lot of overgeneralizations and whatnot, but as far as the district addressing this, absolutely not—no."[33]

One central office administrator observed that it was difficult to translate the training for leadership to the campus level, noting that with respect to districtwide discussions of race:

> We are stuck. And part of that is because as we went through the [Difficult Dialogues] training, I don't think that the district or some of the people who were leading in the conversations were as prepared emotionally for the fallout . . . It's really hard to have a conversation about race in general, and it's much more difficult when you're talking about teaching because that is

personal. And so it was difficult for us at this level until what we realized was, if it was difficult for us at this level, how do we take that out to the schools and [be] able to do it so there is not a much larger fallout from the process?[34]

This person further observes that part of the problem is that central office administrators are not a diverse group, and as a result many administrators and teachers in the district "aren't convinced that it's an issue of race, and they really believe that good teaching will be enough [that] if you just get the teachers in there then all of the problems with the achievement gap will cease. It's really been a difficult conversation for me and others [to] understand that it is about context . . . sometimes racism isn't purposeful, and it isn't done intending to harm, it's done with the best of motives and it's done out of love, but it's from our context and it's from how we were raised, and who we are, and our beliefs and things."[35]

At the campus level, we heard several teachers mention that they had participated in Ruby Payne professional development sessions, based on Payne's book *A Framework for Understanding Poverty*.[36] This book, which is commonly used in districts in Texas as a basis for professional development, has been criticized for presenting a deficit perspective of low-income students, focusing on the "lack" of certain skills that low-income students bring with them to school.[37] The principal of one of our focus high schools, Coolidge High School, mentioned that he was going to incorporate Payne's framework in the professional development training he was holding for teachers that week. We also heard many teachers reference aspects of Payne's trainings in their discussions with us.

Other principals of predominantly non-white, low-income schools made other efforts to help their teaching staff better understand the communities they served. As one principal told us: "At one point after [the] Ruby Payne [training] we actually put our teachers on buses and drove them through some of those areas where their kids are coming from."[38] This effort to drive through the neighborhood, though well-intentioned, provided teachers with little if any face-to-face interaction with community members, and thus limited genuine understanding of the community itself.[39]

One program that has been adopted by many campuses in response to the growing proportion of low-income students is Positive Behavior Supports (PBS), a behavior management system intended to prevent discipline problems by establishing clear expectations and providing effective interventions with students.[40] As a middle school principal described it: "The main thing is that you set your expectations—tell the kids what you expect them to do because you can't discipline them for what they didn't know they were supposed to do. And then make sure they know what they are allowed to do during different activities . . . What's the outcome, what should you be doing?"[41]

The goal of the program is to create a supportive school culture and reduce serious discipline problems and disciplinary actions that are exclusionary.[42] Additionally, we heard several teachers frame the discipline system as a way to make up for deficits in students' home environments. For example, a counselor at Coolidge noted that the PBS program helps them "make up for what the parents aren't doing":

> [It] seems like we have more kids that come to school without having the skills of what's expected of them. And we have to continually teach them . . . "You don't act like that." [The] small portion of kids . . . that cause us the most discipline problems are the ones who have not been taught to value their education. And that is the big link that is very hard for educators to fill because when they come to us at age fourteen and fifteen and they don't value their education . . . Definitely, as the demographics have changed, I will say that the teachers and the staff had to make up that difference, and you all have probably seen this everywhere you went, that we have to make up for what the parents aren't doing. And if you don't do that, you won't be successful as a school.[43]

The deficit perspective of students reflects the lack of a strong diversity training program across the district, which has left teachers on some campuses without the tools to either understand students' home backgrounds or to respond in a culturally relevant way to the changing population at their school.

The district has made an effort to enhance within-school equity for students by adopting the Advancement Via Individual Determination (AVID) program as a tool to open up Advanced Placement (AP) and honors courses to more low-income students and students of color.[44] The program was adopted in 2006, approximately four years before our visit to the district, and we were told that the process of enrolling students in AVID has been relatively slow. One principal stated that this lack of progress stems from the challenge of changing teacher beliefs about students' ability to do more advanced work. Her school is largely nonwhite, but draws white and more affluent students into the campus through a magnet program—and it is the affluent white students who comprise the majority of the AP students. This principal reflected: "Our Advanced Placement program is well below where it should be. I think we have relied too much on certain groups of kids, and my challenge to the teachers is to identify the regular [nonmagnet] student . . . you can't tell me out of two thousand kids, you can't find two hundred of them that can achieve at the AP level . . . I think people have just let it slip. You know the answer is—'Well, they can't do it.' What do you mean, they can't do it? Everybody can do it."[45]

A central office administrator also told us that one of the biggest challenges with the AVID program has been changing the attitudes of teachers in the district who have been reluctant to open up classes to a different demographic of students and to instill in students a belief that they belong: "It's one thing to put students in a more challenging process; it's a whole other thing to prepare them academically, emotionally—to make them believe that they fit there and they belong there. Because I'm sure, as you know, there is huge pushback from teachers when that happens. So we did that immediately and it's taken; and we're still working on that time to really create . . . what I call the mind shift and how we view . . . who are the kids [who are] actually worthy."[46]

In sum, while the district did initiate efforts to create more equitable and culturally responsive learning environments in its schools, the policies were not always translated down to the local level. As a result, teachers on a number of campuses we visited were given little culturally relevant professional development about the growing proportion of nonwhite students they were teaching.

Making Separate "Equal": Resource Equalization

Although the issue of segregation was perceived as too politically sensitive for district leaders to address, the district did attempt to make the increasingly separate schools more "equal" by adopting a resource equalization policy aimed at modernizing the older school facilities, which primarily served nonwhite populations. The focus on resource equity was prompted in large part by a court ruling that changed how school board members were elected.

In the mid-1990s, the district was sued by a local civil rights organization, which charged that nonwhites were underrepresented on the board as a result of the at-large election system. The court ruled in favor of the plaintiffs, ordering a change in elections from at-large to single-member districts. According to the superintendent, this shift led to greater geographic representation on the board, which in turn resulted in a stronger commitment by the district and the school board to equitably distribute resources across the district. As a district-level administrator noted of the lawsuit: "Of all things it was the best thing that ever happened to the district . . . because it made us focus on every area and so we were able then with seven single-member districts to put in an equity plan, like let's say for our bond issues. We put in a billion dollars' worth of bonds and over half of it is really focused on existing schools."[47]

One of the board members who was elected in the shift to the single-member districts says that this resource equalization for the older schools was something that he personally advocated for:

> What I have tried to keep an eye on as a school board member is . . . that we continue to have the resources and keep our school buildings in the older part of the district renovated and actually keep them up-to-date as well as the new ones that we are building in the new areas. Because as the district grows south . . . we have a lot of unpopulated areas in our district south and they are developing new subdivisions out there and then we have to build brand new schools. So one of my focuses has been to try to make sure the district continues with resources in the old part of the district so the facilities would be just as modern and up-to-date as the brand-new schools.[48]

The attention to equity has resulted in a significant rebuilding of many of the older campuses alongside the new construction in the south. As an educator at one of the district's older high schools noted:

> Every time we go out with a bond issue, we have to have new schools typically down south, but at the same time we're going to spend an equal amount of money on the schools that are older and renovating those schools. It's the equity issue. So you can go inside the inner loop, and you'll find schools that are forty and fifty years old that are brand-new. Three-quarters of this school, which is now forty-plus years old, is brand new. This school has more new facilities than Ford High School does now, so that's one of the ways they—back to one of the questions you asked earlier: "How does the school district address that change?" [We make] sure we have equity throughout the district.[49]

We observed the effects of this rebuilding, finding that many campuses in the high-poverty communities were totally renovated. This "separate but equal" strategy was, however, made politically possible only by the court ruling on school board elections.

THE FUTURE OF SOUTHERN ISD

Southern ISD has responded, in many ways, quite positively to its increasingly diverse student population. District-level administrators have been committed to decentralized decision making and local capacity building. They have provided intensive instructional supports to its campuses and have trained teachers in differentiated instruction and meeting the needs of ELLs. Much of this response was driven by state accountability requirements and the desire to keep all Southern campuses designated with the state's highest accountability labels—either "recognized" or "exemplary" (the highest).

While the district has responded proactively to its increasingly diverse population in terms of instruction and interventions, it has been less successful in providing effective culturally relevant professional development to the teachers. This lack of strong diversity training has meant that local campuses, largely staffed by white administrators and teachers, are left to their own devices to institute training or programs to address racial diversity; as a result, at a number of campuses, efforts are weak to nonexistent.

We also found that the district has shied away from addressing within-district racial isolation, a problem that is growing worse in the schools in the north. Instead, the district has adopted student assignment policies that cater to the more vocal upper-middle-class and white families in the southern area who have pressured the district to enact policies that preserve their separateness. The district has also enacted school choice policies that allow middle-class families to flee schools in areas of growing poverty.

Southern ISD has, however, attempted to make the separate schools somewhat equal by using its wealthy tax base to raise bond revenues to renovate and modernize the older schools in the predominantly nonwhite areas of the district. In the short term, this "separate but equal" approach appears to have been the least controversial politically among the voters in the district, who are still majority white.[50] In the long run, however, it may be difficult for the district to sustain this resource-intensive approach. Last year, it was forced to reduce expenditures by more than $60 million when the state legislature failed to allocate promised funding to districts. These cuts will force the district to reduce the additional resources that it has in the past been able to redirect to campuses. This in turn may hinder its ability to maintain high accountability rankings, potentially causing middle-class families who seek out districts with highly ranked schools to reconsider whether to stay in the district. The district may also be forced to rely more on Title 1 funding, which brings with it tough accountability targets, including subgroups accountability that is not included in the state system (ELLs and special education students). Growing racial segregation within the schools in the north will likely make it harder for the district to attain the accountability rankings expected by the community.

There are several potential steps the district could take to address these issues. One important strategy would be to adopt a school choice policy and/or a student assignment policy explicitly designed to foster more diversity across schools in the district by race and/or income. Such a policy may help to stabilize the rapidly resegregating schools in Zone 2 by stemming white and middle-class flight southward, and may also help to deconcentrate poverty in the district's most impacted schools.

To improve how it serves its increasing proportion of nonwhite students, Southern ISD should adopt policies aimed at ensuring that local campuses become more culturally responsive to their changing student population. This would include stronger efforts to recruit and hire teachers with diverse backgrounds and the adoption of more consistent and relevant diversity-related professional development directly to local campuses.

Finally, this case study indicates a need for the district to incorporate more diverse perspectives in decision making at the central office and campus levels. One potential strategy would be to intensify efforts to bring more administrators of color into the key administrative positions. The district also needs to establish more formal channels of communication with communities of color within the district, to ensure that decisions at the district and campus level are more representative of the needs and concerns of all of Southern ISD's increasingly diverse constituencies.

4

Holding the Borderline

School District Responsiveness to Demographic Change in Orange County, California

LORRIE FRASURE-YOKLEY

Orange County, California, is known for its history of political conservatism, affluent coastal beach communities, and its tourist attractions, such as Disneyland. During the last decade, the county became famous, or rather infamous, for the profligate lifestyles portrayed in the popular television series *The Real Housewives of Orange County*, *The O.C.*, and *Laguna Beach*, featuring predominantly white, upper-income suburbanites. However, these depictions of a county deeply segregated by race, ethnicity, and class are far removed from the reality of the internal and external pressures facing this majority-minority county, particularly its public school system.

This case study examines how an Orange County public school district, Azalea Unified (a pseudonym), conceptualized and responded to an increase in low-income, minority, and recently arrived immigrant students; internal pressures related to the collapse of the housing and job markets and nearly $40 million in districtwide budget cuts in less than a decade; and the external pressures of several state and federal mandates.[1] Using data from thirty-four face-to-face, in-depth interviews with county, district, and school officials, as well as U.S. Census and California Department of Education (DataQuest) data, this chapter argues that despite some of its efforts, the combination of fiscal crisis and state and federal mandates made it more difficult for Azalea Unified to respond to demographic change and to adequately address the needs of an increasingly racially/ethnically and economically diverse student population.[2]

The chapter begins with a brief overview of the development of post–World War II Orange County and the state and federal mandates affecting public school education in the county. It then examines the community demographics of the Azalea Unified School District compared with those of Orange County as a whole, and discusses how the community conceptualized demographic changes in the student population in recent years. It next explores how fiscal crisis, coupled with state and federal mandates, influenced how Azalea Unified responded to the needs of an increasingly diverse student population as the district transitioned to majority-minority status in the last few years and also examines the extent to which these actions sought to confront the long-standing racial imbalance in the schools and to create greater opportunities for its minority and low-income students. It concludes with the finding that while some policies, such as targeted magnet programs, *indirectly* addressed racial/ethnic and class concentration and modestly increased diversity and greater opportunities for students in some schools, none of these policy shifts made a significant impact on racial integration in the Azalea Unified school district, which remains largely stratified by race and class.

POST–WORLD WAR II ORANGE COUNTY AND PUBLIC EDUCATION

During the post–World War II era, Orange County experienced vast economic growth as a result of aerospace and manufacturing moves to the region. Specifically, the county benefited from federal government subsidies and tax breaks that helped to create "military-related suburbs" whose postwar local economy was underpinned by the defense-related manufacturing sector.[3] The simultaneous growth in manufacturing and racially/ethnically restricted suburban housing developments produced a predominantly white-middle- to upper-class population in Orange County, a contrast to the more diverse (but still highly segregated) communities of neighboring Los Angeles County. Orange County attracted its "high-value residents" in part by boasting of safe and prosperous school districts with high test scores as well as high graduation and college admission rates. However, the spatial development of the county and subsequent racial and class segregation, largely between whites and Latinos, aided by restrictive covenants and exclusionary zoning laws, reinforced an ethos of privacy, individualism, gated communities, and private property rights.[4] Latino families, including generations working in the agricultural and citrus farming industries, have long resided in Orange County. By 1950 there

EXHIBIT 4.1

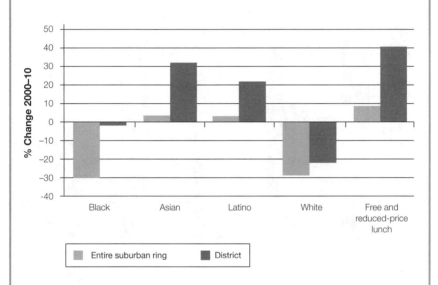

Azalea School District

Percentage change of Los Angeles suburban ring and Azalea Unified School District

Racial and poverty composition of Los Angeles metropolitan statistical area, Azalea Unified School District, and district first grade, 2009–10

	% Black	% Asian	% Latino	% White	% English language learners	% Free and reduced- price lunch	Total enrollment
Total MSA	7.5	10.0	59.4	20.3	29.7	59.7	2,908,252
Principal cities	8.3	9.3	63.7	16.6	32.1	65.3	1,608,368
Suburbs	6.4	10.9	54.1	24.9	26.8	52.8	1,299,884
District	1.7	12.0	35.5	48.6	20.4	29.4	25,920
First grade	1.4	14.2	42.7	37.9	—	—	1,835

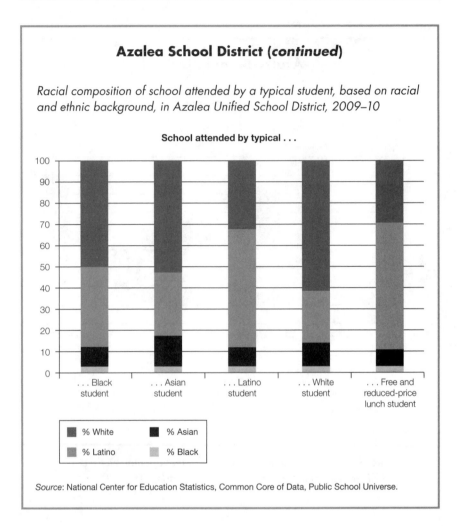

Azalea School District (*continued*)

Racial composition of school attended by a typical student, based on racial and ethnic background, in Azalea Unified School District, 2009–10

School attended by typical . . .

. . . Black student	. . . Asian student
. . . Latino student	. . . White student
. . . Free and reduced-price lunch student	

■ % White   ■ % Asian
■ % Latino   ■ % Black

Source: National Center for Education Statistics, Common Core of Data, Public School Universe.

were reportedly as many as forty predominantly Mexican-American communities in the county.[5] Many of those early settlements still exist today, and most remain ethnically and economically segregated from the neighborhoods predominantly populated by whites and Asians.

The county was the national home of the extreme right-wing John Birch Society, which campaigned to impeach Chief Justice Earl Warren (who authored the decision that declared school segregation unconstitutional) in the 1960s and helped advance the political careers of former Republican presidents Richard Nixon and Ronald Reagan, both of whom undermined integration efforts. Many conservatives in Orange County gained their start in politics through their struggle for power in the Orange County public school system. In the 1960s and '70s, these power struggles "awakened the sleeping giant of right-wing conservatism," resulting in authoritarian tactics and unconstitutional actions such as banning open discussions of religion in the classroom, and allowing school administrators to request teachers to reveal all past political affiliations.[6] Liberal members of the county school board were often removed and replaced with conservatives.[7]

In the late 1970s, the racial/ethnic, socioeconomic, and employment sector demographics of Orange County began to shift rapidly as growing fiscal austerity at the state and national levels created upheaval in California public schools. Following the statewide funding equalization decision in 1971 (*Serrano v. Priest*) and the passage of the property tax referendum, Proposition 13, in 1978, the state has supplied the largest share of school funding in California. Proposition 13 shifted the support for schools from local property taxes to state general funds. The measure rolled back market values to those of 1975–76 and then restricted real estate tax assessments to 1 percent of a property's purchase price. It also limited annual property tax increases to no more than 2 percent yearly for continuing owners and a full reassessed value of the property for new owners.[8] These factors drastically reduced the ability of local governments to raise revenue from property taxes. Since property taxation is traditionally the largest source for local education spending, California public schools were hit the hardest; the state fell from a reported seventh in the country in the 1970s to twenty-seventh in per-pupil spending by 2009.[9]

Scholars trace the struggle to desegregate Orange County Public Schools back to the landmark 1947 *Mendez v. Westminster* case, which ended de jure segregation in California public schools. However, de facto school segregation has persisted for decades, aided by a series of state mandates that have made dismantling the barriers to school integration more challenging.[10] Proposition 1, a state constitutional amendment designed to end mandatory busing, passed in 1979 with nearly 70 percent of the vote. This measure mandated that state courts could not order mandatory pupil assignment or transportation (busing) unless a federal court would do so to remedy a violation of the Fourteenth Amendment's Equal Protection clause.[11] In 1982, the Supreme Court upheld the decision of the lower courts that Proposition 1 was constitutional.[12] The Court's decision added further confusion and complexity to efforts by administrators, teachers, and community leaders to desegregate California suburban public school districts. As Orange County becomes increasingly diverse but remains segregated by race and class, transportation remains an important factor in providing all students opportunities and access to schools outside of their suburban neighborhood.[13]

In 1996, Proposition 209 dismantled affirmative action in the state and affected K–12 education by prohibiting public school districts from explicitly considering race/ethnicity in drawing school zone boundaries. The mandate further complicated districts' decisions regarding the implementation and funding for programs and policies for at-risk student populations, who are disproportionately minority and low-income. In 1998, Proposition 227 dismantled bilingual education in California. While California public schools were already overwhelmed by "low achievement by [English language learner (ELL)] students, confused and frustrated educators, and lack of a consistent curriculum" the federal government issued a further mandate under NCLB, signed into law in 2002.[14]

Despite Orange County's pockets of affluence, many of its school districts were in dire financial crisis, facing continued furloughs, layoffs, and the threat of school closures by the close of the 1980s. In the early 1990s, it became clear that there were long-standing, often hidden, financial problems in the county when its treasurer gambled away $1.7 billion of taxpayer dollars in a Wall Street securities scheme, with the result that, in 1994, Orange County became the largest county in U.S. history to declare bankruptcy.[15]

By the early 2000s Orange County faced internal fiscal pressures as families were pushed out of the county's housing market to neighboring counties in search of affordable housing and job opportunities. The subsequent declining school enrollments resulted in staggering losses in revenue. For example, in 2008 the Orange County Department of Education (OCDE) reported a loss in revenue countywide due to declining student enrollment from $2,125,187 in 2003–04 to a cumulative loss of over $89 million by 2007–08 school year.[16] The Great Recession of 2008 and the collapse of the housing market hit California much harder than the nation as a whole. Following the recession, pockets of growing poverty in the county were further exacerbated by both the housing market collapse and an unstable job market. These factors are coupled with a rise in recently arrived low-income, immigrant populations to the county, residing in rental homes or apartments, often with multiple families to one dwelling.

These internal and external factors underscore the need to examine the responsiveness of borderline school districts (those just transitioning to majority-minority) like Azalea Unified, which for years after Orange County became majority-minority, remained on the whole majority-white. The district only recently transitioned to majority-minority in the last few years. At just 50 percent non-Latino white in 2009, the racial/ethnic demographics of Azalea Unified inevitably tipped to majority-minority status by the close of the decade. Between 1997 and 2010 the white student population in the district decreased by 17 percent, from 63 to 46 percent, respectively; the Latino population increased from 25 percent to 37 percent; and the Asian population increased from 8 percent to 11 percent. Black student enrollment remained around 2 percent (see also exhibit 4.1). By 2010 one-quarter of students in the district were eligible for free or reduced-price lunch (FRL), but this figure varied greatly by school, as some schools served a population with over 50 percent FRL. The next section further examines demographic changes in the county and Azalea Unified and discuss how the Azalea community has conceptualized demographic changes in the student population in recent years.

CONCEPTUALIZATIONS OF DEMOGRAPHIC CHANGE

The demographics of Orange County have shifted as greater numbers of Latinos and Asians moved into the area. As shown in table 4.1, in 1980 Asians and Latinos comprised only 5 and 15 percent of the Orange County population, respectively. By 2010, the populations of Asians and Latinos increased to about 18 percent and 34 percent, respectively. Overall one-third of the county was foreign-born by 2010, including one-half of all Latinos and over 70 percent of all Asians in Orange County. The growth of the African American population in Orange County remained low, rising from only 1.26 percent in 1980 to about 2.0 percent by 2010.

TABLE 4.1

Racial and ethnic demographics in Orange County, 1980–2010

Race/ethnic origin	1980	1990	2000	2010
White	78.2%	64.5%	51.3%	44.1%
Black	1.2%	1.6%	1.5%	1.5%
Asian	4.1%	9.8%	13.5%	17.7%
Latino	14.8%	23.4%	30.8%	33.7%

Source: U.S. Census, 1980, 1990, 2000, 2010.

Several districts in the OCDE remain among the most segregated suburban school districts in the country.[17] Increased districtwide diversity does not necessarily translate to greater levels of integration in suburban school districts, or exposure to non-Latino white students, particularly if these students do not attend the same schools.[18] As suburban school districts become more diverse, such demographic shifts may not trickle down to the school level because of deep-seated racial/ethnic and economic segregation in the housing market, which is often reflected in the prototypical model of the suburban neighborhood school.

Nearly one-third of Latino students in Orange County attend intensely segregated schools.[19] Although Latino students comprise 46 percent of the county's public school enrollment, the typical Latino student attends a school that is 69 percent Latino.[20] Latino students in the county also attend schools where, on average, 65 percent of students are poor, as indicated by the percentage of students receiving FRL; nearly two-thirds of these FRL students are Latino.[21] Black students make up less than 2 percent of the student population. However, they attend schools where two in five students are poor. Southern California's largest concentrations of Asian schoolchildren live in the county. However, just 2 percent of Asian students attend intensely segregated minority schools. White and Asian students in the county are least likely to attend schools with large shares of poor students.[22]

In Azalea Unified, both district- and school-level respondents provided conflicting descriptions of the district's demographic composition, and some differed in the extent to which Azalea was shifting demographically at all. Census data from 2010 underscores persistent disparities between Laneview and Orchard, the two main suburbs that make up the Azalea Unified District: Orchard, in the north, remains homogenously white and middle-upper income, while Laneview, in the South remains more racially mixed with a long-standing Latino and low-income population. Table 4.2 illustrates these socioeconomic and demographic characteristics as compared with Orange County. Some respondents underscored the racial, ethnic, and class-based segregation in the district between Orchard and Laneview. Orchard's Latino population makes up only 14 percent of its total population, while Laneview's Latino population is 36 percent (as compared with 34 percent in the county). Orchard's income, home value, and home ownership rates are higher than both Orange County and Laneview, while its poverty rates and percentage of female-headed households are significantly lower. Orchard's

TABLE 4.2

Orange County select socioeconomic and demographic characteristics, compared with the two main suburbs in the Azalea District, 2010

Data marked with an asterisk from 2008 Census.

	Orange County	Laneview	Orchard
Racial/ethnic composition			
White	44.1%	44.7%	65.7%
Black	1.5%	1.6%	1.2%
Asian	17.7%	14.8%	15.5%
Latino	33.7%	36.4%	14.4%
Language other than English spoken	43.6%	37.2%	21.9%
Foreign born	30.0%	25.4%	16.5%
Family income			
Median household income	$73,738	$77,686	$114,332
Median family income	$83,338	$87,223	$126,746
Family poverty rate*	6.5%	7.0%	1.8%
Individual below poverty level*	9.5%	10.4%	2.1%
Home value and ownership rate			
Median home value*	$653,900	$625,000	$835,000
Ownership rate*	62.0%	66.1%	84.5%
Median rent	$1,312	$1,269	$1,613
Family structure			
School-age child present*	65.2%	65.5%	63.9%
Married	54.2%	57.4%	70.0%
Female head of household	11.6%	12.6%	8.5%

Source: U.S. Census 2008, 2010.

demographic composition is more homogenous and more affluent than both Orange County and Laneview.

The principal of the Allenson High School in Laneview, who has served as an educator in the district for over thirty years, explained that multiple generations of low-income Latino families in Laneview have attended the same schools for decades and proudly return to teach at their former schools.[23] However, increased immigration, largely from Mexico, in the 1990s raised student enrollment numbers at some schools, including

Allenson High School and its feeder elementary schools. Subsequently, as English language learner population numbers increased during the 1990s, test scores at schools in Laneview began to decline rapidly. Moreover, as the number of Mexican immigrant students increased, the long-standing negative stereotypes associated with Allenson High School (and its feeder schools) as low-performing, unsafe, and gang-infested were further exacerbated. In contrast, at the same time that schools like Allenson are struggling to fund desperately needed programs for at-risk high school students, some schools in Orchard are able to plan elaborate eighth-grade "prom-type" dances, supported largely through fundraising, and provide "tolerance training" through antibullying seminars.

Azalea Unified's district superintendent of over twelve years describes his district as diverse but suggests that when it comes to district curriculum, programs, and resources within the Azalea Unified Schools, inequality is not an issue:

> I would describe it [the district] to cover the whole range socioeconomically and ethnically, and it's not a segregated school district in [that] you might view some schools this way, but in other ways they're vastly different . . . About one-fourth of our schools would be Title I . . . These would be lower socioeconomic [areas] and there'd be a fairly high percentage of Latino, very few African Americans . . . But there isn't a sense of the haves and have-nots—certainly not the schools . . . No one in our school district would say there's a different kind of program for certain kids . . . They won't say that the facilities are different and they won't say that the teachers are different . . . you won't hear that. You won't hear it from parents.[24]

However, a district administrator in educational services with over thirty years of service to Orange County Public Schools has a different view:

> This district is a district of haves and have-nots, and they are very—as all of Orange County is . . . segregated. It's unbelievable. I mean, the lines of demarcation could not be clearer . . . In the old days, when this was an orange-growing area, you had the landowners over here and then you had the workers that worked over there, the more Hispanic workers that worked over there, and those lines are clear as day still . . . Well, the Latinos are very carefully put in the one area . . . But that's not unusual; all of our demographics, all of our ethnic groups all go to Allenson High School . . . It's the poor high school. The people from Orchard wouldn't have their kids

go there . . . This is a very segregated community. Very, very segregated community . . . The poor kids go to the poor schools. The other kids go to the other schools. It's the way it goes . . . That's where all the diversity is. All of it is—it goes to one high school.[25]

While this respondent points to persistent segregation in the district, underscoring a clear distinction between long-standing wealthy neighborhoods to the north and low-income neighborhoods to the south, the district is also facing pressure from demographic changes in former solid middle-class neighborhoods experiencing a recent arrival of low-income immigrant students resulting in growing numbers of ELLs and impoverished families in schools that did not traditionally hold these populations in sizable numbers.

Langston Elementary School, located in the middle of the district, provides an example of such a community facing three emerging demographic changes: increasing numbers of low socioeconomic status (SES) students and ELLs; and a decline in overall enrollment, which in turn decreases the average daily attendance and subsequently per-pupil funding to the school. Langston experienced one of the most dramatic changes of racial and ethnic composition of all Azalea Unified District schools. The white population declined from 69 percent in 1997 to 36 percent in 2010, while the Latino population increased from 21 percent in 1997 to 48 percent in 2010. In 1997, only 5 percent of the student population were ELLs, and 15 percent of students received free or reduced-price lunch. By 2010, these figures rose to 13 percent and 22 percent, respectively.

Administrators and teachers at Langston Elementary describe it as the "middle child" of the district, caught between the affluent schools and the Title I schools. A teacher at Langston explains this widely shared sentiment: "I think with the way the budget is in the state, it's sad. Because I think Langston is one of those schools . . . we're not like View Vista, where we have a lot of parents with a lot of money, and we're not like a Parkview . . . a Title I [school]. We're just kind of in between, so we don't get anything from any direction."[26] The dramatic growth in the number of ELLs in the area may be, in part, a result of shifts in the housing market. The number of homes for sale has declined, while the number of homes for rent has increased. This increase of access to rentals has made the community more accessible to low-income families who previously could not afford to live in the neighborhood.

"Middle of the road" schools like Langston are understaffed and underresourced to handle the burgeoning low-income and Limited English

Proficient population. Despite its shifting demographics, the school struggles to provide for the growing ELL population, which has not yet reached a level that would qualify the school to receive Title I funds. It also no longer holds a stable middle-income population to rely on for discretionary funds to fill the gap in resources. The principal further describes the overall demographic shifts at his school and its impact on students in the last ten years.

> I would say we had about 70 percent . . . [of parents with] some sort of formal education that went along with having that job. And about 30 percent were minimum-wage, unskilled labor. And that demographic has almost shifted. I would say that [now] we're probably looking at 50 to 60 percent unskilled or semiskilled labor [in] the community, so that shift in demographics has been a challenge for us and particularly [for] staff members that have never worked with families that are economically struggling. The thought that you can't ask for money anymore for a field trip because they don't have it to give you . . . [that] parents that can't help kids in the intermediate grades because they don't understand the math—those types of things are occurring here that did not when I first got here.[27]

These respondents present a broad picture of the Azalea United District. The picture of a suburban school district serving a white, affluent population has been replaced by a description of long-standing suburban racial and class stratification. The persistent disparities between the two main communities served by Azalea underscore the need to examine how district, school, and community leaders in borderline or recently transitioned districts conceptualize and frame issues related to increasing diversity, and how local educators respond to this trend, particularly when faced with a fiscal crisis and the pressures of state and federal mandates.

DISTRICT RESPONSIVENESS TO DEMOGRAPHIC CHANGE

Students are assigned within their local school boundaries on the basis of place of residence. Those riding school buses must pay transportation fees as set forth by the Azalea board of education, with the exception of students receiving special education services and families qualifying for free or reduced-cost transportation. Transportation fees apply to the first three children in the family, at about $400 annually (both ways) for the first and second child and about $200 for the third child.[28] Transportation for the fourth child and beyond is free. Students can transfer out of their assigned attendance boundaries through an "open enrollment" period through inter-district transfer during the designated transfer periods and upon available space. When the number of transfer requests exceeds the space available, transfers are granted by a lottery selection process. The district's public school choice option, part of NCLB, gives parents the option to transfer their children to another Azalea Unified school that is not in Program Improvement under NCLB, depending on space availability. While transportation for interdistrict transfer students is the responsibility of the parent/guardian, the district provides paid transportation for public school choice transfer students to their new school as long as the student's home school remains in Program Improvement.[29]

Azalea Unified has long struggled with school integration concerns, particularly at the high school level, and the extent to which these concerns could be addressed through changes in school attendance boundaries. However, despite a series of proposals from the Parent Teacher Association (PTA) to desegregate Allenson High School and its feeder middle schools, the demographics of these schools remained largely unchanged during the 1990s. Efforts to integrate schools in the district became especially difficult after California passed Proposition 209 in 1996, which prohibits public institutions from considering race, sex, or ethnicity in deciding which schools students will attend. This may prevent busing or the creation of school boundaries in order to change the racial/ethnic makeup of the schools.[30]

In Azalea Unified, boundary issues reemerged in 2009 and resulted in a missed opportunity to create a greater racial/ethnic balance in the district high schools. The impending opening of a new high school, Orchard High, located in the wealthy, majority-white Orchard suburb forced the district to redraw attendance boundaries for all district high schools. However, the resulting dispute over school boundaries was seemingly not waged on racial imbalance grounds. In fact, reports in the local and regional newspapers included little to no discussion of racial/ethnic integration concerns. Those we interviewed who discussed the boundary debate did not mention the issue either. The two proposals considered by the board largely affected students from the new high school's two feeder middle schools, both with overwhelmingly white student populations. The proposal that was adopted sent all middle school students from one of the feeder schools and just over half of the students from the other to the new high school. The remaining students, who were also predominantly white and lived south of a major thoroughfare, would attend the same predominantly white school, Salazar High, that most students from the two feeder schools previously attended. Under the transfer policy, the district received hundreds of transfer requests and subsequently held a lottery to fill fewer than 150 remaining slots at the new high school.

Opponents of the adopted boundaries, who brought two lawsuits against the district, were made up of largely white and middle-upper-income parents and community groups whose children were not selected to attend Orchard High. The lawsuits contended that the superintendent had violated procedural rules during the school board vote on the boundary proposals and that the district failed to properly consider environmental and traffic impacts when drawing the boundaries. Ostensibly, parents who argued against the adopted boundaries wanted their children to move on to high school with their friends from middle school and contended that the new school boundaries divided Orchard families and their children. According to some parents, children not selected to attend the new high school were ostracized by those children who had been selected. In 2010, both suits against the district were struck down by an Orange County Superior Court judge. The new high school's entering freshman class was predominantly white, and reflected the overwhelmingly white population in Orchard. In the 2010–11 school year, enrollment was 66 percent white, 10 percent Latino, 13 percent Asian, and 1.3 percent black, with only six total ELL students.[31]

Following the opening of the new high school, the demographics of its neighboring Salazar High also remained largely the same at 68 percent white, 17 percent Latino, 10 percent Asian and 2 percent black. Arguably, this was a missed opportunity for the district to ease the racial imbalance among the four main high schools in the district, in part due to the restrictive mandate of Proposition 209, the district's reliance on attendance boundaries based on place of residence, and a lack of affordable and available transportation services.[32] For example, in contrast to Orchard and Salazar, Allenson High School continued to house the largest Latino population of all the high schools in the district, at 59 percent, followed by Asians at 13 percent, whites at 25 percent, and blacks at 2 percent. Approximately 25 percent of students were classified as Limited English Proficient and 54 percent were eligible for the FRL program.

Targeted Placement of GATE/Magnet Academies and Special Programs

My research suggests that the district did little to directly promote racial/ ethnic balance and integration in the district. Instead, the district's actions sought to indirectly decrease racial/ethnic concentration by strategically placing magnet academies, including Gifted and Talented Education (GATE) and International Baccalaureate (IB) programs, at some Title I schools or schools with the most diverse student populations. District officials believed this measure could address racial/ethnic and class concentrations while also raising test scores and halting declining white and Asian student enrollment that resulted when these students transferred to a neighboring district that offered magnet programs that Azalea had previously not provided.

This district policy may not seem revolutionary; yet it did manage to target resources toward some minority and low-income schools despite Azalea's conservative ethos; its long-standing racial, ethnic, and economic stratification; and the restrictive state mandates. One of the assistant district superintendents discussed how the placement of GATE/magnet programs sought to increase diversity and opportunity for all students:

> It would be easy to say, "I don't want my kids to go to that school because there's too many English learners, there's . . . too much diversity and I like my kids to be over here." And we said, no, this is where it belongs. One, it gives all kids access to this school. And then our IB and Allen Tech programs, we put at Allenson High School, which is our most diverse school. Those are two programs that attract students of very high academic rigor. And again, it would be easy to say, "I don't want my kids to go." But if you look, the programs continue to grow and it's created a much more diverse school. And so I think [it says] to our parents, we value all kids in this district. And we believe that the more diverse the school is, the more it replicates what's out there in our community, the better [the chances that] kids are going to go out and be successful in the world because there's no reality of a white school. The more diverse the school is, the better. And I think had we placed those programs at one of our higher socioeconomic schools, we would've missed out on a very powerful opportunity. And there probably still are people who choose not to go there for that very reason.[33]

GATE/magnet eligible students typically attend the magnet school within their feeder school system.[34] However, as discussed above, California has an interdistrict and public school choice transfer policy under NCLB. If space is available and if parents can provide their own transportation, students within the district can attend a program outside of their school boundary and students from outside of the district can apply to transfer into any program in the district. Unfortunately, the district's transfer policies fail to adequately promote greater levels of diversity in GATE/magnet programs, since busing is not provided for students who wish to participate in programs outside of their designated school boundary. As noted, parents must pay out of pocket for school transportation services, with exceptions for parents with children transferring from schools rated in Program Improvement under the NCLB act, as well as special education and students qualifying for free and reduced-cost transportation. Even then, bus services for those exempted students only transport students *within* their school boundary and do not necessarily help to increase student enrollment in the targeted GATE/magnet programs. Additionally, the state legislature continues to reduce funding for home-to-school busing; in 2011, it cut the district's transportation budget by nearly 25 percent, resulting in even fewer stops and available buses.

At the high school level, in order to indirectly increase diversity in the student population, circumvent largely white and Asian high school student flight from the district, and raise overall test scores, in the early 2000s the district selected Allenson High School to house the district's only IB program. Allenson High School continues to fight the persistent negative stereotypes associated with its large Latino student population and the stigmas associated with high poverty—crime, gangs, and drugs. Although Asians only account for 13 percent of the student population, they make up over half of the IB students. Allenson's principal suggested that an increasing number of Asian families are attracted to Allenson because of its rigorous curriculum, contending that Asian students and parents have established a "comfort zone" at Allenson where they feel welcomed, accepted, and supported.

The principal was aware of some claims that while Allenson's IB program attracts a more diverse student population, it potentially creates a "school within a school." Recognizing the need to monitor student enrollment in all academic programs, in 2010 the school administered what it called the Program Participation Study to better understand the number of students in academic programs at Allenson. The study focused on academic programs offered as part of a student's schedule and did not include participation in the number of clubs on campus; it showed that 88 percent of Allenson students are enrolled in at least one or more of the fourteen academic programs offered at the school.

Moreover, in recent years Allenson has allocated resources for special programs though collaborations with the business community, in many cases without funding support from the district. Some of these programs were developed to break the cycle of poverty in Laneview and to provide low-income students with better opportunities after high school. In collaboration with the Building Industry Association of Orange County, Allenson was one of the schools that established the Building Industry Technology Academy (BITA) program in the mid-2000s, a four-year program for students in which students can learn the skills needed to excel in the residential construction trade while reinforcing math, science, and language skills.

Allenson also became the only high school in the district to adopt the Advancement Via Individual Determination (AVID) program, designed for first-generation college-bound students. Most of the participants are minority and low-income students who have the potential to get into the four-year university, but do not have the support at home or a family member who attended college. AVID starts in middle school and is designed to be a six-year program; thus the feeder elementary schools to Allenson High School also participate in the program. Students take a one-period course that prepares them for different aspects of the college prep process, from SAT prep courses to filling out fee waivers and scholarship and college applications. Interestingly, the district does not fund this program. Allenson receives its funding from the principal's budget as well as through dedicated fundraising efforts.

However, the placement of specialized GATE/magnet programs and programs for at-risk students does little to affect change at the middle-of-the-road schools in the district, like Langston Elementary. These schools are neither Title I nor high SES, yet they are experiencing unprecedented growth in the low-income and ELL populations. The budget crisis, as well as the legal and political environment in the state and county, makes it unlikely that programs for at-risk populations will be funded by the district on a large scale.

Restructuring of Bilingual Education Under Proposition 227

Proposition 227, passed in 1998, ended bilingual education programs in California. With some exceptions, bilingual education was replaced by a one-year Structured English Immersion program model.[35] Under the new model, ELLs are instructed in English in a special class for one year, after which they are mainstreamed into regular classes and in some cases given extra support.[36] The implementation of this law was uneven, and school districts throughout California struggled to implement the law. One of its provisions, referred to as a "waiver loophole," allowed parents, after mainstreaming to apply for waivers that would allow their children to return to learning in their native language, if parents of more than twenty students in the school requested the service.[37]

Following passage of the law, Azalea Unified still received among the largest number of waiver requests in the county and the state, despite having a comparatively smaller ELL population. In a newspaper interview in 2003, the superintendent stated that of the district's students who are not fluent in English, one-third were being taught in Spanish (statewide, the rate was 10 percent). For nearly a decade following the passage of Prop 227, the district's reclassification rate and the academic success of its ELLs consistently ranked below the state and county levels, which led to the restructuring of services for ELLs in the district.

Arguably, the waiver loophole made it more difficult to meet state (California's Academic Performance Index, or API) and federal (NCLB) testing and accountability standards.[38] Faced with issues of compliance with Prop 227 as well as the risk of state and federal sanctions, including a greater number of schools placed in Program Improvement under NCLB, Azalea's superintendent sought to curb the waiver system by significantly rolling back the number of waivers granted in the district and to rapidly move a greater number of ELL students toward reclassification and increasing the academic achievement scores of ELL students. Within a year, the number of bilingual kindergarten classes in the district declined from twelve to four. This move sparked objections from Latino parents, advocacy groups, and some teachers, who staged protests at school board meetings. The superintendent discussed his experiences during his first year at Azalea and learning that his district was not compliant with the state law:

> I walked into those classrooms and for the first year . . . I was confused because I saw teachers teaching in Spanish. And I go in the first- or second-grade classroom, third-grade classroom, and then I go the middle school and I'd see that we had kids who were still in ELD [English language development] classes because they hadn't learned English, and [the same applied for students at] the high school. So I was asking about that and they said, "Well, in our district we do the alternative program," which meant that parents signed a waiver so the kids could stay in a bilingual or alternative classroom. So I started to go a little deeper and we found out that these kids were never transitioning out, that the teachers were teaching Spanish . . .
>
> And in the SABE [Spanish Assessment of Basic Education] these kids are brilliant, they were doing really well because they were being tested in Spanish—the SABE test. We don't do that anymore. But in all of the state tests . . . they weren't doing very well at all. So I asked what the question

is and they said, "Well, [in] bilingual education, you teach this percentage at first grade, then you do a little more, then second grade, then the third grade, and by the time you get to third or fourth grade, now they're bilingual and they've transitioned to partial teaching in Spanish to all English.' I said, "Really?" . . . So all hell broke loose. I mean, we had Hispanic people coming, the parents coming, board meeting after board meeting, but we just stuck to it.

Outraged Latino parents spoke out at school board meetings, pushing the district to reverse its decision to curb the use of waivers. ELL parents expressed the need for their children to understand what they are learning, to maintain their cultural heritage, and to be able to communicate at home as well as in school. They argued that essentially they knew what was best for their children.

To address some of the parents' concerns, the district established District English Language Advocacy Committees (DELAC) designed to allow parents an outlet to meet, monitor, and give feedback to the schools regarding the district ELD program. Based on parent feedback, the district restructured DELAC meetings so that topics are presented with simultaneous audio and visual translation. Although academic support for ELLs is now available at all district schools, parents in low-incidence schools, where there are fewer than twenty-one ELL students, are not sufficiently targeted for DELAC participation and feedback. Some Asian and South Asian families, for example, are described as intimidated or otherwise ambivalent about the value in participating in DELAC on their children's behalf. These findings suggest that the district should monitor the participation of parents at low-incidence schools and increase their campaign to reach out to these parents.

In addition to revamping ELD, since 2006 the district has also instituted additional programs to support ELLs and their families.[39] Moreover, all district teachers who work with ELLs hold a Cross-Cultural Language and Academic Development credential or the equivalent. Reclassification rates now far exceed both the county and state levels. However, district data from 2011 show mixed results in its efforts to meet the government's Annual Measurable Achievement Objectives. Azalea Unified's English language learners did not meet the state target for the 2010–11 school year, which measures the percent of ELLs making annual progress in learning English as measured by the California English Language Development Test. However district data shows there has been improvement in the reclassification rate for the district's ELLs. The reclassification rate for 2010–11 was 13.6 percent.[40] District data also shows a trend toward improved academic achievement in English language arts for ELLs, from 17.5 in 2000–01 to 38.9 in 2010–11.

An interview with an ELL program coordinator in the district suggested a need to focus not only on the statistics related to ELLs reclassification and testing performance, but also the district's culture and perceptions of ELL students. However, she also expressed strong opinions about the types of teachers who teach ELL students and their perceptions of the ELL population:

> [We should] value teaching ELD as you value teaching GATE, and make it a privilege . . . They don't assign our EL kids to the best teachers on staff, and that I think bothered me. And I think that also bred some of that animosity . . . it was almost like either it was a new teacher and it would burn out a new teacher if he didn't have the skills and the background or an incompetent teacher they would give the EL students to . . . I would want them to treat our EL students as if they were the most precious things in the whole wide world, that they don't have a deficit. The deficit isn't the children. The deficit [is] the lack of education that our professionals have; it's not a deficit to have a second language, and they treat our kids that way.[41]

Some district officials observed that minority parents do not seem to be prominent players in the overwhelmingly white power structure of the district. The Allenson High School principal emphasized that, despite the sizable Latino student population, a Latino community member is yet to hold an elected or appointed position on the Azalea school board. He discussed what he perceived as the changing relationship of the Latino middle class to the district, suggesting that for the first time the district is receiving demands from the middle-class Latino population:

> I've got a significant Hispanic population, the largest part of my Hispanic population that are second, third, fourth generation, and they are middle-class and they are educated and the thing that the district is having a tough time with is they never had demands from Hispanic community, and they are getting demands from the Hispanic community and I applaud them . . . What they really need to do is they need to organize and get a board member. But you know it's not like it was twenty or thirty years ago, where you have these timid individuals who speak broken English, they don't have any money, they can't communicate, they're embarrassed to communicate, they don't understand the system . . . I think they are much more vocal,

they're not afraid to call the district office, they're not afraid to go to a board meeting, they're not afraid to demand the same things that the kids have at the other high schools.

This quote underscores the need for sustained efforts in the minority community to put pressure on the administration to address the concerns of a student population that is no longer majority-white, but remains racially and economically segregated in the district.

CONCLUSION

This chapter has examined how Azalea Unified, faced with nearly $40 million in budget cuts and the worst economic downturn since the Great Depression, as well as the pressures of several state and federal mandates, responded to an out-migration of the white student population and a subsequent in-migration of low-income, minority, and recently arrived immigrant students to some district schools. Several policy shifts occurred, including the targeted placement of GATE/magnet programs in select Title I schools or schools in low SES neighborhoods; the allocation of resources, albeit uneven, to select programs for at-risk students such as the Building Industry Technology Academy (BITA) program; and the restructuring of ELL programs. While some actions indirectly addressed racial/ethnic and class concentration by modestly increasing diversity in minority and low-income schools such as Allenson High School, none of these measures made a significant impact on the racial, ethnic, and class imbalance in the Azalea Unified District. These responses were intended to adhere to state and federal mandates, which made it more difficult for Azalea Unified to respond effectively to demographic change and to adequately address to the needs of an increasingly diverse student population. State mandates also prohibited targeted spending in the area's transportation services, which are critical for the success of targeted magnet programs designed to attract a diverse group of students from across and outside of the district; magnet schools that provide free transportation tend to be more racially integrated than those that do not.[42]

This research also underscores the complexity of issues facing school districts with borderline or recently transitioned to majority-minority status, highlighting the many ways in which these districts are far from autonomous institutional actors in suburbia. Instead, counties and their school districts operate under conditions of scare resources and amid internal and external pressures that cut off educational opportunities to shifting populations of students. As more historically white suburban school districts change in demographic composition, this research also underscores the need to address the "middle of the road" schools, which are neither Title I nor high SES, but in need of resources and support for an emerging minority and low-income population.

5

Help Wanted

The Challenges and Opportunities of Immigration and Cultural Change in a Working-Class Boston Suburb

SUSAN EATON

Waltham's half-mile commercial strip, Moody Street, showcases the cultural and economic diversity that defines the present and will shape the future of this city-suburb just west of Boston.[1] On warm weekend nights, Moody Street takes on the feel of a multicultural street fair. The Indian grocer on the corner sells authentic corn tortillas and speaks decent Spanish. A Peruvian-owned pizza shop offers oversized slices, meatball subs, and homemade empanadas. An Italian specialty food store sits a few doors down from Chapincitas, a Guatemalan-owned bodega. An upscale ice cream shop, an English-style tearoom, a vast Indian grocery, the bustling Family Dollar store, an eclectic independent bookstore, and a Guatemalan restaurant share one side of Moody Street. Across the way, Tempo American Bistro sells $28 entrees prepared by a predominantly Latino kitchen staff; a few doors down, a Ugandan shopkeeper sells women's clothing.

"Waltham has something for everyone," the city's mayor and native daughter, Jeanette McCarthy, writes on the city's official website. "Waltham is now a diverse community with various opportunities for living, education, work, and leisure."[2] In 2010 Waltham was named the "twenty-eighth best place to live" by CNN's *Money Magazine* (the magazine ranked Waltham's more affluent next-door neighbor, Newton, third).[3]

This case study explores the school-related implications of immigration and cultural change in this historically working-class, formerly white ethnic stronghold. As the cultural fabric continues to change, Waltham's educators express strong support for diversity, and commitment to their students. At the same time, teachers, and in some cases principals, say they feel mostly alone and ill-equipped with little to no guidance in how to respond to the increasing cultural, linguistic, and economic diversity and the challenges such change brings to the surface. Many educators feel they work against a backdrop of unhelpful state policies with regard to English language learners (ELLs) and complain of a prevailing community perception that immigrants are a detriment. Although there has been little history of broad-based cross-sector collaboration here, one program, the Waltham Family School, offers a potentially transferable model.

WALTHAM'S DEMOGRAPHIC CHANGE IN LOCAL
AND REGIONAL CONTEXTS

Waltham, Massachusetts, is home to 60,605 people.[4] Waltham's cultural shifts since 1990 include growing numbers of Latino and Southeast Asian residents who have transformed much of the commercial, social, and educational spaces. The city's white population, most typically of Irish, Italian, and French Canadian ancestry, has been in slow decline over this time. Respondents tend to characterize Waltham as "hardworking" and "working-class." This is certainly true relative to many of the communities that surround it, which for the most part are solidly middle-class and affluent.

In 2010, the city's mean household income was $64,341, nearly matching the state's median household income of $65,401 that year.[5] About 12 percent of Waltham's residents are poor, and poverty has been rising for two decades.[6] (For context, about 10 percent of all people in Massachusetts lived in poverty and about 15 percent of people in the United States were poor in 2010.) The share of residents in poverty is far higher than found in most of the city's neighboring communities, where demographics have remained generally unchanged for at least a decade.[7]

Waltham is a city in its own right and also a suburb of Boston, which lies about ten miles southeast and where 20 percent of people live in poverty. Waltham benefits from a strong commercial tax base, with office complexes, big-box stores such as Costco and Home Depot, and corporate chain hotels

EXHIBIT 5.1

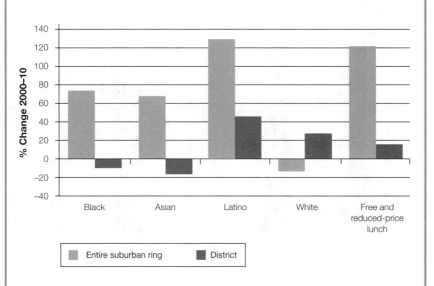

Waltham Public Schools

Percentage change of Boston suburban ring and Waltham Public Schools

Racial and poverty composition of Boston metropolitan statistical area, Waltham Public Schools, and district first grade, 2009–10

	% Black	% Asian	% Latino	% White	% English language learners	% Free and reduced-price lunch	Total enrollment
Total MSA	8.8	6.5	13.4	69.2	5.3	29.6	657,082
Principal cities	26.0	10.2	27.4	33.6	9.9	55.9	107,985
Suburbs	5.5	5.7	10.6	76.2	4.4	24.4	549,097
District	9.3	6.5	28.3	53.6	8.0	31.8	4,763
First grade	6.5	10.1	30.9	50.1	—	—	385

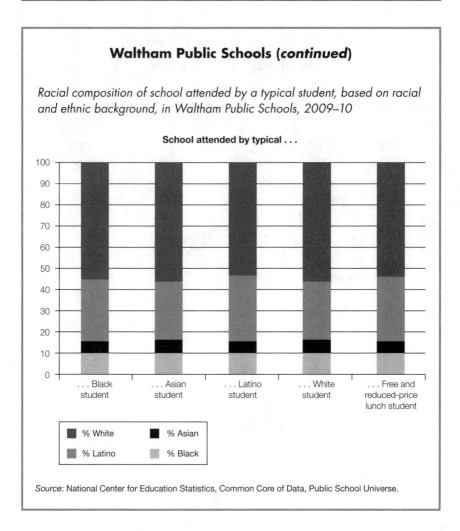

Waltham Public Schools (*continued*)

Racial composition of school attended by a typical student, based on racial and ethnic background, in Waltham Public Schools, 2009–10

School attended by typical . . .

Legend:
- % White
- % Asian
- % Latino
- % Black

X-axis categories: . . . Black student | . . . Asian student | . . . Latino student | . . . White student | . . . Free and reduced-price lunch student

Source: National Center for Education Statistics, Common Core of Data, Public School Universe.

within its borders along a major highway, Route 128. Next to Boston itself, Waltham has the second-largest office market in the Greater Boston area.[8]

The city's southern section is dominated by dense, multifamily rental housing and the vibrant, periodically struggling Moody Street. A transportation hub downtown delivers commuters by bus and train to Cambridge, Boston, to office buildings and hotels along Route 128, and to neighboring suburban communities, including Newton, the affluent job center next door. Immigrant Waltham has tended to live in this section of town, with a full-service supermarket and drugstore close by on Main Street.

The city's northern section, bordering the affluent towns of Lexington and Lincoln, is wealthier and mostly white, dominated by single-family, owner-occupied homes. The east and west sections of town include a mix of rental and relatively modest owner-occupied homes. Well-swept sidewalks connect neighbors in nearly every section of town. Officials have spread public and subsidized affordable housing throughout the city, including its largest development, Chesterbrook Gardens, on the city's north side. A 2011 review of state data showed that Waltham had one of the highest shares of its subsidized housing for Latino and black families in so-defined "high opportunity" neighborhoods, when compared with other communities.[9] Of the 24,923 units of occupied housing in the city, about 53 percent is occupied by its owners and the remaining 47 percent by renters.[10] Well-tended baseball, football, and soccer fields, along with Dunkin' Donuts franchises, dot the city.

In comparing Waltham to surrounding towns, respondents in this study typically characterize Waltham as "grittier," "rougher around the edges," "more like reality," or more working-class.[11] As has always been true, Waltham provides a disproportionate share of the immediate region's housing, educational, and social services to an increasingly diverse, poorer population. In large part because of high housing prices and relatively small shares of rental housing, surrounding communities are more sheltered from the education-related challenges that accompany demographic change. Interestingly, though, several of the surrounding communities devote a larger share of their housing stock to government-subsidized "affordable" housing than Waltham does.[12]

Waltham's diversity is not reflected in the city's civic leadership or in the racial and ethnic composition of the people employed by the public schools, which remain overwhelmingly white. In 2010, every member of the fifteen-member city council and the seven-member school committee was white, as was every top-level level administrator and every school principal.

CHANGE CHRONOLOGY: HISTORICAL PERSPECTIVE ON WALTHAM'S DEMOGRAPHY

Waltham's history of work and innovation began two centuries ago—around 1813, when Francis Cabot Lowell founded his cotton mill along the banks of the Charles River.[13] Lowell's Boston Manufacturing Company (BMC) would be the first factory in the United States to achieve the multistep process for making cloth from cotton under one roof. As a result, many historians consider BMC to be the nation's first modern factory, a distinction that years later would lead city leaders to dub Waltham the "Birthplace of the American Industrial Revolution." At BMC, immigrants from Italy, Ireland, Poland, and Canada cut materials, worked the looms, and packed bolts of cloth for shipping. Waltham's early immigrants struggled. But jobs in the city's mills and factories supported their families. The city prospered along with them. North Waltham—as opposed to the immigrant-dominated streets to the south—emerged as the prestigious neighborhood. Today, an east-west line still divides middle-class, mostly white Waltham from the generally poorer, heavily immigrant section of the city around Moody Street.

As the economy sagged in the 1980s recession, empty storefronts along Moody Street became barometers of distress. In the 1990s, under a strong U.S. economy, businesses downtown began turning the lights back on. As it did in many small and medium-sized cities in Massachusetts, immigration prevented a population decline and in so doing, fueled the economy by bringing in consumer dollars and tax revenues.[14]

By the late 1990s, the basement of St. Mary's Church on Waltham's south side could no longer hold the growing Spanish-speaking congregation. Church officials moved the Spanish mass upstairs, to what one Latina mother called "real church." In 2005, Waltham's Main Street became home to the New Covenant Church of Cambridge, the largest Haitian church in Massachusetts. New Covenant took over the site of a defunct French Canadian church, which had offered services in French to immigrants and their families two generations ago.[15]

CHANGE BY THE NUMBERS

Waltham is home to a relatively young and growing Latino population, within which a declining Puerto Rican population is being replaced by a newer immigrant population, principally from Mexico and Guatemala.[16] The city's black (heavily Haitian) population is growing.[17] The city's white population has slowly declined and is aging but still makes up three-quarters of its residents.[18] Poverty is on the rise both in the city and its schools.[19] The city's resident population has increased in recent years (and only slightly over the last two decades) again, largely because of immigration.

In the schools, Watham's overall *student* population has declined over two decades, while that of its neighboring communities has either increased or remained stable.[20] Waltham's Latino student population has grown by 116 percent since 1990 and its black school population has increased in the last two decades, although the overall share of that population has remained steady over the last decade.[21] Waltham's share of students with limited proficiency in English and the share of students for whom English is not their first language has also increased in the last decade.[22] In 2000, about 4.7 percent of Waltham's students had limited proficiency in English. By 2011, about 10.6 percent of the city's students had limited proficiency in English. In 2000, about 26 percent of Waltham's students reported that English was not their first language. By 2011, that share had grown to 35.7 percent.[23] Similarly, the number and share of students from low-income families is on the rise. In 1995, the share of low-income students in the city was 26 percent. In 2011, that number had risen to 34.3 percent. Waltham's white student population share has declined by nearly one-quarter over the two decades prior to 2011.[24]

Waltham's lower grades are experiencing demographic change at a rate about even with changes occurring overall in the district, meaning that population shifts will continue and that white students will soon no longer be in the majority (see exhibit 5.1).[25] Waltham is still demographically distinct from the closest large city, Boston, where the combined share of black and Latino students in 2010 was 76.1 percent of the total enrollment, 76 percent of students come from low-income families, and 20 percent have limited proficiency in English.[26]

This case study draws on thirty interviews with teachers, administrators, a school board member, staff at nonprofit service providers, realtors, and business owners. Waltham has six elementary schools, two middle schools, and one high school. This study focused on three schools: the high school and two elementary schools. One elementary school sits in the more affluent north side; the other is in a mixed-income neighborhood just outside the city's center.

Residents interviewed tended to see demographic change in Waltham both as a continuation of long-familiar trends and as something that requires adaptation and spurs tension. Longer-term residents of the city often expressed deep pride in Waltham's history as a city that has long housed, served, and benefited from immigrant communities. There was a strong tendency among respondents to view immigration as, in the words of one respondent: "business as usual."[27] Following from this, then, immigration and demographic change were not viewed as phenomena that might require specific responses, but were, according to another respondent, "just life." One high school teacher, who grew up in Waltham during the early 1980s, offered a similar sentiment: "It's just the latest group of immigrants. So, I don't know if there's anything, really to do. There will just be a next group after this one."[28]

Respondents from non-educational sectors commonly perceived that while some white residents were discomfited by racial and cultural change, cultural diversity also attracted young people to Waltham. This was articulated by realtor and Waltham native Michael Greeley, who sells single-family homes and condominiums in Waltham and the more homogenous surrounding communities. Greeley reported that diversity in Waltham is often appealing to potential homebuyers—"a good selling point," adding that clients tend to like it but "not like too much" of it: "People like that it's diverse, I think. . . I've had people say to me about the schools that they know it's diverse and they don't want their kids growing up in . . . Weston or Wellesley, that are all white."[29]

DIVERSITY: A BENEFIT UNREALIZED, A CHALLENGE UNMET

Educators in Waltham, particularly school principals and classroom teachers, expressed consistently positive and enthusiastic feelings about the demographic changes and diversity that characterize the city and impatience with parents or community members who complain about it. Educators are not merely accepting of such change, but are inspired and motivated by it. At the same time, the same educators typically reported feeling ill-equipped to meet the needs of students of color and their families. Excited by the potential for diversity to enhance the teaching and learning, they were also often not confident of their abilities to harness those potential benefits. Some teachers strongly perceived that their desire to respond in a constructive and inclusive, if ill-defined, fashion to demographic change would clash with a community-level passivity, a general mistrust of newcomers, and palpable nostalgia about the days before the Latino and Haitian populations arrived.

Pride and Diversity

Educators uniformly expressed pride about working in Waltham—a place more like the "real world" than neighboring communities. Even educators who initially chose to work in Waltham for reasons not related to diversity— for convenience or coincidence, for example—said they now view cultural variation as one of the best features of their jobs.

One elementary school principal, Evelyn Carr at Southside Elementary, one of the schools included in this study, left her job as a principal in a more homogeneous, nearby district to come to Waltham. Like many of her colleagues, she reported being relieved to leave her old job behind in favor of a more "real" setting. Carr articulated her affection for the school community: "I like the diverse nature of this. It's so much more rich . . . It's so much more realistic than any of the other places I've worked. They are so insular, so white-bread."[30]

Southside, with about three hundred students, sits in a modest, well-kept neighborhood on a quiet residential street about a half-mile from Waltham's downtown. In the immediate neighborhood, which includes a mix of multifamily and single-family homes, residents sit on porches, and children ride bikes and scooters. In 2010, 48 percent of students here were Latino, 42 percent were white, 6 percent were black, and 2 percent were Asian.[31] Nearly half the students here reported that English was not their first language, and 20 percent had limited English proficiency. About 43 percent came from low-income families. Of the forty-two full-time staff members at Southside, only one was Latino.

Southside's educators varied greatly in their levels of past experience with racial, cultural, or economic diversity. For several, teaching in Waltham represented their first sustained experiences with cultures other than their own. Paula Turk, the principal at New Meadow Elementary, another school in this study, grew up in a rural, nearly all-white community in New England, and had discovered a love of multiculturalism and racial and cultural diversity in college. Upon accepting the job offer in Waltham, she eagerly moved to the city's culturally diverse south side: "And this was what attracted me to come to the city and work. . . so that I could have connections with people from all over the place."[32]

New Meadow, in contrast to Southside, sits in a relatively affluent neighborhood in the city's northern section. It enrolls students from the surrounding streets and also from the city's largest housing project. It also houses the Sheltered English Immersion (SEI) program for ELLs in grades 3, 4, and 5. Of the 427 students enrolled at the time of this study, about 69 percent were white, 16 percent Latino, 7 percent black, and about 6 percent Asian.[33]

Typically, the city's teachers and administrators reported that their experiences in Waltham led them to make a career-long commitment to teaching in culturally and economically diverse settings. In other words, teachers are not in Waltham for an interchangeable "job" but are committed to the city precisely because of its diversity. It was common for teachers to say that after Waltham, they would never work in a school that was not racially and culturally diverse.

Fighting Against Perceptions

It was common for teachers and administrators who have been long-term or lifetime residents of the city to perceive themselves as fighting against negative perceptions in the larger community about immigrants and the cultural changes in the city. One veteran educator described an "underlying" resentment about Latino and Haitian immigrants and accompanying false perceptions about the schools. This top-level administrator, who grew up in the 1970s, said he quite often found himself defending Latino and black students to his contemporaries:

> I'm asked, "Well, it must be rough up there." People say things like that or, "How is it to teach now?" But you know, they'll couch it in such a way, phrase it in such a way that they're expecting a negative . . . And when you answer, "Oh, it's the same as ever," or . . . if you answer, "You know, not as crazy as the '70s were," it's an answer that surprises them, and they probably don't believe it or don't want to hear. Because we don't have the drug problems we had in the '70s . . . we don't have the behavior problems that some imagine we would have.[34]

Several educators said they made conscious efforts to reverse fellow residents' negative misperceptions regarding immigrants. Educators at Southside cited examples of manifest resentment and/or anxiety on the part of white parents over the growing Latino population at the school. In one instance, Evelyn Carr recalled, a student's father called to complain about a song sung in Spanish during a Flag Day celebration; another time, a mother complained about the presence of a Spanish-language translator during an informational session. As Carr recounted:

> She said, "I had no idea you were going to have a translator here," And I said, "Well, we have a lot of Hispanic families here, and they need to hear the same information at the same time you do so we know everybody hears the same thing." And she said, "Well, I think it was a total waste of time, and I thought you were going to be able to tell me more information but that took so long that I wasn't able to get the questions answered that I wanted

answered." And I said, "Well . . . this is life here at the Southside School, and anytime you want to ask me about curriculum or any other questions that you feel as though you didn't have time to ask, call me."

Though the principal and teachers characterized such incidents as "uncommon," Carr acknowledged that they symbolize the "separate" nature of Latino and white communities.

Teachers reported that some white parents were uncomfortable about their children being in classrooms with children still learning English. One Southside teacher, Diane Ballenger, told of one mother's reaction to finding a concentration of Spanish-speaking children in her daughter's kindergarten classroom: "She felt that her daughter was going to be held back. She was very upset . . . But as the year got under way and [the woman's daughter] made friends, it improved, because at the beginning of the year she was thinking about putting her in private school."[35]

Challenged by the Change

It was common for Waltham educators to express concern over not having the skills or resources to more successfully incorporate children of color into the schools in a way that would benefit the educational experience of the entire school community. Educators generally said they believed that the racial and cultural diversity of the schools has the potential to have positive, enriching effects for all students in the city, but at the same time, they were simply not sure how to tap into that potential. Teachers often expressed doubt about their skills in talking about difference or moderating discussions that might explore cultural conflict or find common ground amid difference.

Lauren Ellis, who grew up in Waltham and has taught at a middle school for several years, echoed the sentiments of many of her colleagues: "I really feel like there is sort of this idea that people pay lip service to, that diversity is a good thing . . . many of us don't know if we really believe that, or if we do believe it, we're not sure how to make it an asset . . . I do think that diversity in general functions as an asset."[36]

For example, Ellis noted, the requirements of standardized testing and the rules and bureaucratic procedures of public schools did not provide the conditions or space for teachers to come to understand the experiences that have shaped students' lives and worldviews and to think about how to incorporate those understandings into practice: "It's like . . . if you had this really intense life in another country, and then you cross the border in the trunk of a car, and you barely speak English, and your mother is back in Mexico, it's as if none of that matters. The question is, 'Can you read this textbook and be asked about it?' And there's not time in the day or the curriculum. The environment is not set yet where that stuff is recognized, explored, validated, and made an asset."

Educators repeatedly expressed dismay and confusion about policy and practice regarding students with limited English proficiency and stressed the urgent need for "regular" classroom teachers to better understand how to reach and adequately educate children who are not yet proficient in English. Regular classroom teachers not trained in ESL techniques commonly worried about not adequately serving students who would transition into their classrooms out of the SEI program still not understanding English well enough to grasp content; equally, they seemed at a loss for how to best teach students whose parents had opted out of the SEI program and were in regular classrooms without support.

In such cases, teachers said they developed strategies through trial and error, guessing, or seeking assistance from colleagues. One teacher at Southside explained a common method for acclimating Spanish-speaking students: "You find a child [who] speaks the same language, and they help. I have a little girl who didn't speak English—one of the other Spanish-speaking little girls would translate for her. And I sat them next to each other, and that's what saved it." In other words, for lack of bilingual staff, teachers at Southside and elsewhere commonly used bilingual students as informal interpreters.

A middle-school teacher, Kelly Ryan, voiced a feeling shared among colleagues that ELLs are being shortchanged: "It would be helpful to have more aides in my classes with ELL students, especially if they are just coming here and, as I said, we've had a lot of kids from Haiti. And they come here from Haiti from who knows what type of situation . . ."

Teachers typically expressed a desire for more institutionalized assistance in this area and translation services so they could communicate with immigrant parents and so students could articulate their needs or worries or ideas while in school. Teachers, principals, and upper-level administrators were in accord about the need to develop more effective strategies for incorporating Latino and Haitian parents into the school communities. Some educators at Southside, where the Latino enrollment has risen steadily, said they would benefit from Spanish-language classes to make it easier to reach out and involve Latino parents and create a more welcoming environment for families.

Educators consistently expressed dismay about state requirements that even students who cannot read or speak English still take standardized tests in English. Students who cannot yet speak English must take the Math Massachusetts Comprehensive Assessment System (MCAS) in English. After being in school for a year, students with limited proficiency in English are also required to take the English Language Arts portion of the MCAS. Students with limited English proficiency must also participate in the Massachusetts English Proficiency Assessment (MEPA), which consists of assessments in listening comprehension and speaking.

RESPONDING TO DEMOGRAPHIC CHANGE—AND NOT

A skeletal, ad hoc patchwork of policies and programs constitutes school-, district-, and community-level responses to the schools' (and the community's) changing population. As a result, classroom teachers, principals, and central office administrators perceive no focal point from which to initiate system-wide discussion about the implications for demographic change. Neither do people feel that they or district leaders possess the experience or sophistication to respond effectively without assistance. Thus, policy and practice-related "responses" to increasing diversity seem to hinge on the goodwill, instinct, and decency of particular educators.

Constricted Dialogue

Upper-level administrators reported that talking about the implications of demographic change happened frequently at their private meetings and was woven into discussions about achievement and curriculum. Principals also said they often strategized with colleagues about how to reach out to Spanish-speaking or Creole-speaking parents, though they admitted they found themselves at a loss when it came to crafting coherent policy and practice in this area. Teachers often spoke in small groups with like-minded colleagues about how to develop strategies for ELLs or how to better integrate and assist newly arrived immigrant students. But these conversations occurred, as one principal characterized it, "on the side." And "responses" to the changing population were, from the vantage point of most respondents, usually happenstance or isolated examples.

One school board member confirmed the perception of many classroom teachers and principals that issues related to diversity, culture, and changing demographics are rarely, if ever, discussed at public meetings of the elected school committee. If diversity and race or ethnicity are discussed, she said, it would be in the context of test scores.[37]

English Language Learners

Waltham's policy and practice regarding ELLs is dictated by a 2002 voter referendum that outlawed bilingual education in the state.[38] After the referendum passed, Waltham, like other school districts that had offered bilingual programs, was forced to put a new program in place—Sheltered English Immersion (SEI), which the State of Massachusetts defines as: "An English language acquisition process for young children in which nearly all classroom instruction is in English but with the curriculum and presentation designed for children who are learning the language. Books and instructional materials are in English, and all reading, writing, and subject matter are taught in English."[39]

Under Waltham's SEI program, ELLs are evaluated when they register for school. If testing determines that their English is not proficient enough to function in regular, mainstream classrooms, students are placed into the SEI program. There, students take their core subjects with their fellow ELLs but will not take ESL as a discrete subject. The idea is that in a SEI class, every lesson is a "language lesson" in addition to a content lesson. The SEI classes are taught by teachers certified in ESL. In Waltham, students in the SEI program attend homeroom classes, art, music, and physical education with the larger school community. Parents are permitted to opt out of the SEI program and have their children placed in regular classrooms. In September 2010, the district offered no ESL instruction for students whose parents opted out of the SEI program. An administrator who had started her job in 2009, Linda Foley, was putting such classes in place. All elementary schools in the district have an SEI program for grades 1 and 2; by third grade, all students in the SEI program go to New Meadow Elementary School.

Several educators noted that since the administrator Foley was hired, the SEI program and ELL students seem to be getting more attention. For example, Foley strongly encouraged regular teachers to receive training offered by the state in how to assist ELLs. Foley received funding for more bilingual paraprofessionals and hired two more certified ESL teachers.

Administrators explained that they placed the SEI programs on the north side of the city in part to balance out the racial composition of New Meadow School, which still has relatively smaller shares of Latino students than do

elementary schools on the south side. Waltham has never had a desegregation plan per se, nor has it been under federal orders to desegregate. At various times, the school committee has implemented redistricting plans so as to
reduce racial imbalance.[40] The state does identify schools and notify districts
when racial compositions vary substantially between schools and encour-
ages districts to develop plans to reduce disparities, though districts are not
sanctioned for failing to reduce disparities. Among elementary schools, the
disparity between the share of black and Latino students was as high as 30
percentage points in 2010—from 23.5 percent at New Meadow School to 54
percent at the Southside School.[41]

Curriculum and Pedagogy

Educators could point to few, if any, specific curriculum-related changes that
emerged in response to increasing diversity in the district. Rather, they said,
curriculum is largely dictated by the state's mandatory test, MCAS. Some
teachers, though, developed special projects designed, in part, to provide students a healthy forum to discuss culture, find commonalities across culture,
and work with people from different backgrounds.

One teacher, for example, organized a poetry slam at a middle school.
During that event, many students worked in groups and wrote and spoke
about cultural differences, friendships that formed across racial and linguistic lines, prejudice, and other topics. In New Meadow Elementary School, an
ESL teacher from the SEI program and a "regular" fourth-grade classroom
teacher teamed up in a classroom that brought together equal numbers of native English speakers and ELLs. The teachers, strongly supported by the principal, chose to do this "so that native speakers and English language learners
were less separated" in the school for their subject areas and so that both
groups got exposed to in-depth, challenging curriculum.

New Meadow principal Paula Turk, consciously provides discussion forums for teachers to discuss matters related to diversity, cultural difference,
and techniques for assisting students who are still learning English. One
teacher said she was drawn to New Meadow in large part because of Turk's
and other educators' conscious efforts to openly discuss matters related to diversity. New Meadow teachers in particular expressed aspirations to find organizational models and projects so students can work together regardless of
their English-speaking skills. For example, one teacher, who works mostly
with children who are learning English, applied for and received a federal
grant in 2009–10 for a "hands-on" science project, which she felt provided a

forum for Spanish speakers and French Creole speakers to demonstrate their skills in ways that studying content for standardized tests do not. She explained: "They build electrical circuits . . . I had a student . . . he started this year in September. He's new from Guatemala and was in the silent period, beginning speaker . . . didn't talk much, very shy, but during a science lesson was the first one to build a parallel circuit, and the whole class just [looked] over. So, it just proved that the hands-on [was really important]. Maybe he couldn't explain it in English. He could in Spanish perfectly."[42]

Turk said that while she was concerned about the relatively low test scores at the school, she was also concerned about the unfairness of a policy that requires students who are still learning English to take complex tests in English: "If you can't read English, you're not going to pass the test . . . I don't like going to meetings and explaining to parents that one of the reasons why we don't do that well on the test is because these kids shouldn't be taking the test, because for a lot of people, the answer is, 'Well, just get rid of them.'"

In the early 1990s, educators eliminated "tracking" at the middle school level, which had sorted students into high or low groups for learning based on previous performance. Administrators said that this policy change did not come about as a direct response to perceptions that students of color were treated unfairly, but because the academic research suggested less rigid classifications were beneficial.

In the district's one high school, Waltham High School (WHS), classroom teachers and administrators face similar challenges, though the challenges manifest themselves in different ways. The school's principal in 2010, Jack Marconi, who had been principal for thirty-two years before retiring in 2011, said that as demographic changes began to occur, he has increasingly expected teachers to make efforts to reach out to parents who might not be comfortable "advocating" for their kids or might not have the language skills to do so. He offered this story of a teacher who was insensitive to the reality in which increasing numbers of students live:

> I let a teacher go this year . . . and she had a glowing recommendation from her director and department head [but] on further review, I had some concerns about her. I looked at . . . two of her science classes. And over three years, 79 percent of her kids either had a D or F. So the first question that the director had was, "Well, why weren't the parents screaming?" Obviously, these kids just weren't motivated. But then, when you looked at the names it was, Rodriguez, Gonzalez, and these were the parents who aren't going to

advocate. She was being honest with their grades, except, she wasn't reaching out. She wasn't making connections . . . "Well" [she said], "I sent a memo home." Well, you well know that one, the [parent] may not have been able to read it or two, it never got there. [I told her], "You . . . you should have asked us. We would have brought those parents in."[43]

Stephen O'Malley, a teacher in the vocational education program, said that even as he recognizes the "vital" importance of college, it is necessary to "face the reality of Waltham" by providing a vocational path for students who want to get out of school, work, and earn money. He said he thinks that strengthening the vocational track may motivate more students to engage with and stay in school. The challenge, O'Malley and other WHS educators agreed, is maintaining balance between college preparation and immediate need: "You've got a kid coming here who has been out of school in his home country for three years and he's just learning English but he's not really literate in his home language. But you can teach him how to fix a car, design a beautiful brochure, or make prints. Waltham is a hardworking community. It's a city of workers traditionally and I say, let's not forget that."[44]

Student Engagement and Parent Incorporation

Jack Marconi echoed the sentiments of high school teachers who said that it will be crucial in the coming years for the district to consider "keeping children longer;" that is, providing all-encompassing services, including after-school activities, connections to school-supervised internships and jobs, and opening up schools to provide homework help in the evenings. For Latino students in particular, whose dropout rates have increased sharply, he said that creating such programs might help reengage students who are under pressure to quit school to earn money.

Just three years ago in 2007, only 1.8 percent of WHS students dropped out of school, according to state-level data. The rate for Latino students was highest, at 4.2 percent. The share of students dropping out increased to 14.8 percent in 2009–10, and state-level data showed that 27.7 percent of Latino students dropped out (versus 9.6 percent of white students). Also, in 2009, the school reported that 65 percent of Latino students had graduated in four years, while 92 percent of white students had graduated after four years.[45]

Also striking is the sharply reduced rate of "in school" and "out of school" suspensions at the high school in recent years. The school's rate of reported suspensions declined from about 20.9 percent of students suspended in 2005 to 0 percent of students suspended in the 2009–10 school year.[46] These data do suggest that children citied for disciplinary infractions are less likely to be excluded from school or miss substantial amounts of instruction. Marconi said that while this did not represent a major policy change at the school level, he had urged staff members to keep students in school, except in the case of violent, dangerous behavior.

Respondents in this study who had grown up in Waltham said that the racial climate has improved at the high school since they were students in the 1970s, 1980s, and 1990s. During those periods, respondents said, students from different racial groups tended not to socialize with each other. Also, they observed, black and Latino students then seemed less likely to participate in some extracurricular activities.

Broadly stated, the most commonly expressed concern at the high school level is keeping students connected to school who face economic pressures to work and live with parents or guardians who have limited capacities to help with homework or course selections. Like several members of the teaching staff, Marconi stressed the importance for teachers to examine daily practices in the context of poverty and cultural diversity. He came to believe that simply treating students equally would be ineffective if some students' parents might "still be living in another country or working three jobs to put food on the table."

At the elementary school level, meanwhile, principals and teachers struggle to develop ways to better incorporate parents, particularly immigrant parents, into the school community. At New Meadow Elementary, for example, educators express strong desires to better acclimate and incorporate Latino, Haitian, and other immigrant parents into the school community. Turk and her staff are experimenting with translation software that allows users to write e-mails in one language and have them received in another. She hopes to provide transportation for parents who need it to attend school meetings and conferences at New Meadow. Also, Turk and other teachers at the school recently informed the all-white members of the executive committee of the mandated school council that they intended to identify parents of color, as well as parents of special education students, to be members of the school council.

At Southside, the predominantly Latino elementary school, the principal and teachers hosted the school's first potluck dinner in 2010, which was well attended by white, Latino, and black families. Principal Evelyn Carr said that providing many avenues for involvement and socializing is important, given that Latino parents are often hesitant to be deeply involved in academic matters related to school.

Administrators pointed to the district's Parent Information Center (PIC) as an effective and helpful resource for parents who may have limited proficiency in English or who are new to the community. The PIC provides a central location for new students to be tested in English proficiency and to register for school, and as a clearinghouse for information on after-school programs, health clinics, and English classes. Several staff members at the PIC are Spanish-speaking bilingual (there are no Haitian Creole speakers on staff). Two parent liaisons are based at the center and serve as interpreters.

The district employs one Spanish translator for written materials and sends materials out to be translated into French Creole. The city school superintendent, along with other upper-level administrators, acknowledged that services in this area do not adequately meet the needs of the district for example, signage on all school buildings is in English.

Community-Level Responses

In the larger community, several non-governmental organizations offer programs and services for the city's immigrant and minority population. WATCH CDC is a community organization that operates numerous programs designed to assist the immigrant community, people with low incomes, and the community of south Waltham. The organization offers free English classes for adults, with about two hundred people on the waiting list. (Several other venues offer opportunities for learning English, including the local public library and a local church. The city schools offer courses in English and citizenship for a fee.) WATCH CDC also builds, manages and advocates for more affordable housing. As an informal drop-in center, it helps immigrant families with translation, applying for government benefits or housing, and organizing to meet needs and concerns.

A twenty-two-year-old collaborative, the Waltham Partnership for Youth, brings together a variety of social service agencies and representatives from the public schools to collectively assess the need of youth and then to collaboratively develop programs that respond to those needs. The program does not respond specifically to the needs of youth of color, but the director, Catherine Uxbridge, said she recognizes the increasing need for more community-based programming that is accessible to students who live on the city's south side and to make the needs of immigrant and low-income youth a priority.

A Model for Scale-Up? The Waltham Family School Program

Opened in 2003 under an Even Start federal grant, the Waltham Family School is a self-described family-literacy program. Serving eighty to ninety children, the program's goal is to provide high-quality preschool programs to children, while offering parents (mostly mothers) free English classes and instruction in basic job skills such as computer fluency. Parents also attend workshops and informal seminars that introduce them to the workings of the public school system, the importance of being involved in the schools, supporting their children during their school-age years, and being advocates for their children within the system.

Located on Moody Street, Waltham's Family School was the only program in the state in 2009–10 that received Even Start funding. The Family School also raises money within the community, and relies on volunteers. In the program's first year, director Carla Pryor recruited families through her networks within social service agencies and through predominantly Latino and Haitian churches. She also put up bilingual fliers in bodegas and in Creole restaurants around the city and the antipoverty agency. The program is now well known throughout Waltham's various immigrant communities. Pryor is an employee of the public schools, which also contribute funding, though all programming decisions are left to the director. From Pryor's vantage point, Waltham has "enormous" capacity to "rise to the challenge." She explains: "I know that there are people in this town . . . that don't like the changes that have come to this city and don't like immigrants. But . . . once we demonstrated that we were a positive force in this community, I have received nothing but support from the school leadership and from the mayor's office and from folks in the community who really stepped up to make contributions."[47]

At Family School, four mornings a week, the children, ages three to five, attend a preschool class that emphasizes language and literacy development while their parents take ESL classes (two mornings a week), a Life Skills class (one morning a week), and a Parenting Discussion and Parent and Child Together activity time (one morning a week). Along with two home visits a month, families also go on a variety of field trips. Teachers and administrators repeatedly pointed to this program as one that deserves to be expanded. The Waltham Family School receives at least ten inquires a week regarding availability.

School superintendent Peter Azar (now no longer with the district) said he believes the program is successful because clients do not associate Family

School with the city school bureaucracy or as part of government, but as a community-based, safe, and welcoming place: "The reason for that is that many of the families that come here don't have a trusting relationship with bureaucracies. Not with schools, with police. . . They don't trust us . . . And that's why [the Family School] is so successful—because people know, over time, that it is a safe place. They know it's all about kids; they know it's all about learning. They know that no one's going to be looking at whether or not they are here legally or illegally."[48]

CONCLUSION: FINDING A PATH FORWARD

The city's racial, cultural, and linguistic diversity attracts, retains, inspires the dedication of, and shapes the values of a corps of enthusiastic, forward-looking educators who are extremely committed to the city's youth. Nevertheless, educators here need more help. They commonly express a desire for assistance in educating children who are still learning English and for reaching out to and effectively engaging children and parents from different cultural and linguistic backgrounds. Teachers inspired by the vibrancy and diversity of their classrooms are eager to develop practices for harnessing that diversity to enrich the education of all students. Unfortunately, these same educators widely perceive that there is no active, useful forum for discussion or for determining action that might lead to constructive responses to these transformative demographic shifts. There is no plan for preventing linguistic, ethnic, and racial segregation in a city with long-standing housing patterns that have the potential to exacerbate segregation.

As yet, leaders have yet to inspire systemic collaborative dialogue and problem solving around the challenge of responding to student needs in the context of demographic change. Individual educators do indeed explore these issues, but the efforts occur in ad hoc fashion and compete with a variety of needs, such as preparation for high-stakes testing, an English-only state mandate, and the routine demands of operating a school.

That said, Waltham has a recent demonstrated history of engaging a variety of sectors within the community in collaborative discussion, needs assessment, and meeting challenges. Specifically, the model program, the Waltham Family School, is a concrete example of the city's commonsense ability to identify a need and fill it. What's more, the community-level support for this particular program, whose quite public mission is to serve and integrate immigrants into the community, should inspire hopefulness and demonstrate the community's collective ability to meet identified challenges.

A core of deeply committed educators is quite clearly asking that "something" be done to help them respond more constructively to demographic change. If this does not provide enough urgency to act, the sharp rise in the Latino student dropout rate—with nearly 30 percent leaving school in 2009—should.

Waltham's fate is intertwined with the fate of its increasingly Latino and immigrant population. Without immigration, the city's population would be in decline, since the white population is shrinking and growing older. Latino, Haitian, and immigrant Waltham is younger, thereby providing a labor force and generating tax revenues. More than this, though, a community's overall health and well-being hinges on engaged, invested, self-sufficient, thriving residents who care about the place they have made home. Schools, historically, are the social institution responsible for helping to develop these types of residents.

A new economic reality that requires more educational credentials obviously makes the role of schools even more vital. With nearly 50 percent of first-graders students of color, the face of Waltham will continue to change. If Waltham's public school students do not all find paths toward self-sufficiency and success, and if educators do not become better equipped to help them to do that, it is likely that the city too will fail to find its own path to a viable, prosperous future.

6

Dividing Lines

East Versus West in Minneapolis Suburbs

BARIS GUMUS-DAWES, MYRON ORFIELD, AND THOMAS LUCE

Minneapolis, historically one of the whitest of large American cities, began to diversify rapidly in the 1990s.[1] The city's urban core, particularly north Minneapolis, became increasingly diverse, with rapid racial segregation in the schools. During this period of rapid demographic change, families of students of color fled to the suburbs and integrated the schools, including Osseo Area Schools to the north. The period of integration was short-lived. Brooklyn Park, in the eastern section of Osseo Area Schools, was one of the first Minneapolis suburbs to transition from having multiethnic integrated schools into having a cluster of segregated schools. When federal low-income housing was built in already poor and minority neighborhoods in the eastern part of Osseo Area district, segregation in the unbalanced schools intensified.[2] In the west of the district, where the student population remained largely white, residents were resistant to or in denial about changes in their district.

District leadership has employed a variety of approaches to encourage and lead both eastern and western communities to respond more productively to their increasingly diverse student populations. They have relied on choice options to create more balance across the district and have not taken other steps to desegregate the schools.

RACIAL AND ECONOMIC CHANGE IN A LARGE SUBURBAN SCHOOL DISTRICT: COMMUNITY CONCERNS AND EFFORTS

In Independent School District 279 Osseo Area Schools, while enrollment numbers have been stable over the last decade at slightly larger than twenty thousand, the racial and socioeconomic composition of the student body in the district has changed dramatically (see exhibit 6.1). Between 2010 and 2008, the percentage of white students in the district fell from 75.3 to 55.0 percent, the percentage of black students almost doubled from 13.2 to 22.8 percent, the percentage of Asian students rose from 8.6 to 14.5 percent, and the percentage of Latino students tripled from 2.1 to 7.0 percent. Meanwhile, the share of students eligible for free and reduced-price lunch climbed steadily from 18 percent to 35 percent. The share of ELLs also increased, from 2 percent to 9 percent. The composition of the first grade is often a good predictor of racial change in the larger district. Although there was hardly any decrease in first-grade student population from 2000 to 2008, the white first-grade population decreased by –26.1 percent, the black first-grade population increased by 64.2 percent, the Asian first-grade population increased by 80.5 percent, and the Latino first-grade population increased by 208.7 percent.

The distribution of students of color and free and reduced-price lunch eligible students is inconsistent across the district. The southeast corner of the district experienced the first wave of change; the number of students of color and low-income students has increased most rapidly in this part of the district (see maps in figures 6.1 and 6.2). The demographic transition subsequently progressed to the northeast and southwest parts of the district. Highway 169 now represents a well-recognized social boundary within the district, dividing it into a more affluent, predominantly white, western side versus a less affluent, racially diverse eastern side. Residents of metropolitan Maple Grove and Plymouth comprise the western side, while residents of Brooklyn Park, Osseo, and Brooklyn Center constitute the eastern side; Maple Grove and Brooklyn Park are the largest metropolitan suburbs on west and east sides, respectively.

Another factor that has affected the changing demographics in the district is the popularity of charter schools. Minnesota was the first state to adopt charter school legislation, in 1991. The district estimated that of the 4,324 students it lost to other choice options (interdistrict public schools, private schools, and homeschooling) in 2009–10, 1,247 went to charter

FIGURE 6.1

Osseo Area Schools: Race breakdowns for elementary schools, 2009–2010

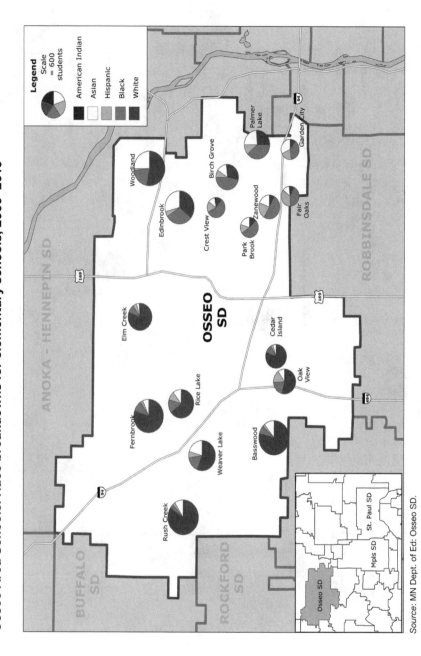

Source: MN Dept. of Ed: Osseo SD.

FIGURE 6.2

Osseo Area Schools: Race breakdowns for elementary schools, 1990–1991

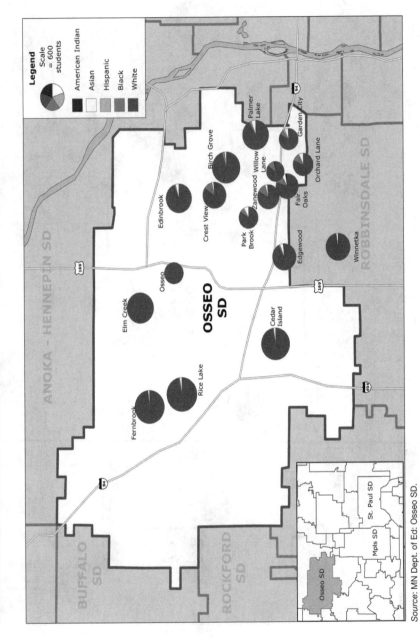

Source: MN Dept. of Ed: Osseo SD.

EXHIBIT 6.1

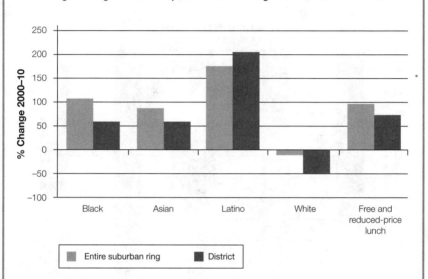

Osseo Area Schools

Percentage change of Minneapolis suburban ring and Osseo Area Schools

Legend: Entire suburban ring ■ District

Racial and poverty composition of Minneapolis metropolitan statistical area, Osseo Area Schools, and district first grade, 2009–10

	% Black	% Asian	% Latino	% White	% English language learners	% Free and reduced- price lunch	Total enrollment
Total MSA	13.2	8.8	7.2	69.4	9.5	33.1	534,873
Principal cities	28.8	16.5	12.8	39.6	22.9	57.3	121,918
Suburbs	8.8	6.5	5.6	78.3	5.5	25.8	412,955
District	22.8	14.5	7.0	55.0	9.1	35.3	20,903
First grade	23.5	16.6	9.7	49.5	—	—	1,538

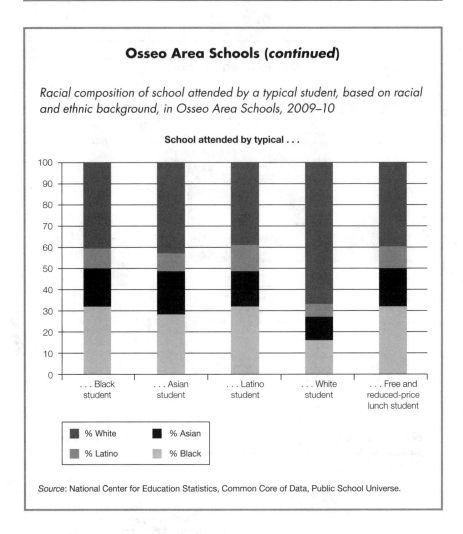

Osseo Area Schools (*continued*)

Racial composition of school attended by a typical student, based on racial and ethnic background, in Osseo Area Schools, 2009–10

Source: National Center for Education Statistics, Common Core of Data, Public School Universe.

schools.[3] The district also found that a larger proportion of students of color than white students were opting out of the district for charter schools, perhaps because of the presence of ethnically themed charter schools.[4]

COMMUNITY ATTITUDES AND RESPONSES TO GROWING RACIAL AND ECONOMIC DIVERSITY

District and metropolitan officials are making deliberate efforts to embrace racial and economic change but also are experiencing some resistance, particularly in the west where residents have tried to halt further diversification. In both eastern and western areas of the district, leaders acknowledge the inter-dependence of neighborhoods and schools for maintaining a thriving community with diverse residents.

The Visibility of Racial Change in the East

Brooklyn Park officials have made efforts to embrace the change by revising their hiring practices and creating programs for positive youth development. However, some in the community also see resistance to change in the form of reduced access to community activities for minority youth and too much emphasis on crime and public safety.

Conceptualizing the Change. Unlike their counterparts in the western part of the district, government officials in the eastern part, including Brooklyn Park and Brooklyn Center, talk about racial and economic diversity because it is part of their reality. Approximately 40 percent of Brooklyn Park residents are people of color. However, residents here, particularly those of color, express their concern that municipal officials do not fully understand the needs of the increasingly diverse community and negatively conceptualize the demographic shift.

A white school board member who resides in Brooklyn Center claimed that "people are pretty tolerant here" while at the same time acknowledging that change has been hard for most people.[5] Reinforcing this opinion, Steve Lampi, the mayor of Brooklyn Park, acknowledged that people in his community "want to strive to embrace the change, but I think it is challenging for them."[6] Mayor Lampi further described the attitudes and concerns of long-term Brooklyn Park residents toward growing racial and economic diversity within the city by citing comments about North Minneapolis, the region's most racially and economically segregated urban neighborhood, with a predominantly black population: "What I hear more than anything is 'We don't want our community to turn into another North Minneapolis.' And I don't know what that means exactly, but we have taken that to mean that we want infrastructure that's in good shape. We want homes that are in good shape. We want people maintaining their properties well, and if you do that and stay quiet, we'll all figure out how to live together."

In addition to acknowledging the challenges associated with changing demographics, some residents focus more on the threatening aspect of diversification. One former Brooklyn Park resident of color described the community attitude as follows: "They feel threatened by the diversity. I have had people say that much to me in those words, 'We don't like these changes. We want our neighborhoods to stay the same. We want our school to stay the same. We want our country to stay the same' . . . As the curiosity about new immigrant populations has faded and they have become more institutionalized in our communities, they become more of a threat."[7]

Keith Johnson, executive director of a community organization advocating for African Americans in Brooklyn Park, suggested that in some instances, city officials view residents of color as problematic threats to public safety and they express a desire to "eradicate them or get them out of the city."[8] Johnson criticized city hall for being complicit in fear mongering by talking about public safety and the need to expand the police force to deal with criminality rather than creating substantial community programs to address the issue. Mayor Lampi stated that he had heard frequent complaints about "groups of kids roaming the streets . . . We do hear a lot about crime, and it seems like there are more minorities involved in crime than not, and I think that that creates some friction sometimes."

Community Efforts to Embrace Change and Areas for Improvement.   Residents and local officials in the district express willingness to embrace the changing demographics but also acknowledge that there is still much more to do. Mayor Lampi said city officials are working to find ways to reflect the diversity of the community in the city government and increase participation of a diverse set of community members. He felt that they have been relatively successful in increasing diversity at the senior management level but not with the larger staff.

In addition to encouraging diversity in the city staff, officials in the east have made targeted efforts to engage with the diversity among the area's young people. In contrast to Keith Johnson's criticisms noted above, several residents suggested that attitudes have evolved from a "safety and crime reduction" paradigm to a "support for positive outcomes" paradigm.

As an example of efforts to address youth crime in a positive way, Steve Lampi cited the Brooklyns Bridge Alliance, a joint powers agreement to promote positive youth development, which was signed by the cities of Brooklyn Park, Brooklyn Center, and a number of other public entities, including the local school district and technical colleges. The alliance grew out of two different efforts: (1) the work of a long-range improvement commission whose goal was to develop more youth opportunities within the city and (2) a police department study showing that most crime happened after school hours.

The first initiative attracted a number of youth of color who teamed up with business entities in order to establish a business enterprise and meeting place called the A-List. The second promoted partnerships with outreach groups to guide more challenged youth in positive directions and prevent them from getting into trouble. Steve Lampi noted that the current struggle within the Brooklyns Bridge Alliance is to balance these two distinct types of needs: the need to deal with troubled youth and the need to provide opportunities so that fewer youth get into trouble.

While city officials present their efforts in addressing youth crime as positive, this view is not universally shared. Keith Johnson criticized the Brooklyns Bridge Alliance's focus on well-to-do youth of color: "Here you create these programs and you do all these public media blitzes to make it appear that you are doing something substantial in the community and you are doing absolutely nothing." Johnson cited the community center on 85th Avenue as another example of the city's unwelcoming actions. He said that once youth of color started going to the community center to play basketball, the center reduced its basketball hours to one hour a day, effectively driving the youth back to the streets.

Community Conceptualization and Response in the West

Residents in the predominantly white and affluent western part of the district tend to be less aware of Osseo's changing demographics. As former superintendent Chris Richardson described the attitudes toward diversity among residents of Maple Grove and Plymouth: "We know it is out there but we don't see much of it."[9] Years of public and private resistance to affordable housing and deceptive practices in real estate markets have isolated this part of the district from the metropolitan area's increasing diversity to some extent. Further, some residents have been actively resisting changing demographics in schools.

Lack of Awareness and Discussion About Race. To the extent that the west is diversifying, "the communities are experiencing mostly racial change but not economic change."[10] In Maple Grove, for example, diversity does not figure as prominently in public conversations as it does in Brooklyn Park. Student demographics in Maple Grove schools were still fairly homogenous in 2008, with the exception of one school described below, making any discussion of race relations less urgent for schools. Assistant superintendent Kate Maguire, a Maple Grove resident, described the attitude toward growing student diversity in parts of Maple Grove:

> When you're in a huge [community, approximately sixty-three thousand residents], you really don't have to leave your community . . . You can live and worship in your community. You go to school in your community . . . There are many people who do not know that we have four high schools, do not know that Brooklyn Park and Brooklyn Center are part of our school community—and oh, by the way, don't care . . . And I know that we have community members in Maple Grove who do not know that we're connected and sometimes have difficulty understanding about how we need to meet the needs of all students and then what that means.[11]

Structural Barriers to Increased Diversity.   In contrast to the growing diversity in the eastern part of the district, much of the relative lack of diversity in Maple Grove can be attributed to its housing policies. In fact, the city of Maple Grove earned a national reputation for its virulent opposition to affordable housing during the 1990s.[12] In the last decade, however, the city has become more willing to build affordable units and it has permitted the construction of a number of housing units consisting of mixed-income developments and apartment complexes in dispersed sites. Maple Grove's mayor, Mark Steffenson, referred to the problems that Brooklyn Park experienced due to its concentration of affordable units in one corridor and emphasized the importance of avoiding similar concentrations.[13] Despite its improving record, according to Brooklyn Park's Steve Lampi, only 12 percent of the housing in Maple Grove is affordable, compared with 28 percent in Brooklyn Park.

The absence of public transportation is another factor that makes Maple Grove a less diverse community. Maple Grove resident and community leader John Williams noted: "I think one of the reasons, . . . that it hasn't changed as rapidly in Maple Grove is we have no mass transit public transportation, unless you are going to the transit centers—to downtown. So for families without transportation, it's very difficult to live in Maple Grove . . . the infrastructure isn't there to necessarily support a lot of that."[14]

Deception and Desire for Neighborhood Schools.   Many residents of Maple Grove move there because of its high-quality schools. Former superintendent

Richardson mentioned that as far back as the 1990s, communities like Maple Grove and Plymouth advocated for neighborhood schools. He argued that real estate agents played a key role in fueling this sense of entitlement to attend neighborhood schools as they deceptively advertised "Maple Grove Schools" in their real estate ads, instead of the Osseo Area Schools. He explained that he had received many irate phone calls from parents who moved to Maple Grove and later became upset when they learned that their children would attend different schools than the realtors had suggested. The phone calls became so incessant that Richardson called a meeting with the Maple Grove Realtors' Association to encourage them to stop advertising Maple Grove schools in their ads.

The Berryhill Controversy. The magnet school approach to diffusing segregation through voluntary movement of students across the district and between districts has also been a source of tension among Maple Grove parents. This tension peaked in 2005 when Osseo Area Schools decided to close Shady Grove Elementary, located in Brooklyn Park, and to move the science, technology, engineering, and mathematics (STEM) magnet program from that building to a larger site in Maple Grove.[15] As a result of this move, the new site for the magnet program, Berryhill Elementary School, was transformed from a predominantly white neighborhood school to a magnet school with a significant presence of students of color. The school, which was roughly 75 percent white in 2000, was just 43 percent white in 2005 after the conversion.

These changes created intense backlash. A large number of parents organized into a group that obtained legal assistance from the Pacific Legal Foundation—a nonprofit organization with extensive experience in mounting legal challenges to school districts' use of race in changing school boundaries.[16] An affiliate of the group, called Families Involved in Neighborhood Schools, also filed a complaint against superintendent Susan Hintz with the Minnesota Board of School Administrators for ethical violations, of which she was eventually cleared.[17]

The superintendent as well as other district and school officials described several instances of "bullying behavior" from residents.[18] Superintendent Hintz received more than twelve hundred e-mails opposing the change. Residents created an Internet blog where they posted various allegations against Hintz and also recruited a local news crew to do an aggressive "exposé" about her. The principal of the magnet program at Berryhill Elementary, reported similar experiences: "My staff got hate e-mail saying, 'Don't come here. We don't want you here. You're not welcome in Maple Grove.' I think much of it was some veiled and some not-very-veiled racism."[19]

Thomas described additional cases in which interracial conflicts between students triggered what she considered "overreactions" from white parents. In some cases, parents bypassed the principal and school district administration to go straight to the police in Maple Grove. Thomas speculated that if the conflict underlying these incidents had not been racial, the police probably would not have been involved at all, suggesting that in these instances the white families were "scared to death" of students of color. In all three incidents, white parents pulled their children from the school.

In addition, a district official and Thomas described a recent case of vandalism at Berryhill: "Somebody got like Round-Up or something that kills vegetation . . . And on the side of the grassy bowl that faces the road they sprayed in 'close this s*** hole.' And it took probably a couple days to burn . . . and then the message was there."

Leaders of the parent group argued that parents who questioned the restructuring of schools and the boundary changes that altered the demographic makeup of several schools had legitimate concerns that weren't about race:

> The parents over here were saying, "I'm concerned that my kid is not going to be challenged as much—get as much attention—because the attention is going to be focused elsewhere." And there is a documented higher incidence of some discipline issues and things like that. Some parents were concerned about that. So that's where [the administrators say] "Oh, it's—now, I understand where you're coming from here. This is all about race." No, it's about my kid's education. I understand that these kids may need more, but I just want to make sure that there's enough that can go around so that my child is not the one that's shortchanged.

Kate Maguire reported that some community members in Maple Grove feel so strongly about making sure resources go straight to their students that they "have suggested that we ought to secede. And we've had people suggest that we form our own school district in Maple Grove so that we don't have a 'financial drain'—their words, not mine—to serve students who have different needs."

Many members of the parent group defined themselves as fiscal conservatives who were critical of the health and human service investments that the district was making in its attempt to serve low-income students who are mostly minority students. They were weary of the financial burden that these "welfare" services imposed on the school district budget.

School and Community Collaboration Across the District

City and district leaders recognize that schools and neighborhoods depend on each other in creating and sustaining positive communities. In an effort to meet the basic needs of students across the district, its leaders have created a collaborative center to provide students and residents with a variety of social services. But the eastern and western areas are sharply differentiated when it comes to dealing with diversification. The east is pursuing the issues of affordable housing plans in the community and the impact of concentrated areas of poverty on schools. In the west, city officials have openly opposed affordable housing and chosen not to provide public transportation—two structural moves that effectively prevent neighborhoods and schools from diversifying.

Acknowledging the Need for Cross-Sector Collaboration in Brooklyn Park. Brooklyn Park mayor Steve Lampi stated his belief in the importance of having good schools in order to have a vibrant metropolis. He emphasized the social and economic challenges that pockets of poverty present, not only for the city but also for the school district. As an example, he described a corridor in Brooklyn Park where 85 to 90 percent of the city's six thousand apartments are located. Most of the units are affordable one-bedroom units that house residents of color. He criticized the Metropolitan Council—a regional government in the Twin Cities with strong land-use and transportation powers—for their lack of leadership in promoting a more equal distribution of affordable housing across the region.

Lampi singled out the issues of high student mobility and turnover as undesirable consequences of such residential patterns: "In the more economically challenged areas of the city, the schools experience a great deal of turnover in students. I have heard numbers that sound like 50 percent of the kids that start school in September will be gone by Christmas time . . . I have got a pretty good idea how that can impact a class." A principal at an Osseo elementary school agreed: "Schools end up with the students and so our society then looks at schools to fix that problem [of the achievement gap] . . . How do you fix that problem without fixing the other problems that created it in the first place, which have been long-standing . . . discriminatory practices in places like housing, employment, other areas?"

Susan Hintz acknowledged the relationship between neighborhoods and schools: "You know, the only way that we would ever really create the balance that I told you about is if we balanced out the neighborhoods, because kids and families want to go to their neighborhood school. And so the changes that we've made that have been so hard—that have been challenging—are paying off in student results. But it's slow and it's difficult . . . There's pretty much a direct relationship [between housing and schools] . . . And we have made some progress in our community to provide stable housing for our families in poverty."

Steve Lampi made it clear that the city and the school district have common interests and that officials of both entities have supported each other in various policy decisions. When Brooklyn Park decided to demolish a large number of inexpensive apartment units concentrated in a small area, the school district was fully supportive of the decision. The mayor mentioned that Brooklyn Park urged the district to better balance its student population in schools and to attract students from other parts of the district through magnet programs like the International Baccalaureate (IB) program, and the district has been responsive.

Northwest Family Services Center.   In addition to housing policies, Osseo Area district has been attempting to address the achievement gap by focusing on the basic needs of its low-income students. Susan Hintz spearheaded a strategic effort to create the (Minneapolis area) Northwest Family Services Center within the district. In an example of cross-sector collaboration aimed at breaking the cycle of poverty that fuels the achievement gap in the district's schools, Osseo Area Schools, along with community partners, successfully secured $2 million in state bond revenue to fund this center. The main goal of the center is to help improve the academic performance of more than sixteen thousand low-income students who attend school in five Minneapolis area northwestern school districts. By integrating a wide array of services in a single location, the center aims to improve family stability—thus diminishing one of the major barriers to student achievement. The superintendent could barely contain her enthusiasm in describing the center: "Well, now we have four million dollars from the county and they're going to set up a medical center with all that. And CEAP [the Community Emergency Assistance

Program] will be there . . . So we'll have the adult education center, the enrollment center, an early childhood center, and a regional family services center with food, shelter, clothes, dental, health, mental health—and we're just really, really excited." Hintz described the center as having "the potential to become a national model for delivery of education, human services, and emergency assistance."[20]

OSSEO AREA'S ATTITUDES AND ACTIONS TO ADDRESS GROWING RACIAL AND ECONOMIC DIVERSITY OF ITS STUDENTS

District officials, administrators, and teachers expressed varied responses to the increasing diversity of Osseo's schools and communities. District officials led efforts to embrace the changes. They implemented a desegregation plan, which led to the development of magnet schools to facilitate voluntary integration, new policies targeting staff diversity and training, and new and modified student support programs. Nevertheless, some teachers and administrators experienced challenges in adapting.

The District's Attitudes

During her nine years as a district administrator, 2001–10, superintendent Susan Hintz advocated for integrating Osseo's schools by citing research that showed the academic advantages of balanced schools, the importance of diverse school environments in preparing students to work in a global economy, and the fact that many universities use attendance in diverse schools as an admission preference. As assistant superintendent, she had urged the school board to make changes to balance the schools, but they were unresponsive to her suggestion at the time.

Currently, however, district-level officials show a high level of commitment to socioeconomic balance in Osseo Area Schools. These administrators view growing racial and economic diversity as part of a regional and national trend. Aware of the equity implications of these demographic trends and the need to effectively manage diversity, they recently introduced a strategic plan that names socioeconomic balance in schools as an explicit goal. Yet, like many other suburban districts in the area, Osseo did not do much to address the growing racial and economic diversity of its students until most of its integrated schools became resegregated. As the proportion of students of color in suburban schools continued to increase, white students began to leave the schools.[21] Currently, twelve of the district's twenty-seven schools are racially isolated, meaning that their enrollment of students of color exceeds the district's overall enrollment of students of color by at least 20 percent.

Greg Howard, a district-level staff member, argued that not proactively addressing racial and economic diversity in the district makes it harder to now address the change. Ironically, as discussed further below, the state relaxed desegregation requirements in 1999 and is currently considering cutting funding for such initiatives, just as Osseo finds the task harder to address:

> What's happened now is the schools are so different, the parents can't conceive—or even teachers . . . Had we been able to manage it in a different way so the differences weren't so extreme, then the changes—the boundary changes, the programming changes, and things—would have been much easier. People would have accepted the programs. Because if you're at Winding Brook [a predominantly white school at the western edge of the district] you say, "We're spending what on ELL?! How can we be spending that much money on ELL?" . . . They don't get that we have kids that move in that have never spoken English. We have kids move in that have never gone to school. [Parents] can't understand it because they have no experience . . . And if somehow then you mix the two extreme schools together, it's a mess. Teachers don't know what to do. Parents don't know how to think about it. Programming's not there properly . . . the rapid change and the localization of the change has made it very, very difficult for the district to manage it.

Howard thought that teachers' attitudes toward racial change are less enthusiastic and more mixed than the attitudes of the district administrators, who do not deal with the day-to-day realities of the diversity. At Berryhill Elementary School, the principal and teachers appreciated the benefits of a racially diverse school, but they were also eager to point out the challenges associated with diversity, including growing student poverty and mobility as well as difficulties of teaching ELLs. Principal Jessica Thomas and her teachers, sometimes citing specific educational research on the verbal deficiencies of preschool children who come from impoverished households, explained the racial patterns in educational achievement by attributing the differences in the students' experiences and school readiness to poverty, not that the parents valued education any less than other families.

Thomas described the attitudes of her staff toward diversity as "mixed." She believes that it is part of her job to mentor her staff and to be a role model as a culturally responsive educator. Although she has no systematic avenues to do so in her school, she has tried to mentor her staff on a case-by-case basis as intercultural issues arise. Further, she emphasized that the challenges of working with a diverse body of students can be extremely exhausting for teachers, especially given the large class sizes at the school. She admitted that both her administrators and her teachers at times fell back to the position of blaming the parents as they struggled with the frustration of dealing with students who had vastly different needs, and particularly of educating their high-needs students, given the inadequacy of their resources.

The staff at Pineville Elementary School, located in the eastern side of the district, is also struggling with challenges as the school experiences rapid demographic transition. Pineville was predominantly white until 2002, when boundary changes resulted in increasing attendance from low-income students of color from nearby rental properties. Currently, one-third of the school's students are Asian, another third are black, and another third are white, and 5 percent of its students are Latino. Approximately 47 percent of the students are eligible for free and reduced-price lunch. A significant number of Pineville teachers are frustrated with growing student poverty, absence of parents, and behavioral issues; however, Pineville administrators contend that a growing number of teachers have accepted the need to learn about the changing needs of their students and assume responsibility for teaching all students. The conversations around minority students are less and less about punitive responses to their behavior but instead focus on trying to problem-solve with them.[22]

At centrally located Oakwood High School, all interviewees acknowledged the challenges arising when the student population has diversified much more quickly than the faculty, and some suggested that not all faculty and staff have adjusted with the same success. However, none of the four interviewees from Oakwood cited instances of strong opposition from faculty about changes in the school. Staff and teachers both emphasized the bottom line—finding teaching methods that engage all the school's students.[23]

Addressing Growing Diversity Through Magnet Schools

Until 1999, Minnesota had a mandatory desegregation plan, which required each school board to report the racial composition of its schools. If any school's minority population exceeded the corresponding population of the district by 15 percent, the district was required to implement a plan to eliminate this segregation or else its state aid was reduced.[24]

In 2000, Minnesota ended mandatory desegregation and introduced voluntary integration through school choice. According to this rule, any school with an enrollment of students of color exceeding the district's overall enrollment of students of color by 20 percent is considered a "racially isolated school."[25] Districts with racially isolated schools are encouraged to develop integration plans that provide options for integrating schools and increasing interracial contact among students. The rule also identifies "racially isolated districts" as those in which the percentage of enrollment of students of color exceeds the corresponding percentages in adjoining districts by 20 percent. Racially isolated districts were encouraged to develop an integration plan with adjoining school districts.[26]

Since adoption, the state's existing voluntary integration rule has been mostly unsuccessful. Legal scholars who criticized it for being ineffective in fostering desegregation summarize the reasons for its lack of success:

> The rules, while certainly *permitting* districts to make pro-integrative decisions, do not mandate or even affirmatively support such decision-making. They also do not explicitly prohibit districts from making decisions about school attendance boundaries or school closings that, in effect, create racially isolated schools. Instead, Minnesota's rules leave the desegregating of racially isolated schools up to the will of local school boards, which face immense political pressure to maintain racial boundaries. Likewise, the rules do not give the Minnesota Department of Education the tools to force school districts to desegregate schools unless the state can prove that the district intended to discriminate against students of color.[27]

Some districts, including Osseo, have tried to implement the new desegregation rule; however, their efforts have achieved only limited success. Working with the new rule and the presence of racially isolated schools, Osseo Area Schools developed an integration plan in 2000.[28] In 2001, the district was deemed a racially isolated school district. Therefore, Osseo Area Schools began the process of cross-district integration with six neighboring suburban school districts to create the Northwest Suburban Integration School District (NWSISD).

The NWSISD was designed to promote integration and interracial contact by facilitating voluntary movement of students across member districts. In order to achieve voluntary desegregation through magnet schools, the NWSISD created several incomplete magnet strands, in which a series of elementary, middle, and high schools, each in a different district, emphasize a particular magnet program, such as IB, fine arts, or STEM. The objective of a strand is to encourage students to cross district boundaries to attend magnet schools in different districts as they progress through grade levels. The NWSISD's magnet school programs currently serve more than three thousand students at fifteen school sites.[29] However, the goal of voluntary desegregation through interdistrict school choice has not been fully realized in the NWSISD. Seven of the NWSISD's fifteen magnet schools are currently considered racially isolated. The Osseo Area district hosts four of the NWSISD magnet schools. The only magnet school in the district that has succeeded in integrating the school building is the Berryhill STEM magnet. There are several reasons for this outcome.

First, the definition of racially isolated schools in Minnesota undermines voluntary movement of students through interdistrict magnet programs. Racial isolation is defined by the percentage of students of color in a school building, and "predominantly white" schools are not considered racially isolated. Districts prioritized creating magnets in high-poverty schools characterized by a predominantly nonwhite student body, and attracting white students to these schools has been an uphill battle for many districts in the NWSISD.

Additionally, the state education funding formula discourages school districts from promoting voluntary interdistrict movement of students because per pupil state aid follows the student when the student leaves a school district. This gave some member districts within the NWSISD an incentive to undermine the original intent of the NWSISD. For instance, Fridley Public Schools violated the original design of the NWSISD by completing a magnet strand within the district, thus encouraging its students to remain in the district through all three levels of schooling and effectively stopping their movement to other districts.[30]

In contrast, Osseo Area Schools honored the original intent of the NWSISD and refrained from completing a within-district magnet strand until recently. As a result, Osseo has been losing students to magnet schools in other districts. In 2009, 561 students left Osseo to attend magnet schools in other districts while only 202 students transferred into Osseo's magnet schools from other districts.[31]

Most senior administrators acknowledge the limited success of magnet schools in integrating school buildings in the district. In discussing the magnet strategy for achieving integration, Susan Hintz stated that the magnets provided "really great programs for the students who were there because of the training that's provided, the staff and the shared vision and all of that sort of thing, but it did not accomplish the movement [of students] to the level that was anticipated." Despite the limited success of magnet schools in integrating school buildings, the district is nevertheless committed to using magnets because of the appeal of school choice.

Policies Targeting Staff

In addition to attempts at choice-based integration, the district has employed several strategies to encourage professional development about diversity for the staff, including teacher collaboratives, professional development workshops, and professional learning communities (PLCs). These approaches attempt to develop intercultural competence among the staff members who are already employed at the schools. The district acknowledges the difficulty of hiring a more diverse staff to reflect the diversity of the community.

Susan Hintz led an initiative to enhance the intercultural competence of the district's leadership. As a first step, she required that district administrators and principals complete the Intercultural Development Inventory (IDI) to assess their individual intercultural competence levels. Over the last five years, district administrators, principals, and school board members have formed cohorts to go through intense cultural competency training. Hintz selected this approach because she believed that "our staff isn't going to change if the leaders don't. And . . . it has to start with the board and the superintendent because . . . you have to be the change that you want people to become."

District administrators regarded the introduction of these standards as part of enhancing the district's "responsiveness" to the diverse needs of its students. Michelle Fisher, a district-level staff member of Osseo Area Schools, described the process of creating standards as one of "moving from intercultural competence, which is awareness and competence building, to responsiveness." Rich Melvin, assistant superintendent for human resources, spoke in similar terms: "And really we see it bigger than just about what happens in the classroom . . . It's not just about 'How do we teach kids?' It is, 'How does our system become more responsive?'"[32]

Osseo is beginning to extend these training efforts to its school-based staff. Currently, the district urges its principals to enhance the intercultural competence of their teachers in any way they see fit. In the future, it intends to enhance the cultural competence of its teachers in more standardized ways and, to this end, is developing a set of specific standards to describe what culturally competent practices would look like at school sites and in classrooms. In three pilot schools—West Creek, Shadow Lane, and Pineville elementary schools—principals engaged their staff in enhancing their intercultural competence with support from the district. The district gave the principals significant autonomy in choosing the specific methods. For example, West Creek opted for teacher collaborative training, while Shadow Lane and Pineville chose a professional development workshop format that enabled teachers to talk and read about racism and white privilege.

The district has also encouraged the development of professional learning communities in every school. PLCs are collaborative teams of teachers who work together in small groups to examine achievement data and discuss ways to improve outcomes. Data are disaggregated by subgroups so that teachers can identify patterns and gaps between and within groups. By analyzing the data in this manner, teachers work with each other to share ideas about how to reach the students who are struggling.

In addition to concerns about developing the existing staff, varying perspectives have emerged with regard to targeted hiring to increase racial diversity among the staff. In a district where minority students comprise nearly 44 percent of the student body, Osseo Area Schools' employees remain primarily white. In 2009–10, 80 percent of the district's administrative staff and 96 percent of teachers were white.[33]

During superintendent Susan Hintz's tenure from 2006 until 2010, the district made hiring and retaining staff of color an explicit priority in its strategic plan. While the district was relatively successful in hiring administrators of color, it made little progress in hiring staff of color. The superintendent believes Osseo has had success with hiring administrators because the district is committed to providing focused, intentional, and systematic leadership training and support for administrators. District officials emphasized the difficulty of recruiting and retaining teachers of color, which they partially attributed to the fact that the district has so far failed to provide a welcoming environment for them. They also mentioned that fluctuating district budgets periodically erode most of the gains made in hiring these teachers, who are usually last to be hired and first to be laid off due to seniority requirements. Other district administrators claimed that the pool of qualified candidates of color was relatively small and the number of districts pursuing those candidates was large.

Many in the community, however, were skeptical of the claim that the problem was a shortage of qualified candidates. Community advocates, including Keith Johnson, suggested that the superintendent's efforts to diversify the district's workforce received pushback from the HR department, which reiterated the need to ensure that candidates of color were qualified and experienced. Johnson suggested that the issues of qualifications and experience were used as excuses to avoid hiring candidates of color.

Rich Melvin, who heads the HR department, acknowledged that it was sometimes difficult to simultaneously meet the goals of hiring the most qualified candidates and hiring more staff of color. He expressed his reluctance to hire staff of color just for the sake of increasing their numbers in the district:

> When we talk about hiring practices, I've not been as eager to just hire staff of color so that we can say we have more staff of color because there have been times when we've done that. They haven't been successful, and that has been worse . . . I think that's been a more difficult situation than if we hadn't hired them because when . . . you've got some entrenched thinking or behaviors, stereotypes, that just reinforces that and puts actually more pressure on the next person of color that you hire to perform at a higher level than other people. And I'm really sensitive to that. Now I don't want to be so overly sensitive to say [that] we're not going to hire any people of color unless they're the very best.

Nevertheless, the district has been successful in creating two specific staff positions: bilingual staff to support new families and students; and cultural liaisons, who later became student learning advocates. The new bilingual staff members assist non-English-speaking families and students as they learn to navigate the school system. Unlike the student learning advocates, who are based in specific school buildings, the bilingual staff members are centrally located in the district's enrollment center. They provide the first point of contact for new families coming into the district and also respond to the needs of families and students with limited English at various school sites. Given the rapid proliferation of foreign languages spoken by its students—currently more than eighty languages—the district is clearly far from being able to respond to the needs of all the non-English–speaking families but tries to respond to the needs of the largest non-English–speaking groups within the district.

The cultural liaisons initially came into schools to do presentations about the culture of different groups, such as important holidays and foods. However, the district soon realized the limitations of cultural literacy activities and shifted its focus to student achievement; therefore, district administrators transformed the role of cultural liaisons to student learning advocates, who work directly with students of color by providing support for them and their families in racially isolated schools. They reach out to families who do not have relationships with school staff, tutor students in academic areas, and mentor students regarding social and emotional issues. Susan Hintz expressed additional appreciation for the student learning advocates because of the diversity they have brought into an otherwise predominantly white workforce.

Programming to Provide Student Support

In addition to taking steps to target staff needs, the district has also created new and modified existing programs to provide support to the increasingly diverse enrollment. Hintz focused her organization's attention on poverty-related sources of the achievement gap. The district reviewed existing research on strategies to address this gap and implemented two strategies districtwide. Osseo has doubled its capacity to deliver early childhood programs, especially in the southern part of the district, where the need was highest. This initiative involved reconfiguring several schools in the south to expand all-day, every-day preschool programs already offered. As part of this plan, the district over-hauled three elementary schools into a campus system. Two schools became preK–3 schools that would feed into a third, which housed fourth through sixth grades. This configuration gave the district the opportunity to expand its preK services in the southern part of the district and brought the schools' socioeconomic composition more in line with the district averages.

At the same time, the district recognized that imbalances remained and streamlined its resources to help schools with the highest need. To accomplish this goal, the district used what Greg Howard called a "pile deep" method:

> Rather than trying to spread things out thin across the whole district, we take the special resources we have, like Title I, and focus it on a small number of really, really high-need sites. And so that really puts them in a good situation. We have not had flight of teachers from those sites. We have not had an emptying of those sites. And I believe we have some of our most effective principals at those sites, and we really do hold them up as examples . . . We have twenty-seven schools [that have high low-income percentages]; it goes to five. And so that's what I mean by . . . pile deep. And they still have tremendous challenges in those schools, but we are trying to be equitable, not equal.

By targeting resources on the highest-need schools, the district allowed those schools to reduce class size—a factor that contributes to the relative absence of high teacher turnover in these racially segregated, high-poverty schools. Thereafter, students' academic performance at those schools improved. Howard noted that these highest-need schools "often are the sites that have the highest percentage of the kids making their individual [academic growth] targets."

Recognizing the need for culturally responsive behavior management systems, schools across the district have implemented various programs to attempt to build community and teach character rather than rely on overly punitive systems. At Berryhill, responsive classroom strategies became a part of the magnet school's curriculum because they were especially pertinent to the diverse population there. The principal described the approach as follows:

> It is a series of beliefs, philosophies, strategies, and practices that say that the social curriculum in a classroom and in a school is as critical to learning as the academic curriculum, and that until you have established the social curriculum, you will not be able to move kids forward in the academic curriculum. So we sent our teachers to training; almost all of our teachers have been through one to two full weeks of training in responsive classroom [techniques]. And then we spent a significant amount of time building our discipline and expectation system—like a full year—based on the philosophies and practices of responsive classroom.

At Oakwood High School, interviewees acknowledged that there were significant racial differences in the incidence of disciplinary action against students. Black students, particularly black males, were more likely to be involved in such situations. The school instituted a "pyramid of interventions" to guide teachers and staff through graduated responses to disciplinary issues, with the goal of minimizing the need for more severe, higher-level administrative interventions. The school also provided training in a program known as Love and Logic, which emphasizes providing students with choices rather than confrontations. Reaction to these programs is somewhat mixed, with some teachers more likely to reach the top of the pyramid of interventions—sending the student to a vice principal for discipline—more quickly than others.

At Pineville Elementary School, where staff members adjusted relatively quickly to the school's rapidly growing racial and economic diversity, the administrators implemented a proactive behavioral support system. They moved away from simply reacting to behavioral issues with the limited goal of ensuring students' safety. Instead they implemented two new programs: ENVOY, a nonverbal communications training program for teachers successfully used in districts like Minneapolis to reduce escalation of problems between teachers and students; and Productive Recess, a program that involves structured rather than free play during recess, where the students are given the option of participating in eight different small-group activities. In the last two years, the school's discipline incidences decreased by 60 percent.

CONCLUSION

Community responses to increasing diversity in the Osseo Area Schools have been mixed, with residents in the east more aware and accepting of the change than residents in the west, where resistance has been expressed by an outspoken group of parents, deceptive real estate practices, and structural barriers to the spread of diversity, all of which have contributed to making the district's job of desegregating the schools more difficult. City officials, particularly in the east, have acknowledged the importance of working with school district administrators to develop policies that are beneficial to the community at large, recognizing the importance of good schools to supporting a good community and the reverse. Cross-sector collaboration is evident in the development of the Northwest Family Services Center, which is aimed at providing comprehensive services to students and families in need—an attempt to break the cycle of poverty that fuels the achievement gap. In another effort at cross-sector collaboration, there have been attempts to provide more affordable housing, though its concentration in the east has resulted in more concentrated groups of low-income students at schools in the east. In contrast, there is no real evidence of cross-sector collaboration to proactively plan for making the western part of the district more accessible and welcoming of diverse students.

When most of its previously diverse schools became segregated, Osseo Area Schools implemented a strategic plan to remedy the unbalanced distribution of students of color across the district. The district developed a magnet school plan, hoping that choice options would lead to voluntary movement of students across the district (as well as between Osseo and surrounding districts) and thus result in more balanced schools. This hope, however, was not realized, and choice options were appealing to parents because of the programming they offered rather than the integration of students that was desired. The district also employed a variety of professional development models, all of which were geared toward increasing intercultural competence of the staff. Facing difficulties in hiring more diverse staff, the district's teaching force remained primarily white, although new staff positions addressed the needs of minority, low-income students and added diversity. Programming changes to address poverty-related sources of the achievement gap included increasing early childhood education programs and targeting funding toward the schools with the highest need. Recognizing that students of color are often overrepresented in special education and in disciplinary actions, schools across the district implemented tiered interventions and culturally relevant behavior management systems to prevent such overrepresentation. In many cases, school staff members had difficulty adjusting to their school's changing student populations, but most have come to accept the diversity and strive to serve all students to the best of their ability.

While these efforts at desegregating the district and serving the needs of a more diverse student population are commendable, they have been less successful than desired in accomplishing the goal of balancing the racial and socioeconomic distribution of students across the district. Despite Minnesota's state desegregation policies and the collaborative efforts of NWISD to move students across district lines in an effort to desegregate several districts, schools within Osseo Area Schools remain segregated. If the district had implemented these strategies earlier in the process of resegregation, it is likely that it would have realized more success, because once schools have transitioned to become racially isolated, it is very difficult to reverse the trend and to build understanding and political support for the need for such policies when parts of the district have very little exposure to overall demographic change.

7

Conflicting Mandates Amid Suburban Change

Educational Opportunity in a Post-Desegregation Florida Countywide District

KATHRYN WILEY, BARBARA SHIRCLIFFE, AND JENNIFER MORLEY

Beach County Public School District (BCPS) is a large countywide district in Florida, the county lines of which encompass a major city, smaller municipalities, and unincorporated rural and suburban communities.[1] With a residential population of nearly 1.2 million, these communities include the entire matrix of suburban typologies, including exurbs, exclusive enclaves, and at-risk bedroom communities.[2] Historically, Beach County has been part of a racially and ethnically diverse geographical area. Multiple colonizing influences, including the Spanish, French, and English, and the importation of Africans as slaves, brought waves of settlers to the indigenous area. The nineteenth and twentieth centuries saw the establishment of African American communities; later, industrial development attracted Cuban, Spanish, and Italian immigrants. An increasingly diverse population continued to emerge as World War II brought military installations and wartime industries, most notably shipbuilding, which facilitated road construction, urban growth, and a diversified economy. During the 1970s and '80s, as other job opportunities opened up, white and African American farm workers were replaced by Mexican American laborers, which increased the area's Latino population.[3]

Beach County is part of a larger metropolitan area that has experienced rapid population growth in the last ten years. Growth has brought increasing diversity to suburban and rural areas but has generally been uneven. The vast majority of the county's growth has occurred in areas unincorporated by city governments. As a result of this growth, suburban and rural areas have shown increases in racial and ethnic diversity, particularly among Latinos, as construction opened opportunities for better-paying jobs in the skilled labor market outside the central city. Beach County's population demographics, and thus those of the district, have also been changing over the last ten years; since 2000, the population has increased by approximately 230,000 residents, to nearly 1,230,000 according to the 2010 U.S. Census. As of 2010, Beach County's population remains majority-white, but whites have become a smaller percentage of the total population, while the percentages of Latinos, African Americans, and Asian Americans have all grown.[4] Latinos represent a quarter of the population, and African Americans make up 17 percent.[5]

Population growth is attributed to a variety of factors: increased opportunity in construction and finance industries, affordable housing, and lack of a state income tax, as well as the traditional lures of a tourist economy such as warm weather, low-skill/credential jobs, and promises of a new start or better life. The increased need for housing and infrastructure for population growth correlated with increased job opportunities. Opportunities were plentiful, the labor force was growing, and unemployment hovered between 2 and 3 percent for most of the late 1990s and early 2000s.[6] Industries related to housing—construction and trades such as air-conditioning, plumbing, windows, mortgage and finance, and real estate sales—flourished. Other businesses— retail, restaurants, mega-malls, corporations, and hospitals—followed population density, creating employment centers in the outer rings. Other factors accelerated movement of the diversifying population into the suburbs. Shifts in federal and local public housing policy brought recipients into suburban apartments via Section 8 housing vouchers. Locally, whole communities of "projects" were razed, dispersing previous residents into other areas.

During the mid-2000s, several factors combined to diminish this explosive growth. In 2004, a particularly devastating hurricane season led insurance companies to double and triple home insurance rates, and sometimes cancel policies altogether. As the housing market cooled and ultimately crashed, industries associated with housing sustained losses and businesses eliminated positions and laid off workers. From April 2008 to April 2009, for the first time since the end of World War II, Florida experienced a loss in population.[7] The national financial collapse was the final nail in the coffin. Local unemployment soared, and was over 12 percent in 2010. Housing values plummeted, causing some residents to be "under water," where the payoff price for the homes exceeded the actual home value.

EXHIBIT 7.1

Beach County Public Schools

Percentage change of suburban ring of Florida metropolitan area and Beach County Public Schools

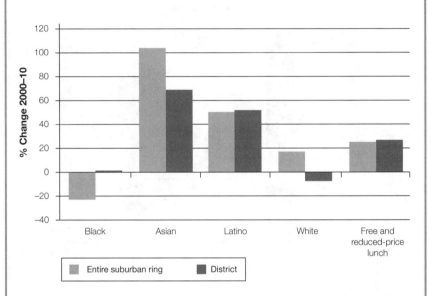

Racial and poverty composition of Florida metropolitan statistical area, Beach County Public Schools, and district first grade, 2009–10

	% Black	% Asian	% Latino	% White	% English language learners	% Free and reduced-price lunch	Total enrollment
Total MSA	18.2	3.3	21.5	56.6	7.7	51.7	388,551
City/ Suburbs*	21.9	3.6	22.9	51.2	8.8	51.8	298,503
Suburbs	6.2	2.3	16.6	74.5	3.9	51.4	90,048
District	23.0	3.3	29.9	43.5	11.5	53.7	193,265
First grade	21.1	3.4	30.4	38.8	—	—	15,170

Note: Not all enrolled students have race/ethnicity specified for this district.

*County-wide districts including both central cities and some parts of suburbia within the district boundaries.

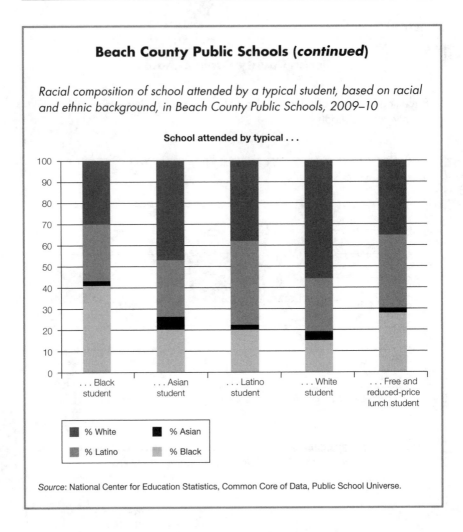

Beach County Public Schools (*continued*)

Racial composition of school attended by a typical student, based on racial and ethnic background, in Beach County Public Schools, 2009–10

School attended by typical . . .

...Black student　...Asian student　...Latino student　...White student　...Free and reduced-price lunch student

■ % White　■ % Asian
■ % Latino　■ % Black

Source: National Center for Education Statistics, Common Core of Data, Public School Universe.

In its 2008 report to Congress, the Federal Housing Finance Agency indicated that Florida showed the greatest drop in home values of all states in the Atlantic South and, along with California, saw some of the greatest increases in foreclosures nationwide.[8]

SUBURBAN DIVERSIFICATION: INTEGRATION OR RESEGREGATION OF BEACH COUNTY PUBLIC SCHOOLS

Historically, white suburbanization had frustrated efforts to integrate schools. Yet suburban diversification seems to provide a new frontier of racial integration, although it is unclear whether such schools will remain diverse. The increasing diversity of suburbia, however, has shown patterns of resegregation in older suburbs (inner rings) as private interests and government policies promote development in the outer rings. For instance, suburban expansion in Florida has been largely characterized by "leapfrog development"—where developers pass over more expensive land in the urban service area to purchase less expensive land in rural areas, resulting in congested roadways, oddly placed u-turns, strip-mall development, and a homogenization of community aesthetics. In addition, hostility toward inclusionary zoning among developers and pro-development lawmakers has largely prevented ordinances designed to create more stable and integrated communities, leading the more recent inner-suburban–outer-suburban divide to replicate the urban-suburban divide.[9]

All these changes create paradoxes for those committed to school diversity as a key to promoting educational equity. In the current policy context, suburban diversification has done little to alleviate patterns of segregation in the urban core and inner-ring suburbs, and may be reproducing isolation in some outer-ring schools. Even more detrimental, these changes are taking place in a federal and state policy context that is focused on trying to close the achievement gap through accountability and choice without crafting housing and educational policies to alleviate social economic isolation and the class divide between communities.

BCPS is an important place to explore these complexities and how school leaders confront them. The district was released from court supervision over a decade ago and had used court-approved policies designed to integrate schools for over three decades (including suburban-urban busing and magnets). The desegregation experience continues to resonate in district officials' conversations about the value of diversity. Yet the larger national and state policy context promoting school choice, including charter schools, coupled with local political constraints of community mobilization to protect class and racial privilege, *constrict* district responses to tackling suburban resegregation as well as the resegregation that has already occurred in city schools despite huge investments in magnets/attractors, transportation, and the use of noncontiguous zoning. This chapter describes the ways in which the district leaders have grappled with these dynamics, which have resulted in contradictory decision making; for instance, busing poor, black children to schools in middle-class suburbs to promote desegregation, while in other instances backing away from similar proposals to assign students from wealthy suburban areas to more diverse schools, ultimately reinforcing segregation. District responses to the demographic change in the suburbs have largely been informed by past efforts to desegregate urban schools such as locating themed or high-track academic programs that serve as magnets to attract or retain "high-achieving" students in schools experiencing turnover, while simultaneously promoting policies to expand opportunities to traditionally underserved groups.

This chapter describes district and community responses to demographic changes. The development that the county has undergone and the increasing diversity of its student population offer a unique site to explore demographic change in suburban schools. Twenty-nine interviews were conducted with district- and school-level educators, as well as several external actors in the community, to provide insight into the multiple perspectives on the significance of suburban change for educational opportunity. These interviewees spoke of community backlash against efforts to integrate suburban schools, fears that choice will lead to racial turnover in suburban areas undergoing demographic change, and how the larger policy context complicates their response, such as Florida's accountability system of grading schools diminishes the academic image of certain schools. The initiatives highlighted in this chapter represent only several of many new programs being introduced in the district. Interviews come from a small sample, and may not represent the entirety of the Beach County district, which comprises hundreds of schools.

SUBURBAN DEMOGRAPHIC CHANGE, CHOICE, AND RACE-NEUTRALITY

The increase in Beach County's population over the past decade necessitated the construction of more than fifty new schools. As of 2009 the county operated over 250 schools, enrolling nearly 200,000 students. In the 2008–09 academic year, over 100,000 children, or nearly 53 percent of the BCPS pupil population, attended suburban schools.[10]

Reflecting the surrounding metropolitan area, Beach County school district has continued to become increasingly diverse. Latino and Asian student populations have increased, while white and black student populations have remained stable or declined (see exhibit 7.1). Despite the downward trend in percentage, non-Hispanic white students still comprise the largest percentage of enrollment, followed by Latino, black, Asian, and Native American students. Also in these ten years, the percentage of low-income students, as measured by free and reduced-price lunch (FRL) has increased. The percentage of students who are ELLs has also increased by approximately one percentage point.

In order to better contextualize student demographics in Beach County, it is helpful to look at how it compares with neighboring districts. The district is directly "boxed in" by four neighboring districts. Of these, Beach County is demographically most similar to its eastern neighbor, though it has the lowest percentages of white students and the highest percentage of Latino and ELL students of all five (see table 7.1). Districts west and north of Beach County have higher percentages of white students, lower percentages of students of color, and much lower percentages of ELL students.

Beach County's response to increasing suburban diversity is to focus largely on improving student educational outcomes, and in particular, reducing academic disparities between white students and students of color, often framed in terms of reducing the achievement gap. While increasing student diversity offers hopes for improved racial integration in suburban schools, it has done little to alleviate patterns of segregation in the urban core and inner suburban rings and, as interviews with a district administrator suggest, may be reproducing economic isolation in some suburban schools.

Currently Beach County uses a voluntary integration plan, without either the racial or SES desegregation standards found in other controlled choice plans. Integration, or at least the avoidance of resegregation, depends on strategically placed magnets and other themed programs to attract students to schools outside their attendance area. The district hopes that a voluntary choice plan will help maintain integration, despite evidence that school choice plans are associated with increases of racial and poverty concentrations within schools.[11] Indeed, district-level administrator Bob Tuttle

TABLE 7.1

Beach County and neighboring districts, demographics, 2009–10

	Beach County	East	South	West	North
White	41.4%	49.6%	53.9%	62.0%	71.1%
Black	21.9%	21.7%	15.1%	18.9%	5.5%
Latino	28.5%	23.1%	25.4%	9.5%	16.4%
Asian	3.1%	1.5%	1.7%	4.0%	2.4%
Native American	0.3%	0.2%	0.2%	0.3%	0.4%
FRL	53.7%	63.0%	51.8%	39.0%	50.1%
ELL	11.5%	9.4%	9.5%	3.9%	4.3%

Source: NCES Common Core Database, 2009–10.

says, the choice plan has already begun to result in the concentration of poverty in neighborhood schools. According to Tuttle, in 2000–01, the county had eight or nine schools that were considered high poverty (90 percent or above poverty), but in 2004 the choice process increased the number of high-poverty schools to twenty "overnight."[12]

Currently, the district has eighty-nine Title I elementary schools, twenty-four Title 1 middle schools, and ten Title 1 high schools. In the last decade the number of Title 1 schools in suburban areas has grown; at the elementary level, the percentage of Title 1 schools that are classified as suburban increased from 27 percent in 2000–01 to 43 percent in 2009–10. In recent years, Beach County has also seen an increase in the number of public schools with a majority Latino or African American enrollment. Since the implementation of choice in fall 2004, the number of elementary schools with a 50 percent or greater majority of African American students has risen from sixteen in 2003–04 to twenty in 2009–10, and the number of middle/high schools has increased by twelve. Elementary schools with a 50 percent or greater majority of Latino students have nearly doubled, from eleven to twenty-one schools in the same time period.[13] Currently, there are thirty majority-Latino schools (all grade levels). These racial groups represent only 22 percent and 29 percent of the district's enrollment population, respectively, clearly revealing racial disproportionality and increasing isolation. Most of the schools with 50 percent or greater population of African American children are urban. However, about half of schools with a 50 percent or greater Latino population are classified as suburban, reflecting the broader demographic change in the metropolitan area. This movement toward racially identifiable schools suggests that an unregulated choice plan may decrease integration.

In the 2007 *Parents Involved in Community Schools vs. Seattle School District No.1 (PICS)* case, the U.S. Supreme Court affirmed the goal of integrated education as a compelling interest but restricted the means many school districts use to maintain integration.[14] Beach County administrators had been opposed to using social class indicators in student assignment under choice, and now assumed that using race in student assignment was unconstitutional under the *PICS* ruling (an assumption shared by many districts, given the ambiguity of the *PICS* decision) and were reluctant to take any measures that might lead to a lawsuit. Only in December 2011 did the federal government release guidance on school diversity clarifying how race could be used by school districts to pursue integration.

Though racial integration is no longer a driving force behind district policy, several interview respondents suggested continued recognition of the benefits of diverse schools. District- and school-level educators described increasing diversity in suburban areas as "good for public education." District-level administrator Robert Tate, who has been with BCPS more than thirty years and has seen the district transition from desegregation to the current choice policy, continues to affirm the value of diverse schools: "If you can have a diverse student population, that benefits everyone."[15] Tate believes that an increase of minority students into suburban areas through federally subsidized housing has lessened the need for "artificial" means of creating "racial balance." Several teachers reported that diversity of their students is one thing they like about their school; two white teachers at a suburban school said that their school needed "more diversification." Uniform, casual comments, such as calling a school "balanced" when there is a diverse student body, demonstrate the remnants of a culture dedicated to the idea that exposure to differences is an important part of schooling. In regard to racially isolated schools, administrators see increasing segregation as a problem in that it creates more social isolation, which is seen as an educationally unsound way to prepare children for a diverse society and global economy. Yet, without a clear protective framework to prevent segregation or explicit policies to promote racial or socioeconomic diversity, amid rapid suburbanization and demographic change, it remains to be seen how BCPS can achieve diverse schools.

EFFORTS TO CLOSE THE ACHIEVEMENT GAP

As demographic change affects suburban schools in BCPS, the efforts to retain white and/or affluent students that often typified desegregation plans now focus on increasing schoolwide achievement in the context of high-stakes testing under Florida's public school accountability system and NCLB. As a result, programs that explicitly encourage diversity (e.g., the previously mentioned desegregation policy) have been submerged under those aimed at monitoring and rating schools on disparities in test scores associated with race, class, and exceptionality. So although the district has been released from the desegregation order, district and site based administrators still monitor very closely school demographics for children counted as subgroups under NCLB. As one district administrator put it, "high schools [are] accountable to every cell [subgroup] under the sun because they've got a diverse population in our high schools. So that's why our high schools—not even [elite high school] is making AYP, you have so many cells that you're accountable to."[16] BCPS has been quick to embrace a variety of federal, state, and privately supported programs to boost student achievement and reduce achievement gaps.

The benefits and drawbacks of such programs are not straightforward. For instance, BCPS seeks to broaden access to a more rigorous curriculum for traditionally underserved groups, while at the same time creating academically oriented programs such as the International Baccalaureate (IB) to increase enrollment of traditionally privileged students in schools undergoing class and racial change. During the 1990s, BCPS placed IB programs at two high schools in inner-ring suburban areas undergoing racial change. More recently, IB programs have been extended to two high schools, one that has witnessed an increase in Latino enrollment; the other a new school in an area outside the city limits with a significant Latino population. In addition, the BCPS sited Advanced Placement magnets at a rural high school and a suburban high school, both with high enrollments of low-income Latino/a students. Such programs have the potential to expand educational opportunities to underserved students if such higher-track options do not reinforce social advantage.

Ironically, the placement of attractors in schools outside of the urban areas may further undermine efforts to diversify urban schools. As the only African American school board member described it, the philosophy behind magnet programs was to create racially balanced schools, thus encouraging white suburban parents to enroll their children in urban schools. However, she observed:

> What sometimes has been kind of a contradiction to that whole philosophy is that many of the programs . . . some of the programs that were unique in those schools are now in our suburban schools. And so now why should a person who lives in [white suburban area] come into [a high school in a low income predominately black urban area] when some of those courses or those activities or those programs are right in their community? So we have to be very careful with that balance. If the goal is still to make our schools more diverse and get kids who ordinarily would not come into urban schools, we have to be careful not to make those offerings so available and accessible all over the district. Otherwise I think you contradict, or counteract, what you're trying to do.

In addition to encouraging specialty attractor schools, Beach County is also focused on improving opportunities within the traditional schooling context for students whose access to more challenging curriculum has historically been limited. Beach County is a strong supporter of expanding enrollment in AP and honors classes to students who have been traditionally excluded from advanced college prep courses, primarily students of color and low-income students. This large-scale effort has been in partnership with the College Board, which is working with Florida to improve the availability of AP and SAT exams to students. In addition to the state effort, Beach County has welcomed a curriculum reform initiative from the College Board, which also aims to provide extra support and college-readiness coursework to traditionally excluded students and to support the work of students new to AP rigor. This program includes a scripted math and language arts curriculum, written by the College Board, which has been implemented in every middle school and high school across the district. Part of this implementation includes a college skills class, so students can "participate in enrichment and motivational activities that make college seem attainable" and focuses on developing organization and study skills, critical thinking, and provides assistance from peers and college tutors.[17] The program targets traditionally excluded students as well as students whose academic performance lands them somewhere in the general academic "middle."

As part of identifying the academic middle, every ninth- to eleventh-grader takes the PSAT exam at no cost, and the scores are used as one indicator of AP potential in accordance with College Board's guidelines. This model is perceived as a more objective measure of ability and is believed to prevent the kinds of informational gatekeeping among teachers and counselors that has been long associated with entrance into advanced coursework. Paul Curtis, a district-level academic administrator who has been with the district for more than twenty years, now oversees programs like those from the College Board. He describes what he sees as the benefits of using this model: "We're going to give a PSAT to every kid in ninth, tenth, and eleventh grade and we're going to say at the end of that test . . . 'Eric, you have the potential—based on your reading scores of being successful, scoring at 3, 4, 5 in AP American History . . . You know, you're sitting in regular classes. Let's try you out in honors. Let's try you out in AP because you have the ability to do it. Here's a test that shows from the College Board that you have the ability to do it.'" Curtis recalls his early experiences as a teacher, when gatekeeping practices were more visible: "Twenty-four years ago, AP and honors were kind of a mystery to most kids. There was a lot more of what I would call gatekeeping, where teachers and counselors made decisions about who took what. You had to have recommendations to get into classes . . . You either were in or you weren't."

Interview respondents describe the AP push as a positive change, and the College Board suggests this program has had a positive impact on increasing AP enrollment as well as PSAT- and SAT-taking for students of color.[18] Curtis compares the population of students he sees now in AP courses with those of his earlier teaching days: "I had probably, out of teaching five classes a day, maybe one or two African American kids or one or two Hispanic kids in my honors classes. In my Fundamentals class, it was almost exclusively minority . . . There is still room for growth, but that has changed tremendously. You now see Hispanic and African American students in honors and AP classes and in fact, I think it was last year a nearby high school had the first African American valedictorian ever in the history of the school."

Max Reilly, principal at Palm Crest High School, describes his experience with racially stratified AP classes: "When I came here, the first thing I did, was I looked at AP classes and I saw the lack of minorities in AP classes, so we held a forum. And we invited forty-three minority parents to come to the forum and out of those forty-three, thirty of them enrolled their kids in AP this year coming up. It's all information based."[19]

Reilly adds that he has faced resistance to "detracking" AP: "I've had more resistance from teachers than I do from the community . . . because teachers are used to getting those top-level kids—not saying that the other kids are not top level as well, but now you have to work a little harder instead of just saying, 'OK, here's chapter 1. You're going to get this done, and then we'll come in on Monday and we're going to go over it.' Now you have to do a little bit more work."

District teacher and department head Steve Davis says resistance to opening up AP is not uncommon, and that resistance has racial overtones: "You could call it a race issue. I'm not saying teachers are racist, but [it's] under a guise of 'this person can't read.'" He additionally notes that resistance is wrapped up in worries about pass rates on exams administered to AP students: "It's the exam, it's the pass rate; [teachers are] worried about the pass rate, and particularly now with the way school grades are changing to incorporate AP participation into the state grade."[20] Bonus pay to teachers is based on the number of students who pass the AP exam, not who participate in AP courses.

Bruce Cartwright is a local lawyer involved in real estate development and primarily represents developers and landowners. From his perspective as an external actor, Cartwright describes the district push to expand AP as weakening academic standards: "We're watering down their opportunity because we don't want to offend others . . . the more they try to make everybody feel special, the more they may start losing some of the best and brightest, because what would kill local schools here is if a private school were to build a satellite campus here. Boom. If there was one, people would be willing to drive there [to attend]."[21]

Students still may face limitations in access to advanced coursework, namely the PSAT. Obtaining a high enough score on the PSAT is one way to gain AP placement. Other routes include past participation, student-parental requests, and teacher and counselor recommendations. Practices may vary from school to school. However, implementing a multiple-choice benchmark as the entry into advanced coursework is problematic because such a test arguably selects for students who have already experienced coursework that contains the types of information relevant to the exam. This model may work well for students whose academic trajectory and life experiences have prepared them well for the PSAT, but what about students who have not shared these opportunities?

There may be serious implications for ELL students. The PSAT is offered only in English, thus excluding ELL students whose English ability does not yet allow high-enough performance on the PSAT for admittance into AP courses.[22] However, Paul Curtis did offer anecdotal descriptions of Spanish-speaking ELL students being placed in AP Spanish, and that this effort has helped to "open the eyes people at those sites [to the fact] that just because a student doesn't speak English doesn't mean that they aren't intelligent and able to do rigorous work."

One teacher and a school psychologist separately suggested that the College Board programs, said to assist traditionally excluded students, actually assist and recruit students who are *already* college bound. This criticism is captured in an interview with an ESL teacher: "[It] is not a program that is meant for lower-level ESOL [English for Speakers of Other Languages] students . . . it's really for those students who have a higher GPA, are doing well, and want to go to college. Maybe nobody else has gone, but they want to go. It's not really for a student who has struggled, has had problems . . . Unfortunately we're not targeting the population that might need it. We are targeting that population that would probably be able to go to college on their own."[23]

SHORT ON ELL RESOURCES

Beach County's population of ELL students is the highest of the surrounding districts, approximately 12 percent, which represents more than twenty-two thousand students. Several interviewees expressed concerns that resources for ELL students remain limited, including a lack of non-English curriculum materials for ELL students. Although district actors spoke of a commitment to ELL students and the recruitment and retention of bilingual teachers and training, this support does not appear to be institutionalized by a specific policy.

Problems developed at two elementary schools because no one in either front office spoke Spanish, which necessitated pulling the ELL paraprofessional at one school and the exceptional student education (ESE) teacher at the other school (who happens to be bilingual) from their classes to translate. Donna Star is principal of the former school, which is situated in a rural, low-income area undergoing demographic change. Star explained that the problem was solved when the school hired a data processor who spoke English and Spanish, although she acknowledged that it was "only coincidentally," rather than "a concerted effort." Star reported that this hire improved relationships between the school and Spanish-speaking parents: "We have seen more and more people coming to the office now, coming to our events now. They feel more comfortable. They feel more welcome seeing her, knowing that they can walk in and communicate effectively with the school."[24]

The other elementary school still did not have a Spanish-speaking person in the front office, nor Spanish-language options on its call-prompt system. Both schools each had three ELL personnel but only one had a permanent ELL resource teacher. One area high school had one full-time ELL resource teacher assisted by several part-time translators. Teachers at several schools reiterated the need for increased ELL teachers. The absence of support for ELL students highlights a tension between the reality of available resources and Beach County's goal of improving educational outcomes, particularly at a time in which suburbanization has worsened economic conditions for migrant workers in the county.

Title I funds are a source of ongoing assistance for qualifying schools. The district is a strong advocate of using Title I resources for personnel to assist with student achievement goals and believes that Title I resources are most effective when they are dedicated to classroom, rather than administrative, support. Donna Star describes the additional resources that Title I status affords: "At this particular school . . . we get Title I money so that we can provide some additional services to all of our students, and we do that pretty much in the form of people—so we currently have on staff . . . a full-time reading coach the district gives us, and we also have an academic intervention specialist." As a result of school budget cuts and limited resources, acquiring Title I status is becoming an increasingly appealing as a way to acquire resources. Julie Baxter has been a fifth-grade teacher for five years at Oakwood Estates, a non-Title I elementary school. She describes faculty discussions about becoming Title I, given that such status is perceived as providing teachers the necessary resources to improve student progress. Baxter's comments suggest that "becoming Title I" has been unintentionally incentivized: "We are almost at 46 percent free and reduced lunch, so we are almost a Title I school . . . I wish that they would bus in fifty more kids to put us over that mark because we need to get some more help. So you're at 46–47 percent you get nothing, whereas if you're at 51 or whatever it is, you get [it]."[25]

To summarize, the administrators and teachers interviewed see recent changes in Beach County's practices as increasing educational opportunity for traditionally excluded students and middle-of-the-pack performers. The AP push and the new College Board courses, particularly the college skills class, are positively perceived, though expanding AP enrollment has been met with some resistance from teachers. No one in our interviews questioned the use of the PSAT as a potential gatekeeper in AP course enrollment. Title I resources are being put to use in hiring resource teachers to support student learning—resources coveted by nonqualifying schools—and ELL resources seem scarce. The access concerns raised by these changes, as well as the continued need for support in compensatory program funds, highlight tensions between improving educational outcomes for students and the availability of resources to do so.

COMMUNITY RESISTANCE TO DIVERSITY: SCHOOL ZONE POLITICS

Interviews also describe tensions related to school zone attendance lines, which often involve differences in class and race. The Beach County district and its communities have felt the impact of a new state law requiring class-size reduction, which has resulted in the sometimes tumultuous experience of school zone reassignments and student transfers.

In 2002, and with strong support from suburban areas, voters amended the Florida Constitution to require school districts to reduce class sizes by the 2010–11 school year. The amendment established state standards for the maximum number of students permitted in classrooms at all levels of schooling: elementary school (eighteen students), middle school (twenty-two students), and high school (twenty-five students).[26] Prior to the amendment, Beach County officials considered a school overcrowded if it was at 120 percent capacity; now a school is considered overcrowded at 95 percent capacity.[27] Rapid growth and the Class Size Amendment have resulted in school attendance areas that must be continuously reconfigured to adjust for capacity goals; there have been frequent boundary changes in the last ten years. Some minority students have been assigned to majority-white suburban areas through the use of noncontiguous zoning, a remnant of bus routes from older desegregation days. Zoning and transportation related to growth and overcrowding have helped to increase diversity in suburban areas, but they have often created conflicts.

Changes in attendance zones elicit community tensions along both economic and racial lines. Administrators explain that high-status communities, or communities that perceive themselves as affluent, tend to mobilize and resist boundary changes that increase the number of low-income students transferred or rezoned into suburban schools, especially targeting black and Latino students.

District-level interviewees also agree that more-affluent parents demand assurance that diversity will not reduce educational quality, and these demands appear to get a response—or at least attention—from the district. These parents are characterized as concerned about school quality, rigor, and support services; and decisions made by these parents are perceived as rooted in these values. Bob Tuttle reflects back on his experience as principal at a school serving a small population of wealthy children and a larger population of rural, migrant students. He describes feeling like he had to "make sure those parents coming from homes that were $400,000 [know] that their child is going to be just as challenged academically, instructionally, as any other child on that campus." Otherwise, he explained, those parents will "want to take advantage of choice options somewhere else, where they feel like 'I'm going to put my child into a school that I think the children are a little bit more like the background of my particular child.'"[28] School-level response to the needs of lower-income Latino and black parents with children attending suburban school has largely focused on off-campus sites for school-community engagement, sharing information about academic programs, hosting parent teacher conferences, providing tutoring, and pursuing recruitment and retention of diverse faculty, particularly African American males and bilingual faculty.

The biggest outcry from resistant parents is that an increase in diverse students (perceived as a decline in white students) will reduce school quality. White (along with wealthy African American) parents may not perceive a school that is less than majority-white as balanced—even if the student population mirrors district demographics, which, as described earlier, are no longer majority-white. Several officials describe a tipping point at which too many students of color cause white parents to be less attracted to magnet schools.

When low-income students transfer to a more affluent school, the poverty status of the students increases the school's percentage of FRL, tipping it toward Title I status. The head of federal programs observed that there is a stigma associated with a school becoming Title I, and that school personnel must convince suburban parents that standards will not be lowered to meet the needs of lower-income students. One suburban schoolteacher says that parents from the nearby affluent subdivision would "freak out" if the school received official Title I status. She indicates she even knows parents of several children in the area who now qualify for free and reduced-price lunch due to a parent being laid off, but that they would never apply for assistance, perhaps because of the attached stigma.[29]

The story of Oakwood Estates Elementary School provides an example of the racial and class tensions involved in school boundary disputes. When Oakwood Estates first opened under desegregation, the school had an African American student population that declined soon after the choice plan was implemented. When two predominantly high-poverty and black schools about eight miles away became overcrowded, the district transferred some of their students to two less crowded suburban schools. Oakwood Estates received a number of these transfer students. The principal calmed fears about the busing program by stating publically that she, along with her PTA president, were "in lockstep with integration." She said the school had received children from similar low-income neighborhoods in the past without losing its focus on academics. She did describe needing to meet separately with two parents who did not believe it was *fair* that Oakwood was chosen to receive the students because other suburban schools were even less demographically diverse. The principal speculated: "I really felt like there was some racism among the families but they would never come out to basically say 'we're worried about the school becoming more black and less white.' But I think people were really thinking that but did not know how to articulate it."[30]

Teacher Julia Baxter describes resistance from parents, as well as the tension she felt in the midst of the transfer: "A lot of parents were upset. I think they felt like . . . 'These kids are going to ruin our school.' I had a hard time dealing with parents like that because . . . wait, they are just kids . . . I think the parents were really afraid these kids were going to bring guns and there was going to be fighting." Resistant parents insisted the school lacked resources to provide for "at-risk" students and that such students would reduce school quality. This resistance is noteworthy and perhaps ironic in a community that campaigned against school overcrowding. Ultimately, these parents were unsuccessful in overturning the transfer, but the school board did vote to change its procedure so that in the future boundary changes would be presented to all parents involved rather than just transferring families, as the previous policy required. Some interview respondents suggested this resistance represents only a vocal minority, which the media magnified.

A separate incident at a nearby school provides a different outcome, in which affluent parents successfully resisted the transfer of their own children into a nearby school attended by students from a Section 8 housing development. To relieve overcrowding, a new elementary school was built in the northern part of the district, situated between the affluent community and a Section 8 apartment complex. The new school was intended to draw students from both communities. Students from the affluent community were attending an overcrowded elementary school. Parents of this community pressured the district to halt the upcoming transfer, preferring overcrowding to enrolling their children in a school with students from the Section 8 area. Robert Tate recalls that at the time a state representative—whose daughter lived in the affluent community—was brought in to apply added political pressure against the district's plan: "We ended up not moving that affluent community into that particular school, which was the right thing to do. It was done for political reasons. And I understand the reality of that, but to this day that [affluent] school is still overcrowded and to this day, seven years later [the newer school] is still substantially under capacity."

Given the over fifty new schools that the district has opened in the last decade, it is not surprising that concerns and protests involved in zoning shifts would be a frequent topic of conversation. Despite a general observation that "nobody likes change," school officials explain that most resistance originates from more affluent communities. Frank McCourt, a veteran teacher before moving to the central office, is responsible for school boundaries and communicating with those affected by boundary shifts. Speaking about disputes over school zoning, he comments: "It is a stock expression in my world: 'to move those people.' And 'those people' could be the apartment people, the black people, the Spanish people, the trailer people, the people in the houses that cost less than half a million dollars—any and all of the above."[31]

In general, those who resist boundary changes are typically characterized as homeowners/taxpayers. Conversations with school leaders suggest most resistance comes from middle- and upper-class whites who fear that an increase in economic and racial diversity (particularly an increase in low-income black students) will lead to lowered academic expectations and a decline in test scores. These fears are disguised and rationalized by meritocratic rhetoric that delineates between a "deserving us" and an "undeserving them." For example, those who resist increasing racial and economic diversity in their neighborhoods insist that they pay more for their homes, pay higher taxes, want to maintain neighborhood cohesion, have concerns about safety, and are more involved in schools than others; they also wonder whether newcomers will invest through donations and volunteerism.

Changes in boundaries are not the only phenomena eliciting community tensions around increasing socioeconomic and racial diversity. Other policy factors are in play, namely state and federal accountability policies. Each school is assigned an annual grade, such as A, B, or C, based on student performances on state standardized assessments. The consequences of such policies extend beyond the school. Because school characteristics and nearby home values have been historically associated, those who resist demographic change worry that diverse students will lower performance averages on state assessments, in turn lowering property values. For example, if a subdivision is zoned for an "A" school, homeowners believe their property values will decline if the attendance area is shifted to a school with a lower rating. Additionally, parents of children in an "A" school also feel threatened if students are zoned in from lower-performing schools.

Under federal accountability policy, students attending a "failing" school have the option to transfer to a better-performing school, meaning a child would have to be transferred from the familiar, neighborhood school to a new suburban school. This has been met with resistance by some urban parents, who prefer their children to remain in the current school. Bob Tuttle finds it "ironic" that of the one thousand students receiving transfers under NCLB choice, half the parents requested their children be reassigned back to the "failing" school, a phenomenon not uncommon in other districts across the country.[32] Tuttle goes on to say, "We can't always put a finger on it. It was just that parents [we interviewed] for the most part . . . felt as if their child was accepted better [in their neighborhood school], and felt they more comfortable as a parent at the school where they resided in that neighborhood."

SUPPORT FOR CULTURAL COMPETENCY?

Beach County requires a diversity component to be fulfilled as part of the induction program for new teachers, yet in our interviews with teachers there was little mention of cultural competency. Further, efforts to make schools more attractive to wealthy parents focused on academics without a corresponding focus on making schools more welcoming for lower-income parents. Formal district responses prioritized increasing test performance and college readiness over improving cultural competency. Such prioritization reflects the influence of state and federal accountability policies, which leave little incentive, time, or funding for programs aimed at improving cultural competency and school climate. Some teachers felt that schools could do more to incorporate diversity in the curriculum and activities, whereas others felt that it would be too much to add and might detract focus from the state mandated curricular goals. Tensions related to culturally competent teaching are nonetheless a salient issue. Julia Baxter, who is white, describes an experience with an African American parent: "You have a lot of people that are African American who don't trust white people; they just don't trust us. I had a parent tell me that her child was in trouble all the time because I didn't know how to teach little black boys. She had no respect for my profession, she had no respect for what I was trying to do and what I was trying to help her son do . . . It was because I was white, so that's been a big hurdle as well; it happens a lot."

Sonia Alvarez is the program director of an outside organization that works to promote dialogue and respect among all cultures, religions, and races by cultivating leaders to change communities. In previous years, she has been brought in to consult with the district about school climate and culture. Alvarez offered an outsider perspective on the school district. She reported that she had tried to address how culturally relevant, culturally competent instruction impacts academic achievement but found: "It's not a priority. The priority is FCAT [Florida Comprehensive Assessment Test]."[33] The district's focus has been inconsistent, according to Alvarez, and despite her working with some of Beach County's administrators and board members, she believes the district has failed to connect improved cultural relevancy with increasing student achievement: "They can't see the investment that understanding culture has on preparing students for success." Though she has been brought in to address issues such as bullying, for example, Alvarez says she does not see administrators receptive to her view that there might be deeper issues underlying the bullying that need to be addressed: "When we show up, we can assess or notice if there are other issues to address . . . 'If I look at . . . referral issues on your school, is it incidents of bullying, or is it issues . . . that may be manifested through things you want to call bullying?' . . . I may bring it up to the administrator or to the liaison and they'll say 'thank you for your services.'"

One interviewee did describe an informal opportunity being developed to educate up-and-coming administrators about working in diverse schools. Steve Davis describes how an area high school is being used as an informal "training corps" for future administrators. Because of the school's diversity, district officials see it as a good place for new administrators to "get their feet wet." The problem, says Davis, "is the lack of stability in leadership."

One of the challenges of desegregation for decades has been the lack of welcome that minority students and families have felt from majority-white schools, often in neighborhoods distant from their own. Recognizing this, city-suburban desegregation transfer programs have explicitly focused on making schools receiving urban transfer students more receptive through teacher and administrative training and a range of other initiatives.[34] Given the statements of teachers about teacher professional development around diversity, it is perhaps not surprising that so many urban students offered NCLB choice decide to remain in racially isolated schools.

EQUITY CONCERNS FOR THE FUTURE

Policies like the Class Size Amendment and meeting state and federal accountability standards exacerbate tensions around demographic change in suburban communities where there has been a growth of Title I schools and where resources cannot fully meet the needs of these students. Lacking a more comprehensive desegregation plan (e.g., making sure the school choice offered has controls for diversity; requiring magnet and charter schools to make diversity a part of their goals and admissions) makes it harder to ensure equitable opportunities for students because of ensuing racial and economic resegregation. Like other districts across the country, Beach County is under intense pressure to comply with state and federal mandates and to meet testing standards. The district has implemented several initiatives to improve educational outcomes, and the focus of these initiatives is reflective of pressure to meet high-stakes annual yearly progress goals under state standards and federal NCLB mandates. This pressure influences the everyday life of the classrooms. One teacher describes how testing has narrowed the curriculum and efforts to promote diversity: "I was on the Diversity Committee and I just felt like we had really pulled some great ideas together for . . . Black History month and I really wanted to go all out and have like an assembly, schoolwide for the kids to come to . . . After selecting the dates . . . we were told that that wasn't going to be . . . that we don't want to interrupt the flow . . . with tests coming up."[35] That the district's focus is largely shaped by state and federal accountability mandates is made especially clear by the decision to make standardized tests the lynchpin of academic opportunity.

Administrative and school-level interviews show that recent changes to improve educational outcomes for traditionally excluded students and middle-of-the-pack performers are seen as largely positive. There has been resistance from teachers in expanding AP enrollment as well as criticism that these new programs actually only target students who are already college bound—that students who could especially benefit from additional resources are being overlooked. It is especially concerning that a standardized test is being used as the primary entry point to advanced coursework, particularly as it excludes ELL students whose competency in English may hinder performance on the exam but who could still benefit from more challenging coursework with the language assistance of an ESL teacher.

Federal funds for low-income students are being used to add resource teachers, a spending decision seen as wise by many of the interviewees. Schools that serve high percentages of low-income students, but not enough to qualify for Title I funding, could use additional funding resources but remain ineligible and unable to provide additional services. Schools also face a lack of funding and institutionalized commitment to increasing the number of bilingual school faculty and teaching staff to accommodate an increasing number of ELL students and families. Improving cultural competency does not emerge from interviews as a priority, despite racial and class-based tensions in local communities and schools. Educational opportunity in this post-desegregation district is largely shaped by state and federal policies, particularly assessment standards, as well as new changes like the Class Size Amendment, which in turn affect the everyday reality of suburban communities and elicit tension around demographic change. This manifests in debates around attendance zones, student transfers, school grades, and property values.

After thirty years of court-ordered desegregation, Beach County has placed the hopes of maintaining integration on a voluntary choice policy. Absolved of the responsibility to ensure racial diversity through desegregation, BCPS is now in the precarious position of watching once-integrated schools possibly backslide toward racial and economic isolation. The threat of racially and economically resegregated schools must be taken seriously, as such schools would undermine the equitable intentions of recent changes. However, it remains to be seen how school demographics will shift and, in turn, the kinds of educational opportunities that will be available to students.

8

High Civic Capacity, Low Demand for Integration

Rapid Demographic Transition in Suburban Atlanta

ELIZABETH DEBRAY AND AIN GROOMS

Until recently, the South has had the lowest segregation for black students, partly because of countywide districts, which often encompass city and suburban areas. As Gary Orfield and Erica Frankenberg write, "Partially because of desegregation orders and plans, the South was the most integrated region for black students for a quarter century until it fell behind in the 2005–6 school year."[1] School segregation in the South today affects more school systems than those that were historically under court order. Many districts now within major metropolitan areas never had mandatory busing because they were predominantly white and largely rural in 1971 when the Supreme Court decided *Swann v. Charlotte-Mecklenburg*.[2] Many of these systems have undergone rapid population growth and increases in racial diversification over the past ten to fifteen years, raising important questions about how and whether policy makers address the changes, both within schools and the communities overall.

This chapter presents findings from a county we will call Sewall County, situated in suburban Atlanta.[3] Geographically, it represents the "outer edge" of suburbia, with very little possibility of whites fleeing any further. The county is distinctive first because of its extremely rapid growth; its population more than doubled between 1990, when it had 58,741 residents, and 2000, when it had 119,341, making it one of the fastest-growing in the United States for several years consecutively. Its population in 2010 was 203,922, an increase of 70.9 percent since 2000. It is also distinctive for the high education levels of its black middle class. According to census data, the median education levels of black residents of Sewall County are higher, on average, than those of white residents; 26 percent of black adult residents hold a college degree, compared with 21 percent of whites. It is also the metropolitan area county with the highest projected increase in employment by 2030 and the highest net jobs gain in the area over from 2001 to 2010.[4] The presence of a black middle class is nevertheless offset by indicators that poverty and unemployment are fairly equally divided across both races. For instance, in 2010, 55 percent of the families receiving food stamps were black, while 44 percent were white. In August 2009, 49 percent of new unemployment claims were white, and 48 percent were black.[5]

The county enjoys a high level of cooperation between the Chamber of Commerce and school district, as well a reputation as a relatively high-achieving school district overall. The school system includes twenty-eight elementary, eleven middle, and ten high schools, and was recognized in 2009 as the Georgia large school system with the greatest Title I gains. (On the other hand, it was designated by the state in 2010–11 as having not made Adequate Yearly Progress, and had four high schools not making AYP targets).[6] There is strict enforcement of neighborhood schools, with no approved charters or magnets, and virtually no transfers being granted in recent years. While the schools are increasingly segregated by race, with the northern part of the county having the highest concentration of majority black schools, the black middle class has not mobilized politically to demand that school segregation be reversed where it is occurring. In the one area of the county with racial, ethnic, and income diversity, the high school (profiled later in this chapter) has increased graduation rates to 90 percent and been nationally recognized for high Advanced Placement (AP) exam participation by all groups. The business community, school board, and school district administrators have all adopted race-blind educational policies; a stated ethos of high academic standards for all; and policy makers' articulated commitment to equality of resource distribution among schools rather than to achieving school-level racial balance targets. While residents describe racial tensions as minimal, there are indications (for instance, a recent redrawing of school board zones in the state legislature) that white residents are attempting to protect their political power.

EXHIBIT 8.1

Sewall County School District

Percentage change of Atlanta suburban ring and Sewall County School District

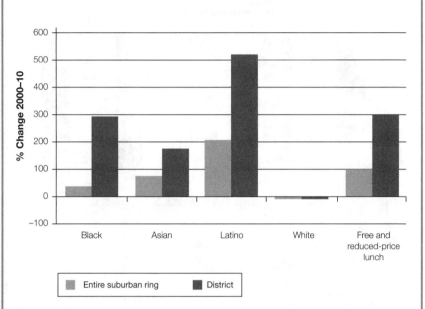

Racial and poverty composition of Atlanta metropolitan statistical area, Sewall County School District, and district first grade, 2009–10

	% Black	% Asian	% Latino	% White	% English language learners	% Free and reduced- price lunch	Total enrollment
Total MSA	38.8	4.8	13.2	40.1	6.5	51.0	929,094
Principal cities	45.6	5.5	12.6	34.5	6.4	49.2	254,831
Suburbs	36.2	4.6	13.4	42.2	6.6	51.7	674,263
District	44.7	2.7	7.1	41.2	2.1	43.9	40,951
First grade	39.9	2.9	8.5	42.9	—	—	2,821

Note: Not all enrolled students have race/ethnicity specified for this district.

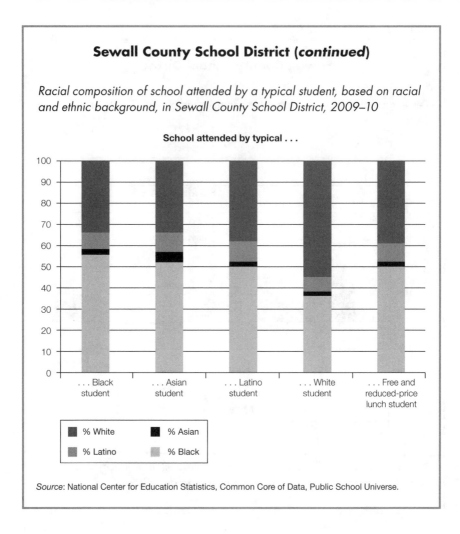

Sewall County School District (*continued*)

Racial composition of school attended by a typical student, based on racial and ethnic background, in Sewall County School District, 2009–10

School attended by typical . . .

... Black student   ... Asian student   ... Latino student   ... White student   ... Free and reduced-price lunch student

■ % White   ■ % Asian
■ % Latino   ■ % Black

Source: National Center for Education Statistics, Common Core of Data, Public School Universe.

RATIONALE FOR INCLUSION IN LARGER STUDY
AND RESEARCH METHODS

Sewall County was chosen for study for several reasons. The first was the clear importance of studying a southeastern county in a major metropolitan area. Erica Frankenberg and Chungmei Lee's 2002 report, *Race in American Public Schools*, indicated that the most rapid resegregation in terms of black exposure to whites was occurring in some southern districts. They wrote, "southern suburban districts also [were] declining sharply in the exposure of black and Latinos to whites; for example, three of the districts with the most change since 1986 were located in suburban Atlanta."[7] Sewall County also experienced very rapid racial change in the composition of its overall population. Between 2000 and 2010, the proportion of white residents declined from 80 percent to 60 percent, and by 2010, the school system was only 41 percent white. In addition, the county had three or more racial groups represented in the schools—Latinos constituted 7 percent of enrolled students in 2009–10.

This chapter, which draws primarily on policy maker and school system leader interviews, explores two of the prominent themes of the suburban change study: how policy makers and community leaders conceptualize rapid growth and increased diversity; and what policies and strategies they adopt. Between October 2009 and June 2010, we conducted nineteen interviews with district-level policy makers and community members, as well as selected school-level interviews with teachers and administrators at two elementary and one high school (which is profiled in greater depth later in this chapter). These schools were selected in collaboration with district officials and selection was based on school demographics and enrollment, level of school integration or segregation, and level of poverty. This permitted comparing schools with different patterns of race and poverty. We made site visits to these schools and interviewed the principal, other school administrators, teachers, and parents. We also collected a wide range of documentary evidence regarding demographic change, enrollment patterns, educational expenditures, and relevant documents about school policies and programs. We were unable to obtain an interview with any members of the local NAACP or other representatives of the civil rights community, which we acknowledge as a limitation of our data. All interviews were conducted in confidentiality, and the names of interviewees are withheld by mutual agreement.

GEOGRAPHICAL CONTEXT: RAPID GROWTH
AND DEMOGRAPHIC CHANGE

Sewall County is geographically large, bisected by the north-south interstate; in 2010, only 50 percent of the land was developed. There are five incorporated towns, including the county seat. In the late 1950s, the north-south interstate system through Atlanta was completed. The interstate system of travel, plus the desegregation of the Atlanta schools, affected the first large wave of white migration out of the city in the late 1950s through the mid-1960s. The political agreement between the business community and the schools to avoid attempts at busing for desegregation in exchange for increased power of blacks on the school board contributed to an exodus of whites out of Atlanta, mostly to the near southern suburbs. However, Sewall, as a farther-out and mostly rural area, was not particularly affected in this wave.

Located only thirty miles from Atlanta, Sewall is a convenient place from which to commute into the city, which 69 percent of its working residents do. Explained the president of the Chamber of Commerce: "The people who are coming to Sewall all want the same thing—it doesn't matter whether they are black, white, or Asian: affordable housing, safe neighborhoods, good schools, access to health care, good recreation. They all want what we consider the ideal suburban life."[8]

The county school system did not develop a voluntary desegregation plan until 1971 (when the county population was 58 percent white and 42 percent black), though some black students did gain access to formerly all-white schools as early as the mid-1960s. As in many southern school systems, it was a token, "freedom of choice" desegregation plan. The school system steadily became whiter, peaking in 1989 at 82 percent white. Whites were continuing to move into the county, while blacks were also moving out of the county back to the city to pursue jobs there, as the main options in the county were mainly low-level service industry jobs or teacher positions.

The second suburban exodus occurred in the early 1990s, when the black middle class began to populate the near southern suburbs immediately north of Sewall, to which whites had moved in the late 1950s and early 1960s. But the third exodus—and the one that affected Sewall—is when in the mid to late 1990s, blacks moved *farther out* from those closer-in suburbs. Following a national pattern documented by Frey, this economically driven wave consisted mainly of middle-class blacks who were moving to Sewall not just from the near southern suburbs, but from all over the country—all were seeking the availability of affordable housing and convenient access to the expressway.[9] By 2010, the county population was 62.7 percent white, 30.5 percent black, 4.7 percent Latino, and 2.7 percent Asian.

Demand for additional housing moved southward, where land and space were available. The growth, however, has differed from that of some of the other metropolitan suburbs; land values were among the cheapest in the area. Local school revenue is built mainly on residential property taxes because there is very little industry in Sewall County. The constantly declining revenues over the past years, a result of the housing market crisis, have meant that the school district's per-pupil expenditures are among the lowest in the state, as are its administrative costs.

Between 1999 and 2010, the county school system saw a 100 percent increase in enrollment, from 20,185 students to 40,951 (see exhibit 8.1). The growth of the school system slowed once the recession hit in 2006. However, despite projections of no growth in 2009, there were 800 new students. In 2009–10, the county schools were 41 percent white, 45 percent black, 7.1 percent Latino, 2.7 percent Asian, and 4.0 percent multiracial. The same year, 43.9 percent of the system's students were receiving free and reduced-price lunch and 2.1 percent were English language learners. Two-thirds of the schools in the county are majority-nonwhite (37 of 51 schools). According to the 2010 NCES Common Core of Data, the countywide school dissimilarity index for white and black students was .40 and for whites and Hispanics was .37. The dissimilarity for black and Hispanic students was .19. These indices reveal moderate levels of segregation for whites from black and Hispanic students, and low levels of segregation for blacks from Hispanics. Approximately 7 percent of students in the county attended private school in 2010.

THE CONNECTION BETWEEN SCHOOLS
AND THE HOUSING MARKET

Sewall County experienced the highest rate of housing growth in the metropolitan area between 2000 and 2009, with 87 percent of construction of single-family homes (the second-highest proportion among metropolitan Atlanta counties).[10] As noted above, higher average education levels of blacks relative to whites have given them access to the housing market. A local, longtime realtor explained how many members of the black middle class have been able to afford some of the county's higher-priced houses:

> Well, they're starting out in that same market like somebody graduating from [a major local university] or anyplace else: they're coming out of school, they've got a good job, they're well prepared for the workforce, and they want to buy a house. You've got to get close into your job and then you've got to get where you can afford to move. I've sold a large number of homes to double-income families, black families who have been able to afford those two hundred– to three hundred–thousand dollar houses—they were dime a dozen and so they had a lot of opportunity to buy.[11]

The chair of the cultural diversity committee for the Chamber of Commerce reflected on how the on-average higher education levels of black residents as a percentage of population with a bachelor's degree relative to whites have ensured equitable access to the county's housing market: "That in itself is probably minimizing or mitigating some of what may naturally happen from a real estate perspective [in terms of racial discrimination]."[12] However, blacks in Sewall were more than twice as likely as whites to take out risky subprime mortgages, meaning more black families than whites are struggling to keep their homes.[13]

Between 2000 and 2010, most growth occurred in the northern, formerly majority-white part of the county. In the northernmost city, the white population has decreased 35 percent since 2000. The pattern has been that whites have moved in a south- and westward direction, with countywide white residence patterns resembling a backward "L." Poverty rates correspond to these changes; by fall 2011, the elementary schools in the northern part of the county had free and reduced-price lunch rates ranging between 62 and 81 percent, whereas in the southern, mostly white part of the county, those rates ranged between 30 and 65 percent.

There have been some attempts at mixed-income housing developments. However, they have largely not attracted middle- to upper-income whites or high-income blacks. For instance, one residential live-and-work community in the northern part of the county, with various-sized homes that range from modest to more expensive, has an elementary school within its borders that is now only 8 percent white. According to one policy maker, the modest-sized homes were near the subdivision's entrance and sent the wrong signals to prospective higher-income buyers.

Where there are racially balanced schools, it is attributable to the influx of black middle-class residents buying mostly modest-sized homes, resulting in residential integration, at least temporarily.[14] However, an elementary school administrator in the most residentially integrated part of the county told us that with the economic downturn, "a lot of the homes that were normally selling have now become rental properties . . . more minorities are moving into the rental properties than are buying homes," and adds that "there have been a lot of white families selling their homes in these subdivisions because of the rentals."[15] So these pockets too may become more segregated as whites have continued to move to the southernmost parts of Sewall County. Explains one former school district official, pointing to the southwestern-most corner of the county map: "If you're looking for relative peace and quiet and relatively modest land prices, this is a great place to live. If you also just want to be around white folks, this is where you're going to live."[16] Another former school district official said:

> It's the politically correct thing to say "Oh yes, we welcome and embrace diversity," but when you look at some of the data, it tells you that many times individuals aren't embracing diversity as much as they may espouse. You are able to see patterns where neighborhoods were initially predominantly white, and then you begin seeing the neighborhoods becoming more diverse with African American families moving in—over time those became predominantly African American neighborhoods. And of course then our schools reflected the racial composition of those neighborhoods those schools were serving.[17]

While we did not hear that it was a pervasive trend, one former district policy maker stated that some realtors are less than honest with parents about school zoning; for instance, occasionally implying to prospective buyers that the new home would be in areas zoned for the two whitest high schools, when in fact they were zoned for one that was 85 percent black.

POLICY MAKERS' AND COMMUNITY MEMBERS' CONCEPTUALIZATION OF CHANGES

Consistently throughout our interviews, district policy makers, school administrators, and community members showed awareness of the dramatic demographic changes that had occurred in the county over the past decade. We also often heard that the understanding of increased diversity is conceptualized more broadly than along racial lines. As much of the growth in the county has come from the North and Midwest, native inhabitants must adjust to neighbors with different religious backgrounds and styles of communication—not to mention the linguistic barriers sometimes present with Latino, Indian, or Pakistani immigrants.

We also heard, however, that policy makers and community leaders alike see themselves as taking a proactive approach toward the rapid changes; they define themselves in opposition to a county to the north, where they believe change was not as well anticipated and planned. The superintendent who led the district until 2008 explained that the school system anticipated the magnitude of the change before the business community did:

> Certainly, we recognized the need for having a more diverse workforce that was reflective of our student population. So we made efforts—very deliberate efforts—to recruit teachers who were as diverse as our student population. As a member of the Chamber of Commerce board of directors, I kept trying to explain to people that we all need to be preparing for a different type of population here in our county than we have had previously.
>
> It took a longer time for some of those businesses to recognize that—even though we could tell you with a great deal of certainty exactly how our population was changing each year—when, in fact, we would be a majority student of color school district versus one that was a majority white school district. And I don't know that everyone quite understood that. They would see the data and they would not dispute any of it, but I don't know that they saw it as quite as plainly as we did.[18]

He added, "We would have opportunities to meet with various groups in the community [and] parent groups at schools and ask them to tell us ways that we could best make that transition in a proactive way of moving from a fairly homogeneous population to one that was far more diverse."[19] A school board member agreed: "Once we knew that the climate was changing in the northern part [of the county], we just didn't sit there to watch it change . . . What I do is, I do stay in contact with the people in the community like the NAACP, the Ministerial Alliance. We talk and . . . we see what's going on and what's on their minds."[20]

As described in greater detail in the section on cross-sector collaboration, many of our interviewees also discussed the activities sponsored by the cultural diversity committee of the Chamber of Commerce. In the recent past, the chamber helped organize trips for county leaders to Birmingham, Alabama, and Charlotte, North Carolina, to engage them in what the chamber viewed as necessary conversations about the ongoing changes in the county. Said the previous school superintendent:

> One of the last events or activities of which I was a part before I left the district was a trip to Birmingham. We took about fifty individuals from the business community and other governmental leaders in the county on an overnight trip to the Civil Rights Museum there. It was an opportunity to have some of those very open, candid discussions that are necessary. Often,

people aren't interested or aren't comfortable in talking about the racial changes that occur. That was a barrier I was constantly trying to knock down and say, "We have to be comfortable with it, and we have to be open about it, or things will never change so that we can progress in a positive direction."[21]

The responses of those we interviewed reflected a split in perceptions about the consequences of the rapid rate of racial change in both the county and the school system. In the opinion of the assistant superintendent for curriculum and instruction, whites were beginning to understand that racial change did not equate to degraded school quality:

I honestly believe the racial climate is positive and getting better . . . I've always sort of assessed the climate in the school system because I watched the white flight out of the middle school [in another county] where I was principal. And it's disheartening because you know that you've got this great school and these great children and you see people move because of race.

And I think that over time what is happening is people are getting it. They are seeing—once that white flight happens—those schools are not falling apart, they continue to achieve . . . I think we have done a very good job, first of all ensuring that we have our strongest leaders in the schools where people anticipate the greatest challenges. And those leaders have made quality decisions to ensure that student performance does not decline in those buildings.[22]

On the other hand, one long-time white resident and former school official took a far more pessimistic view when asked about how the broader white community perceives the changes:

I'm afraid that whites in the county see it as deteriorating, they see that these are African Americans they think that are moving from the inner city into their suburban community that are depressing housing prices—this is before the economy went bad—that are causing schools to deteriorate in quality. Certainly all of that is wrong thinking, in that they perceive [these are] poor ghetto children and families that are moving into Sewall, and that's not knowing the history of the exodus to the suburbs—that these are middle-class African Americans moving further out from the suburbs, not from the city.[23]

As is the case with many suburbs undergoing rapid growth, we heard about a split between pro–further growth and anti–further growth elements of

community. The superintendent, when asked about how the broader community perceived the changes, stated, "I think there are two sides of that."
One group wants change to slow down—even welcomes the economic
downturn—to retain the slow pace and uncrowded roads they moved there
for. Another group that also moved to the county for the slow pace and convenient commute nevertheless wants all the city conveniences of sidewalks,
sewers, and good roads.[24]

The leadership within the school system acknowledged that raising teachers' expectations of students, within the context of the broader community's
perceptions, was a continuous challenge. According to the assistant superintendent for curriculum and instruction, many classroom teachers, whether
black or white, have no previous experience with "those kinds of students"
and struggle to develop new skills "to meet the needs of learners with whom
they may not have been accustomed." Teachers need help "to make that transition . . . It's overcoming that barrier and I think it's just, probably more than
anything else, cultural influences where people tend to believe that there are
certain types of students who do not learn at very high levels."[25]

One theme that we heard frequently was that teachers and parents were
wary of the growing school-level poverty rates as an indicator of declining
quality. Said one assistant superintendent, "[Some parents think] that when
there are more children in a building who fall below the poverty line based
on free and reduced lunch, that there is something inherently wrong in our
building in terms of our not being as good a school as we could be if our
numbers of those students were lower. Sometimes that's a perception in the
community and sometimes within our buildings among teachers . . . there
are teachers who do not want to teach at Title I schools."[26]

Across the interviews in various sectors of the community, we consistently
found an overall lack of pressure for the racial integration of schools; for example, demands that the school board make different zoning or transportation decisions that might halt the growing trend toward racially identifiable
schools. In large part, this was attributed to the residential preferences of individual races. The assistant superintendent for curriculum and instruction
commented, "I don't think the community is concerned about that. I think,
just by nature, people enjoy what they believe to be their comfort zone, and
that sometimes means being around 'people like me.' So whether these are
schools like in [an elementary school] where it is predominantly black, or
maybe in [the southern part of the county] where it is predominantly white,

I don't believe that we get challenges from the community to say, 'Let's look at a redistricting plan so that we can balance our schools.'"[27]

To summarize, we find that, overall, there is a strong theme of embrace of change, as well as significant civic capacity to address these changes. That is, the business community, county leadership, and community organizations have worked together to try to address challenges posed by rapid demographic change. There is also a characterization of a lack of community pressure on policy makers to achieve greater racial balance in the schools. At the same time, there is fairly wide variation in how citizens and policy makers characterize the overall racial climate: while some believe it is positive and getting better, others perceive that whites see the county schools as deteriorating.

FORMAL POLICIES

In terms of formal school district policies, we discovered three major patterns: (1) there is no formal set of policies to try to achieve racial or socioeconomic balance (this also includes an absence of choice policies, whether magnet, charter, or other transfer beyond neighborhood schools); (2) policy makers have mixed feelings about the importance of hiring to achieve a diverse staff; and (3) the primary county response to diversity is teacher training programs.

Student Assignment

Throughout the 1990s, county school district officials followed growth patterns, rather than race, in student assignment policies. There have been numerous re-zonings, and we heard some indications that white parents have protested periodically against their neighborhoods being combined with majority black areas. Describing one such high school rezoning around 2006, the former superintendent for administrative services said:

> *Former superintendent:* These parents didn't want to go to this high school that was going to be populated . . . It didn't matter that this is a middle-class black population, it was simply the prejudice that if they are black, they're gangbangers who don't particularly value education, and we don't want our white children leaving this wonderful white school—that must be wonderful because it's white— to go to this school that's going to be a little white, a little black, but it's going to be much blacker than this school.

Interviewer: So what happened?

Former superintendent: Well, they went, or they left. They were re-zoned into that school. It's been a wonderful success story, this [high school]. It's been a strong academic school. I'd have to look at my numbers exactly, but it's a racially diverse school. The overwhelming majority of parents, black and white, are very satisfied with this school.[28]

An occasional parent or civil rights activist will note the racial resegregation, but racial balance is not the Board of Education's priority. Says the former assistant superintendent for administrative services: "The Board of Education's response is, we don't draw attendance lines based on the color of skin, we draw attendance lines to alleviate overcrowding."[29] The current assistant superintendent for administrative services confirmed that there were no policies that took race or socioeconomic status into account in school assignments: "Our zoning is based solely on student populations or local populations. It's numeric. . . just rezoning for population. So once we determine that, then we have the general idea of which schools we're trying to relieve and with that general number, what proportion from adjacent schools is a ballpark number we're looking for, based on overcrowding at different levels at each of those schools."[30]

A school board member concurred: "We try to keep the kids out of the trailers. We try to keep them indoors, so if we can relieve one school from having trailers by building another school that will benefit some of the other kids, that's what we do."[31]

Staff Diversity: A Diffuse Goal

District-level policy makers and building-level leaders confirm that hiring a more diverse teaching and administrative staff is a critical goal, but one that has been difficult to achieve in practice. Most are also quick to state, however, that attracting high-quality candidates remains their top priority. Particularly at the two elementary schools, the principals told us that they had made inroads in hiring a more diverse teaching staff, only to have those teachers relocated due to lack of building-level seniority during the budget crisis.

The assistant superintendent for human resources explained that there has also been flight of white staff from predominantly minority schools: "From an HR standpoint, there are two different schools of thought. You know, do you want your teaching staff to, quote, 'look like the population that they are teaching,' or should that not matter at all? We struggle with that; we try and make best choices based on that." She also has seen white flight of staff at primarily black and minority schools. "We've seen white staff say they want to leave—they want to get down in [a majority-white] area, so that's just a phenomenon, it's a reality that goes on."[32]

The assistant superintendent for human resources was asked whether the county had adopted recruitment and retention programs to bring in new administrators who have experience working with this new demographic of students. She replied: "I think it definitely goes along with our selection process. We have an applicant pool that's very large in all areas, so we don't specifically go out recruiting, say in New York, for inner-city, savvy kind of folks, but we . . . definitely structure an interview around, if it's a multicultural school, we make sure that they have multicultural gifts and experiences."[33]

The assistant superintendent for curriculum and instruction explained that a routine periodic review of the state's school systems by the Equal Employment Opportunity Commission had identified recruitment as a goal. However, balanced hiring is difficult: "Sometimes people lean toward preferences, I think—I know that when I became principal of [a middle school in northern county] it was very important to me to have a balanced staff in terms of race, but it became more and more challenging as our student population became more African American. I would have more African American applicants who would come to the school as opposed to white applicants . . . You simply want the best teachers."[34]

We frequently heard at the school level that more diversity in the teaching force would be welcome. The literacy coach at one of the elementary schools that had 48 percent white students, 30 percent black students, and 22 percent Latino students, stated: "We don't have any [Latinos] as teachers or blacks as teachers here," with the exception of herself.[35] While the school principal and assistant principal had recently succeeded in hiring an office clerk and clinic aide who were both bilingual, they acknowledged that "it's very, very difficult" to find applicants who fit the job descriptions. Administrators also reported using Title I funds to hire translators, which they can do, since they are a targeted assistance school. They characterized this as an antidote to the state's policy of no bilingual education; said one, "I feel it would be so much more beneficial to our children to first have the ability to read in their native language, because those skills will transfer."[36]

Teacher Training for Cultural Diversity

Formal professional development via the Respecting Equally All Cultures program stands as the county's primary response to increased school-level diversity. According to the county's director of professional learning, who administers the program, its purpose is "to recognize personal bias and how it affects interactions with other people, and to get schools to value diversity and improve inter-group relations so all individuals recognize, understand, and appreciate their diversity and the value that they contribute to the school system."[37] Facilitators are trained by the Anti-Defamation League's A World of Difference program; they in turn go into the schools to hold conversations about diversity—dialogues that, in the words of the director, "allow staff opportunities to have courageous conversations about difference through job-embedded professional learning."[38] In 2009, 85 percent of the county schools participated and the goal for 2010 was 100 percent. Every school in the county system is required to include a goal for Cultural Proficiency in its School Improvement Plan. Further goals are to promote multiculturalism through collaborations between community organizations to open dialogue regarding diversity issues of prejudice, personal bias terminology, and racism, and to close the achievement gap between identified groups of students.

School leaders were mixed in their response to this training. At the high school, the training received positive reviews. However, at one racially balanced elementary school (41 percent black, 40 percent white, and 19 percent Asian, Latino, or other), the principal said that the program's message, which he characterized as "accepting people as they are," did not resonate well with his faculty. "I think some people have—I don't want to say resented it—they felt like it was a waste [of] time, because we're past that."[39] At the other elementary school, the administrators emphasized that programs that dealt with the culture of poverty had been far more beneficial.

THE CASE OF SILVERN HILLS: CHALLENGING ACHIEVEMENT PATTERNS IN A RACIALLY MIXED HIGH SCHOOL

Having heard accounts from many in the school district about high expectations in the face of such change, we were interested in learning about the actual experiences inside one high school. We selected it both because of its location in the most socioeconomically, ethnically, and racially mixed residential area of the county, but also because of the rapid increase in the black student population over the past six or seven years. We did, in fact, find evidence there that both student achievement and attainment were not only improving but gaining recognition in spite of the rapid changes, and that these achievement patterns did not follow patterns that would be typical nationally in terms of an "achievement gap" between blacks and whites.

Adjacent both to a country club and multimillion-dollar homes that were once predominantly white, as well as some low-income apartments, Silvern Hills High School (a pseudonym) is one that has undergone a rapid demographic transition. In 2009, it had twelve hundred students in grades 9 to 12, with 40 percent receiving free and reduced-price lunch; the student population was 54 percent black, 30 percent white, 7 percent Latino, 4 percent Asian-American/Pacific Islander, and 5 percent multiracial or other. By all accounts, the teachers and administration pride themselves on their high academic expectations and strong family support. There is a very strong black middle-class presence. The principal says that when you walk halls, you "can't tell or see airs from one group to another," and that you can't say that one racial or ethnic group is better off. He says the school is "the way society should be," in that it mirrors the increasing diversity of society, and calls it a "unique environment." Between 2005 and 2010, enrollment has remained stable, but between 2000 and 2005, the high school was "torn apart" three times with the successive openings of new high schools.[40]

The school has dropped its restrictions on AP enrollment, and it was designated an AP Access and Support school, with 30 percent of the program being minority and at least 30 percent scoring between 3 and 5 on the examinations. The mathematics department is especially strong, boasting a 99 percent pass rate in AP calculus exams from 2002 to 2009. Silvern Hills has also had a greater than 50 percent pass rate on all AP exams in 2007, 2008, and 2009, and was one of two high schools in the county named by *Newsweek* as one of the sixteen hundred best high schools in America in 2010. The principal also noted that in eleventh-grade English/language arts on the state test, blacks are outperforming whites—"a different achievement gap." The chair of the English department, who teaches both ninth-grade and honors English, explained how data-driven the department is:

> For some faculty meetings, what we do is get into smaller groups—and this is not just departments, this is different content levels getting together—and we look at different test scores and we look at data, we look at who is doing better and who is not, socioeconomic levels, and which students are

struggling. We try to come up with ideas and different plans and remediation and how can we target these kids. It's not about targeting the [Latinos] or the African Americans; it's always about kids who are struggling, like how can we get these kids to do better?[41]

The school received recognition from the state in 2010 for its 90 percent graduation rate, which was an increase from 70.6 percent in 2008, and far exceeded the state average of 80.8 percent. The school's graduation coach, interviewed for the local paper, attributed the success to academic remediation, credit recovery opportunities, and teacher-student tutoring.

The guidance counselor characterized the staff as very open-minded and welcoming of cultural diversity training. Of note is that the school is an Anti-Defamation League "No Place for Hate" zone, and a group called Students for Change also facilitates dialogue about embracing diversity. Overall, the message at Silvern Hills is one of pride in academic achievement and expectations in the face of rapid racial change. Somewhat indicative of the county's rural history, the vocational/agricultural track is overwhelmingly white. The principal said that some parents who had previously sent their children to private schools are coming back due to the school's strong academic reputation.

The guidance counselor believed there had not been significant white flight out of the county schools, largely due to the administration's maintenance of high academic expectations:

> We have not seen a huge white flight. I have seen a huge black flight coming to our school and I think that speaks well of our school . . . because [the county leaders] are open to change. The philosophy is to do what is necessary to meet the needs of our students where they are at—like I said previously, our academic standards have not changed. We expect our students to rise to the expectations; in addition, we do offer academic support to assist students to be successful. The county has allowed our administration to do what is needed . . . they're giving our school leadership the permission to do what we need to do to meet our students' needs, regardless who they are.[42]

Thus, we found evidence at Silvern Hills that some of the typical patterns of race and socioeconomic status being correlated with achievement were being successfully defied by teachers and administrators. This was not the case at other Sewall County high schools; for instance, at a majority-white (67 percent, compared with 30 percent at Silvern Hills) high school in the southern part of the county, both black and lower-income students failed to make Adequate Yearly Progress for academic performance in 2010–11. One possible reason is Silvern Hills' relatively smaller size, which offers more personalization, but equally important is its overall press for academic achievement and its strong principal. However, Silvern Hills faces a challenge in maintaining this progress; by fall of 2011, the percentage of students receiving free and reduced-price lunch had increased from 40 to 51 percent.

CIVIC CAPACITY: CROSS-SECTOR COLLABORATION

In Sewall, we found evidence that there was particularly strong collaboration between the school system and the Chamber of Commerce. Beginning in 2007, the chamber spearheaded a One [Sewall] initiative that involved an economic strategy plan. It convened intracounty governments, commissioners, mayors, city council members, development authority, hospital authority, and also key businesses in the community to focus on an economic development comprehensive plan. One of the task force areas was education and workforce development; it involved about twenty leaders and eighty community members overall. The superintendent describes the linkage that has been made between a strong education system and a healthy economic system: "We're working with our chamber in developing a parent engagement, community engagement piece that will be coming out shortly . . . and one of the top issues is education and workforce readiness, 100 percent graduation."[43]

The school system's director of professional learning describes the effort to develop the Respecting Equally All Cultures initiative as one that was broad and inclusive of many stakeholders. The initial committee consisted of the superintendent, board members, school administrators, teachers, parents, representatives of the faith-based community, and business people. The chair of the Chamber of Commerce's cultural diversity committee similarly describes proactive, rather than reactive, efforts: "We think [the cultural shift] is happening in a way that will evolve as opposed to [becoming] a revolution—evolve in a way that will make us a better county." When asked about how his efforts at the Chamber might translate into change in the school system, he cited "creating awareness" through student diversity councils, and establishing "No Hate" zones.[44]

The county also has a local nonprofit agency, Connect [Sewall], whose mission, according to the executive director, is "to network social service-based organizations and government in the service of children and families.

We do that by targeting four specific areas: success for students, economic development, cultural diversity, and community outreach."[45] Connect has provided outreach in areas like gang prevention in high schools and outreach to homeless families.

Many leaders credited the former superintendent's efforts to reach out to the county's civil rights leadership during a period of rapid change. As the assistant superintendent for curriculum and instruction reflected:

> I do give [the former superintendent] quite bit of credit for having the foresight and the vision to see that the change was coming. He established tremendously strong relations with the NAACP and the Black Ministerial Alliance and groups like that in the community that really supported the school system during a time when it could have been a very different kind of relationship. They could have been looking at it in terms of "us versus them," and it was not that way; they were partners with the school system to say, through this change what do we do to assist? How do we help? And I just feel that it's been one of the smoothest transitions that could possibly have happened.[46]

The chair of the Chamber's cultural diversity initiative mentioned the idea of neighborhood associations and leadership development as one that would facilitate better communication about racial and cultural differences within neighborhoods. He reported that in 2008, the diversity initiative conducted facilitation training for around twenty people drawn from city and county government and the school system, with the goal to "create awareness and engagement now in order for leaders to have the ability to facilitate cultural discussions," and thought that would be promising for building leadership in neighborhoods.[47]

The membership of the Chamber of Commerce's education committee also reveals significant cross-sector collaboration. The committee of twenty includes representatives from banks, the Development Authority, the school system, and the power and electric municipal cooperatives. It is engaged in a wide range of activities to support the county schools, from hosting the annual STAR (Student Teacher Achievement Recognition) breakfast to hosting a teacher induction program that welcomes all new teachers entering the school system. Yet another program pairs community executives with high school principals over the course of a year so that, as the education committee chair says, "you get to share each others' worlds over a year."[48]

The business community remains concerned that Sewall is the largest county in the metropolitan area that does not have a technical college, so there is a recognized need to form a public-private partnership to build such an institution. As the education committee chairwoman stated, "We feel that it would definitely increase our graduation rates, just because students would be more interested, and it's a steppingstone [to] getting some type of technical certificate or diploma as they pursue the long-term postsecondary education."[49] Improving school readiness, increasing dual enrollment programs, enhancing mentoring for high school students, and achieving a 100 percent graduation rate by supporting graduation coaches in middle and high schools are also major goals of the education committee.

CONCLUSION

The president of the local chapter of the NAACP was quoted in a 2009 newspaper article as saying: "There used to be a lot of racial tension here, but everybody knows that we need each other to survive this recession. People now, they seem to be starting to care for one another."[50] Both the business community and school system leaders have emphasized the importance of cultural dialogue and antiracist discussion in both schools and neighborhoods; whether these strategies will prove to be adequate interventions to meet the needs of increasingly segregated schools remains to be seen. Although we did hear throughout our interviews that the racial climate was "positive and getting better," it is inevitable that demographic transition eventually brings some political tensions. In 2011, after we had completed our fieldwork, we learned of such tensions that surrounded a school board zone redrawing, in which a black board member was placed into a majority-minority district, despite having built a constituency base in a more racially mixed district.

While the relationship between the business community and school district is a positive one in Sewall, it has played out against the context of an almost total adherence to neighborhood schools. What makes it different from the patterns in other suburbs in this study, however, is that the strong black middle class, with its access to affordable housing, has so far not exerted any significant political pressure for school desegregation. Regardless of their race/ethnicity, participants were fairly constant in their expressed belief that "all children can succeed regardless of race" and said that they felt "positive" about the changes in the county. There was very little acknowledgement of racism by the interviewees, including blacks, when asked about racial tensions in schools or in the community.

With the emphasis on neighborhood schools, there has been a lack of public school choice. While there have been some charter school applications to the school board in the past decade, none has been approved. There is one advanced career technical academy within a high school that accepts applicants countywide, but it is not characterized as a "magnet." There are some school leaders and community members who are strongly supportive of charter schools, but the school board clearly does not share this as a priority.

Despite the undisputed color blindness of the student assignment policy, neither community nor county officials in Sewall have tried to avoid either the changes or their school-level implications. Jeffrey Henig and his colleagues wrote in their study of civic capacity urban education reform: "As parents, communities, schools, business, government agencies, and so on learn to cooperate and trust one another, by acting together they can accomplish goals that could not be accomplished either separately or competitively."[51] Indeed, we find that that business and community leaders from various sectors across Sewall have deliberately communicated and worked together to address the needs of the schools. The net effect so far does indeed appear to be a community and school system where, relative to other suburbs of this city, there is a serious effort to embrace change rather than flee from it—after all, the community's residents are living at the outermost fringe of suburbia, with the next nearest city an hour to the south.

Our interviewees overwhelmingly said that the racial climate was positive and getting better. What remains to be seen in suburban districts undergoing rapid change, however, is whether schools like Silvern Hills, with its fragile racial balance and increasing poverty rate, are able to maintain the sort of academic environment that exists now—one that has defied, at least for a while, national and regional patterns of achievement and attainment gaps.

9

"The Oak Park Way" Isn't Enough

*Lasting Diversity Achieved, School Challenges
Remaining in Suburban Chicago*

GARY ORFIELD

The Village of Oak Park is a suburb bordering the west side of the city of Chicago.[1] It is among the first generation of suburban communities, created by railroad stops and street railways near to central cities in the 1800s.[2] The Union Pacific Railroad opened a station in Oak Park in 1848, connecting it to the Chicago Loop, only about twenty minutes away. The community began to develop in the 1850s as Chicago was becoming a great city. After the great Chicago fire, its growth accelerated in the 1870s and it became an independent municipality in 1901. It is a pre-automobile city with considerable urban density along some corridors. It is served by two mass transit lines and a large freeway, creating excellent connections with downtown Chicago.

For more than a century, Oak Park was a virtually all-white community. It had 40,000 residents by 1920 and reached 66,000 in 1940, remaining at about that level until 1960. Since 1970 it has been quite stable, around 52,000 to 55,000 people.

Oak Park faced its threat of major racial transition in the late 1960s. Just across the street from a rapidly declining section of Chicago, near the center of one of the nation's most hypersegregated housing markets, it was predicted to resegregate at a time of severe racial tension. In dramatic contrast to the other communities studied in this book, Oak Park mobilized a comprehensive campaign against resegregation, effectively using a wide range of local powers, and created an island of lasting integration in a sea of resegregation.

In 2010, the population was about two-thirds white (63.8 percent), a little more than one-fifth black (21.7 percent), with 6.8 percent Latinos and 4.8 percent Asians.[3] It has also maintained this significant diversity with remarkable stability—the product of a dramatic local initiative more than forty years ago. Since the average American household moves about every six years in normal times, Oak Park has replaced its population several times over the past forty years without disruption. Both blacks and whites have continued to move in as its aging housing stock has become much more valuable.

Thus, what was a massive community mobilization to deal with a crisis has become an established successful community where diversity is often taken for granted and gentrification is a more serious threat than resegregation. In her classic *Death and Life of Great American Cities*, Jane Jacobs wrote in 1961 about the way a fascinating and affordable neighborhood, full of artists and intellectuals, became so successful that it drew in people with money who did not share the vision of those who made it unique.[4] Thus Oak Park has become a more typical successful suburban community where the cost barriers to housing have risen greatly. But challenging racial issues remain. Oak Park offers much stronger schools than Chicago and a number of nearby resegregated suburbs, but the outcomes are still far from equal. Stable diversity makes true integration possible but success requires deeper changes in schools and communities. Oak Park shows both the possibilities of lasting diversity and the fact that there will always be challenges and the need for sensitive and thoughtful responses to racial inequality. Schools are central to these issues. Though they do not have the power to resolve and repair all the inequality that comes from out-of-school differences in families, peer groups, and other forces, continuous efforts to narrow gaps and equalize opportunities must be seen as a high responsibility of school leaders.

THE RESEGREGATION CHALLENGE

As the civil rights movement reached its peak in the mid-1960s, Oak Park was a white community that seemed like part of the problem of suburban segregation. In 1966, Martin Luther King Jr.'s last major campaign, the Chicago Freedom Movement, focused on the brutal wall of residential segregation confining the city's black community. King wrote that the intensity of the resistance he faced in Chicago exceeded anything he had confronted in the South.[5] King moved his family into a home on the West Side of Chicago, the city's poorest ghetto. Though Oak Park, directly to the west a few miles

EXHIBIT 9.1

River Forest School District and Elementary School District 97

Percentage change of Chicago suburban ring, River Forest School District, and Elementary School District 97

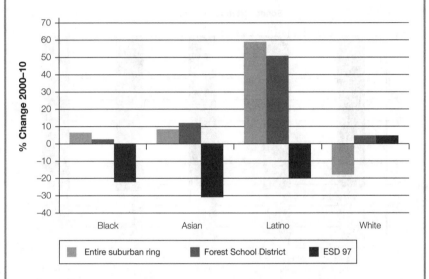

Racial and poverty composition of Chicago metropolitan statistical area, River Forest School District, ESD 97, and ESD district first grade, 2009–10

	% Black	% Asian	% Latino	% White	% English language learners	% Free and reduced-price lunch	Total enrollment
Total MSA	22.4	5.2	27.9	44.3	10.8	43.5	1,590,247
Principal cities	38.1	5.4	37.7	18.6	13.2	66.4	564,726
Suburbs	13.6	5.2	22.3	58.8	9.5	31.0	1,025,167
River Forest	29.2	3.3	5.7	61.6	0.3	19.0	3,182
ESD 97	27.4	4.7	4.9	62.9	1.7	18.8	5,421
ESD 97 first grade	22.5	6.0	5.5	65.8	—	—	550

Note: Not all enrolled students have race/ethnicity specified for this district or metropolitan area.

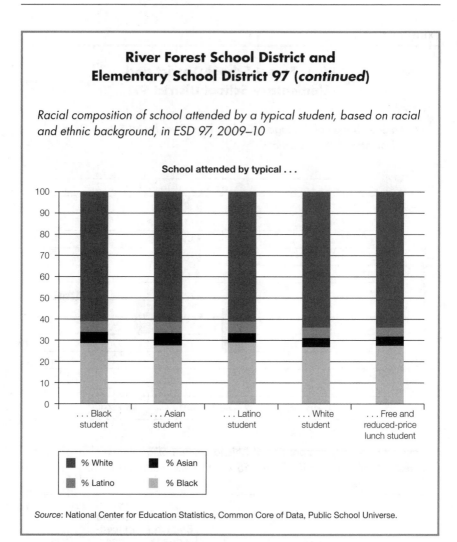

River Forest School District and Elementary School District 97 (continued)

Racial composition of school attended by a typical student, based on racial and ethnic background, in ESD 97, 2009–10

Source: National Center for Education Statistics, Common Core of Data, Public School Universe.

away, was not a major target of the campaign and did not mount the violent resistance encountered elsewhere, there were marches during the campaign that went through Oak Park.[6] The West Side's black community was expanding rapidly and approaching the Oak Park boundary. There had been virtually no record of stable integration in Chicago for a half century, so the expectation was that the ghetto would continue to expand outward and that once communities were significantly integrated they would rapidly resegregate. The dominant pattern was block-by-block change of white areas to black areas, with whites fleeing and blacks hungry for better housing steered into the new area.

Demographer Pierre deVise was well known for his 1967 study, "Chicago's Widening Color Gap," when he issued projections suggesting that Oak Park was soon going to face significant resegregation.[7] In 1968, deVise predicted that "the Negro corridor" would penetrate Oak Park within five or six years. He noted that there was affordable housing in Oak Park and that "the approaching wave of Negro population" was just a mile away and "advancing at the rate of two blocks per year," forecasting that a region of dense affordable rental housing near the mass transit lines would resegregate as the ghetto expanded.[8]

This prediction, published just months after the assassination of Martin Luther King Jr. and the West Side riot that had immediately followed, shocked Oak Parkers. The resegregation process in other communities had been fast and ugly, and the West Side communities were devastated. People could see what was happening five minutes away and what had happened in the Chicago area since the great migration from the South began during World War I.

The Oak Park community mobilized to prove deVise wrong. Residents invented a number of strategies and later created bonds with similar communities across the country to compare experiences and develop strategies. Kathryn Divine studied the village a decade after the process began, describing a "consensus-building political process that involved citizens in the defining of goals and strategies while it also drew upon the expertise of talented business, political and administrative leadership."[9] The village supported "cooperative planning by the elected officials, citizens on appointed boards and committees and village administrators. In addition . . . many church, business, and other civic and social groups and individuals presented ideas to the Village Council."[10] Participation surged and "some citizen initiatives like the Housing Center and the Frank Lloyd Wright Historic District have become village institutions."[11] The village brought in public relations experts and very aggressively moved against signs of deterioration near the Chicago border, even moving the village hall there to show confidence. There was an intense, multidimensional, and long-term involvement in the housing market and everything that could influence it, including community conditions.

Oak Park leaders forcefully addressed various forms of housing discrimination and the conditions that tended to accompany racial transition. A 1981 Chicago Urban League study of a number of the many racially changing communities in Chicago noted that they faced central problems including increasing crime, "inadequate police protection . . . decline in city services . . . and a trend toward commercial disinvestment [which reinforced] stereotyping of transition areas as areas of economic decline."[12] Another problem was that "housing maintenance and rehabilitation" often suffered and "a physically deteriorating community produces dissatisfaction and a sense of helplessness in area homeowners."[13] At the core, there was serious discrimination: "A pervasive pattern of racial steering by real estate brokers is obviously present in transition areas . . . Black families are offered housing choices limited by racial discrimination, and are often trapped in a resegregation process which denies them the opportunity to live in an open, racially diverse environment. They are subjected to economic exploitation and the pressures of poverty and unemployment. They are denied equal access to government services and private capital."[14] These were the conditions that Oak Park set out to change.

In 1950, Oak Park had been deeply embarrassed by overt discrimination against Percy Julian, the first black resident of the village and an eminent scientist who would became the second black member of the National Academy of Sciences. Julian's home was firebombed, which created a national scandal.[15] This helped change attitudes, and the police department began protecting black homebuyers, unlike some other area police forces. The community passed a fair housing ordinance in collaboration with local realtors in 1968, the year Congress enacted the federal Fair Housing Act.[16] Sociologist Juliet Saltman writes: "In 1971, community trustees created one of the first community relations departments in Illinois to enforce the fair housing ordinance. A year later, as the first blacks began moving in, the Oak Park Housing Center was founded by the village trustees to ensure that the community maintained a mix of black and white residents." The Housing Center "initiated programs to ensure economic and racial stability" and "above all, the commitment to racial diversity and integration maintenance permeated their programs."[17] The Housing Center worked with realtors to be sure that the housing shown to whites included more heavily black areas closer to Chicago, and that blacks were shown housing in the heavily white parts of the village, a policy described as "reverse steering" by critics and defended as enlarging integrated choices by supporters. No potential buyer or renter was limited to such housing options and the intent of this practice—to support integration—was continually made clear. The community actively monitored and aggressively prosecuted residential steering, including revoking the licenses of guilty agents. There was a very concerted effort that integrated the staff of the city and school board offices. The effort, which included human relations training for the city's realtors, received national attention and recognition from the U.S. Department of Housing and Urban Development.[18]

Oak Park took a very active role in fighting neighborhood deterioration and impoverishment in the blocks near Chicago's ghetto. The community focused very intense policing in a vulnerable area near the Chicago border and used building code enforcement to force upkeep of property and avoid signs of decay. It actively discouraged the location of the typical "ghetto-style" storefront businesses and focused local dollars on rehab and maintenance in areas where disinvestment might have occurred. Eight hundred units of subsidized housing were scattered around the village to avoid the kind of problems associated with Chicago's profoundly segregated and dysfunctional public housing.[19] Oak Park invested in subsidizing private upgrading of housing stock and even provided a financial incentive to owners of rental buildings to intentionally integrate their buildings.[20] To assuage potential homebuyers' fears about possible declines in housing values, the village offered insurance to protect values, a highly controversial move that few buyers ever took advantage of, but that perhaps contributed to confidence in the housing market in the early period. The schools cooperated with leaflets on the local school programs and a policy of welcoming home seekers wanting to visit. No school was permitted to resegregate, but there was no need to implement a major desegregation plan because of the success of the housing strategy. With a small number of schools and the ability to create new attendance areas when the grade structure was changed, the community did not let school resegregation take hold.

The community mobilized on many fronts, some of which were criticized as excessive by some civil libertarians and black advocates. In retrospect, perhaps more was done than was necessary, but no one really knew how much was enough or even if preventing resegregation could be done so close to a large expanding ghetto.

Communities are shaped by self-fulfilling prophecies. A comparative study of neighborhoods across Chicago, which was designed to show the impact of crime on neighborhood change, found that it was not the amount of crime that was a central cause of transition but what people believed about the future of the community. They were much more likely to make long-term commitments if they expected the future to be better. And commitments by major institutions, such as universities, were very important.[21] What Oak

Park did in the 1970s was to break the dominant self-fulfilling prophecy in the Chicago area real estate market and create a very different and positive set of beliefs. A systematic comparison of different patterns of transition and stable integration in the metropolitan Chicago area showed that resegregating Census tracts were treated much as ghetto communities were by banks and businesses, but areas that proved to be stably integrated had outcomes in terms of housing and jobs very similar to those in white communities.[22]

The strength of the Oak Park approach made the community prominent in the movement for housing integration.[23] Juliet Saltman writes: "By the end of their first decade, the Oak Park [Housing] Center had counseled over 40,000 clients . . . The center had . . . a staff of seven full-time and five part-time people . . . They received coverage in national media . . . and had formed a nationwide federation of other suburb communities trying to achieve stable integration, the Oak Park Exchange Congress."[24] It was clear within a few years that Oak Park was not following the projected pattern of resegregation but becoming a very different kind of community. After the initial changes bringing the village to about a one-quarter black population, the ratios stabilized. Unlike a number of neighborhoods with residential integration in Washington, DC, Chicago, Los Angeles, and other cities, individual schools did not resegregate. Serious attention was focused on maintaining school quality and race relations, but there was no need for major student assignment efforts requiring extensive busing. The reputation of the schools remained far above that of Chicago and of resegregated suburbs. It was an astonishing and lasting success in terms of residential and school integration under difficult circumstances. It is a testimony to the power of effective community mobilization and skillful, determined use of municipal powers to produce very different outcomes. The irony, of course, was that the success made it very safe for people to move into the village who did not share any intense identification with or dedication to the integrationist beliefs of community pioneers. Over time, since the success was achieved, integration didn't have to be worked on so hard.

In retrospect, critics sometimes point to the success as the by-product of unique historic assets—relatively affluent residents, the Frank Lloyd Wright connection, and serious citizen involvement. But other well-endowed communities experienced a very different destiny. What was truly unique about Oak Park was the leadership and mobilization of municipal, community, and school leadership in pursuit of a positive vision of the future, a vision that became reality to such an extent and for so long that it is now largely taken for granted. Communities that experience long-term integration and economic success come to be seen as desirable by all groups and are treated by major institutions in fundamentally different ways than resegregating communities. They have successfully replaced the vicious cycle of resegregation with a kind of balanced integration-gentrification that can be sustained over generations and create a very different lifestyle even in the midst of hypersegrated housing markets.

DEMOGRAPHICS

Significant black migration to Oak Park began in the 1970s. The civil rights movement and the integration policies adopted in the 1960s to avoid "white flight" facilitated this migration of black residents to all parts of Oak Park even while a strong white presence in the housing market remained.[25]

In 2000, Oak Park was two-thirds white, 22 percent black, 5 percent Latino, and 4 percent Asian (see table 9.1). Between 2000 and 2007, the population and the share of white residents in Oak Park stabilized.[26] There was a slight increase in the number of residents between 2000 and 2007 and the percentage of the white population was virtually unchanged between 2000 and 2007. When interviewees were asked how the population has changed in the last ten years, respondents said that the make-up of the community and schools has not changed. That perception is generally consistent with the data.

Although Latinos represent the fastest-growing minority population in the Chicago metropolitan area, Latino migration to Oak Park has been limited, perhaps because of housing costs (there are numerous other areas of Latino suburban migration, including adjacent Berwyn and Cicero). Latinos have traditionally been deeply segregated from both blacks and whites in Chicago and there are stark lines separating the communities on the West Side. The largest Latino community is further to the south.

Oak Park has been among the most integrated municipalities with populations over twenty-five thousand in Illinois.[27] In 2000, the village's dissimilarity index for white and black residents was 38.4, a low level of racial separation, vastly lower than Chicago or the metropolitan area (see table 9.2).[28] Nonetheless, some census tracts are more integrated than others, with somewhat higher shares of black residents concentrated near the border with Chicago.[29] The Chicago metropolitan housing market has consistently been one of the nation's handful of most rigidly segregated. On a scale in

TABLE 9.1

Population and percentage change, Oak Park, 1970–2010

	1970 Population	%	1980 Population	%	1990 Population	%	2000 Population	%	2010 Population	%
Total	61,149		54,887		53,648		52,524		51,878	
White	60,558	96.9%	46,738	85.2%	41,313	77.0%	36,124	68.8%	35,121	67.7%
Nonwhite	591	0.9%	8,149	14.8%	12,335	23.0%	16,400	31.2%	16,757	32.3%
Black	190	0.3%	5,929	10.8%	9,804	18.3%	11,788	22.4%	11,233	21.7%
Native American/ Alaskan native	—	—	74	0.1%	73	0.1%	81	0.2%	93	0.2%
Asian/ Pacific Islander	—	—	1,339	2.4%	1,785	3.3%	2,194	4.2%	2,527	4.9%
Latino	—	—	153	0.3%	1,915	3.6%	2,374	4.5%	3,521	6.8%
All other	401	0.7%	654	1.2%	673	1.3%	2,337	4.4%	2,904	5.6%

Source: Reproduced in part from Village of Oak Park (2010), U. S. Census Bureau, p. 19; DemographicsNow. Calculations by the authors.

TABLE 9.2

Residential segregation (indices of dissimilarity), Oak Park

	1980	1990	2000
Black to white	58.2	49.5	45.1
Black to Latino	59.2	47.4	45.7
Black to Asian	63.3	53.5	47.8
Latino to white	47.3	38.7	35.8
Latino to Asian	57.3	49.0	46.6
Asian to white	50.5	42.9	42.6

Source: J. Lewis, M. Maly, P. Kleppner, and R. Tobias, Race and Residence in the Chicago Metropolitan Area 1980 to 2000 (Chicago: Institute for Metropolitan Affairs, Roosevelt University, and Office for Social Policy Research, Northern Illinois University, 2002).

Note: Zero=perfect integration; 100=perfect segregation.

which 100 is total apartheid, metropolitan Chicago has been in the 80–90 level for many years.

Keeping neighborhoods and schools diverse, of course, did not mean that that the village now had a society of true equality. Oak Park's income level has long been relatively high, and it grew dramatically after the mobilization of the community, tripling between 1979 and 1999. In 1999, the median family income in Oak Park was 47 percent higher than that for the state of Illinois. In River Forest, the adjacent community that shares the high school, the median family income was 120 percent higher than the state average.

Poverty in Oak Park and River Forest is very low, with little change over time. Oak Park's poverty rate was dramatically lower than the national and state averages, and remained low even during the Great Recession, less than 5 percent. Nevertheless, there are substantial differences by race in income and poverty levels. The poverty rate of black and Latino households was about three times the white or Asian level, and average black household income was less than half the white or Asian level.[30] These class variations are doubtless related to some of the variations in school outcomes that have been controversial in the village. Recent research documents a high and growing relationship between income differences and educational outcomes, differences that are by some measures even higher than racial differences.[31]

Housing in Oak Park is expensive, registering large increases in the value of housing up to the time of the Great Recession. The median housing value increased more than 77 percent from 1990 to 2007, after adjusting for inflation. Oak Park lost over thirty-three hundred affordable rental units since 2000, either through condo conversion or rent increases.[32] This was a negative factor for maintaining diversity.

Respondents indicated that high housing prices were a deterrent to minorities moving to Oak Park. White homeownership rates increased from 64.3 percent in 2000 to over 70 percent in 2007, while black homeownership declined, from 35.8 percent in 2000 to about 32 percent in 2007.[33] During this time, Asian homeownership also increased, while the rate for Latinos declined. The median household income of black families declined between 2000 and 2007, putting these families at a disadvantage in the housing market. The 2010 Census showed a significant decline in the proportion of black residents in the city. Across the country, a disproportionate share of the black middle class works in the public and nonprofit sectors, where employment was deeply affected by the economic disaster.

THE VILLAGE OF OAK PARK AND ITS RESIDENTS

Oak Park has high property taxes and provides an array of services to the community. It's served by two distinct government entities—the village government and the township. Each has separate budgets, staffs, and functions under Illinois law. The village provides municipal services such as fire, police, housing, parking, and streets while the township provides human and social services (i.e., mental health, senior, and youth services). The village has an elected council (board of trustees) consisting of a president (i.e., mayor) and six trustees.[34] The village board hires a village manager to oversee the day-to-day operation of government services and programs. The township board includes four elected trustees and a supervisor and is the policy-making body. In addition, the township includes an elected clerk, assessor, and collector and an appointed township manager. A management council made up of the six appointed heads of the village, the two school districts, park district, library, and township facilitates communication and collaboration between the two governments and other public agencies. There is also the council of governments that represents the taxing bodies for Oak Park and River Forest.

In 2011, a random sample of village residents were surveyed as part of the National Citizen Survey. The overall quality of community life was seen as excellent or good by 90 percent of the residents, and four-fifths had plans to stay in the community for at least five years. Almost half had done volunteer work in the community, 92 percent had helped a friend or neighbor, and more than one-fourth had attended a local government meeting in the past year. Most residents gave the local government and local officials positive marks. Attitudes about both the village and the respondents' neighborhoods were even higher than in the past. The percentage saying "acceptance of diverse backgrounds" was increasing (over 80 percent) and more than 90 percent of Oak Parkers saw the area as a good place to raise children.[35] A tax increase referendum for the public schools garnered a very tangible measure of citizen support; though times were difficult and there was opposition, the increase passed with 55 percent support in April 2011.[36]

OAK PARK ELEMENTARY SCHOOL DISTRICT 97 AND OAK PARK-RIVER FOREST HIGH SCHOOL DISTRICT 200

Two school districts—the Oak Park Elementary School District 97 and the Oak Park-River Forest High School District 200 (comprising just the single high school)—serve the residents of Oak Park. The high school also serves residents of River Forest and enrolls over thirty-two hundred students. It is a comprehensive public high school with about 90 percent of graduates pursuing post-secondary education. The campus, situated on four blocks, has over 1 million square feet of building space, a five-thousand-seat stadium, a field house, and two swimming pools. The main classroom building includes three gymnasiums, science and computer laboratories, a digital imaging lab, television studio, art studios, and a music and drama wing with multiple auditoriums/theaters. The school has 243 faculty members, 86 percent of whom have a master's degree. The enrollment is majority white (57 percent) but with a substantial share of black students (27 percent) and relatively low poverty. Both districts are well resourced. Operating expenditures per pupil for the high school district was $16,562, compared with the state average of $10,417 (37.1 percent difference) and $12,680 for the elementary district (21.7 percent difference). Compared with the many communities that have experienced major cutbacks and economic and institutional reverses, Oak Park has been very fortunate. It is a very different world from the schools in Chicago or adjacent suburbs.

Elementary School District 97 enrolls over five thousand students. In the mid-1970s, the district converted its ten K–8 schools to eight K–6 schools and two 7–8 schools. The district located the middle (grades 7–8) schools so that the student population was fairly racially balanced. In 1999, a referendum passed to build two new middle schools (on the same location as the previous schools), resulting in the current configuration.[37] The composition of the elementary school district and the Oak Park-River Forest High School have shown continuing diversity with only modest changes in racial proportions over the past two decades, while the overall metropolitan population and the population of the suburban ring have changed substantially. The percentage of whites in metropolitan Chicago has fallen from 53 percent to 43 percent, the proportion of blacks has declined from 28 percent to 22 percent, and the share of Latinos soared from 15 percent to 29 percent since 1990.

Enrollment in Elementary School District 97 changed very little between 1999 and 2009. Whites comprised 56.9 percent of the district enrollment in 2009, and blacks, 25.8 percent. Since 2000 the white share of the enrollment in both districts gradually rose; the changes are particularly notable in the first grade, a good predictor of future enrollment trends (see exhibit 9.1). The school statistics show that the share of black students both in the elementary district and the high school rose significantly from 1990 to 2000 but fell during the next decade. The percentage of poor students qualifying for free and reduced-price lunch has increased over the ten-year period from 1999 to 2009, from 12.2 percent to 17.1 percent. The share of students on free lunch was far below the metropolitan area or even the suburban average (see table 9.3; see exhibit 9.1 for metropolitan area and suburban figures). However, since 2004, the poverty rate has fluctuated between 16 percent and 19 percent. A slight increase in enrollment and poverty in 2009 was attributed by a district-level administrator to the addition of children who had been in full-day kindergarten and parochial schools now using the public schools because of the economy.[38] The trends do not suggest resegregation; on the contrary, they suggest that the community is now gradually gentrifying.

While most of the schools reflect the district averages, a few are outliers. Two schools with the highest percentages of minority students—Irving and Longfellow—also have the highest percentages of low-income students. Irving Elementary is the only majority-minority school in the district, with 58.5 percent minority students and 41.5 percent white students. It has the highest percentage of low-income students, at 26.2 percent. Longfellow Elementary has the second-highest percentage of minority students, at 47.7 percent, and the second-highest poverty rate, at 18.8 percent. Longfellow is also the largest elementary school, with 527 students in 2009. Mann

TABLE 9.3

Student Enrollment and Demographics, Oak Park Elementary School District 97, 1999–2009

Year	Enrollment	Asian	Black	Latino	White	Multiracial	FRL	ELL
1999	5,171	2.7%	35.1%	3.3%	58.7%	—	12.2%	1.5%
2000	5,075	2.6%	34.7%	3.6%	58.8%	—	14.5%	1.4%
2001	5,035	3.1%	34.4%	3.8%	58.4%	—	10.6%	1.7%
2002	5,013	3.7%	30.2%	8.5%	57.5%	—	12.5%	1.5%
2003	4,923	3.6%	31.7%	4.0%	60.4%	—	13.3%	1.3%
2004	4,938	3.5%	31.8%	4.1%	60.5%	—	16.3%	—
2005	4,969	3.6%	29.8%	3.9%	55.6%	6.9%	16.3%	1.2%
2006	4,973	3.5%	29.2%	4.0%	55.9%	7.4%	17.9%	1.1%
2007	5,001	3.7%	28.2%	3.8%	56.5%	7.8%	18.4%	1.6%
2008	5,040	4.0%	26.6%	3.7%	57.1%	8.4%	19.2%	1.7%
2009	5,247	4.3%	25.8%	3.8%	56.9%	9.2%	17.1%	1.6%
Ten-year percentage point change	1.5*	1.6	−9.3	0.5	1.8	2.3**	4.9	0.1

Source: Illinois State Board of Education, *Interactive Illinois Report Card*, http://iirc.niu.edu/Default.aspx.
*Percent change in enrollment, 1999–2009.   **Percentage point change, 2005–2009.

Elementary has the highest proportion of white students, at 78.7 percent, and the lowest poverty rate, at 3.1 percent. The distribution of race and poverty across the other schools is more reflective of village totals.

As with the elementary district, the enrollment and the racial/ethnicity composition of Oak Park-River Forest High School District 200 has been stable since 1999 (see table 9.4). Enrollment increased 13 percent, from 2,721 in 1999 to 3,076 in 2009. White students represented 59.1 percent of the enrollment in 2009; little changed from 1999, when white student enrollment was 60.6 percent. The proportion of black student enrollment has declined since 1999, from 31.9 percent to 26.7 percent in 2009. Similar to the elementary district, the introduction of the multiracial category may account for some of the changes in the black student enrollment as students reclassify themselves into the new category. Poverty fluctuated from a low of 5.6 percent in 2002 to a high of 17.4 percent in 2009. The 2009 rate may reflect the

TABLE 9.4

Student Enrollment Demographics, Oak Park-River Forest High School District 200, 1999–2009

Year	Enrollment	Asian	Black	Latino	White	Multiracial	FRL	ELL
1999	2,721	3.5%	31.9%	3.9%	60.6%	—	13.9%	0.4%
2000	2.727	3.3%	30.7%	4.5%	61.4%	—	9.6%	0.7%
2001	2,830	3.1%	30.3%	4.0%	62.4%	—	5.8%	0.7%
2002	2,921	2.5%	27.5%	5.2%	64.6%	—	5.6%	0.4%
2003	2,962	2.6%	26.9%	4.3%	65.6%	—	5.8%	0.4%
2004	3,023	2.9%	26.0%	4.7%	66.0%	—	9.7%	0.2%
2005	3,087	2.8%	25.3%	4.1%	61.9%	5.3%	12.0%	0.1%
2006	3,076	3.0%	24.9%	4.0%	62.2%	5.5%	12.5%	0.3%
2007	3,139	3.1%	24.9%	4.7%	61.6%	5.2%	11.9%	0.2%
2008	3,098	3.0%	26.4%	5.0%	59.7%	5.6%	11.6%	0.2%
2009	3,076	2.8%	26.7%	5.6%	59.1%	5.6%	17.4%	0.1%
Ten-year percentage point change	13.0*	−0.7	−5.2	1.7	−1.5	0.3**	3.5	−0.3

Source: Illinois State Board of Education, *Interactive Illinois Report Card*, http://iirc.niu.edu/Default.aspx.
*Percent change in enrollment, 1999–2009.   **Percentage point change, 2005–2009.

economic downturn, since there had been little change in the poverty rate between 2005 and 2008.

The distribution of students across schools shows a highly desegregated pattern. The average black student in the district attends a school with 61 percent white students while the typical white student attends a school with 27 percent black and 5 percent Latino students (see exhibit 9.1).

In a period of deep national concern about the high dropout rates for the nation's black and Latino students, Oak Park's data are very positive. Nine of every ten black and Latino students are graduating, according to the district's statistics, as are almost all white students (see table 9.5). The dropout rate is many times higher even for Chicago's white students than it is for black students in Oak Park, where black students are graduating far above the national rate for white students.[39] In spite of all the difficulties reflected in the persisting test score gap in Oak Park's school districts, this is a remarkable record.

TABLE 9.5

Graduation rates for Oak Park-River Forest School District
calculated using CPI

	2000	2007
Black	73.0%	91.4%
Asian	66.0%	84.8%
Latino	81.1%	88.9%
White	94.8%	95.1%
District	87.1%	96.2%

Source: National Center for Education Statistics, Common Core of Data

DIVERSITY AS A LEGACY SOMETIMES TAKEN FOR GRANTED

Most Oak Parkers hold a perception of Oak Park as a diverse community, but since little has changed in terms of the racial and social economic makeup of the community since the 1970s, they have not conceptualized issues as related to *increasing* diversity. Diversity within the Oak Park community is primarily defined as black-white diversity. The proportion of Latinos and Asians is much smaller than the black population, though the Latino numbers have grown significantly.

The dramatic changes and successful initiatives in the 1970s created an image of Oak Park as a community sharing a positive vision of diversity. One administrator described this perspective, known as the "Oak Park Way": "They have a phrase called the Oak Park Way. It really started in the early '70s when they made a strong commitment to welcome diversity in the community and to make sure that no one felt like they couldn't live in any neighborhood in the community."[40] According to a community respondent, "There was a generation . . . where people were moving in [to Oak Park] by choice because they wanted to live in the diverse community, they were committed to the social change and the social stands that were being made at the time. That generation, that guard, has moved on and there really hasn't been a generation to replace it at this point."[41] The community survey in 2011, however, showed a very broad positive feeling about the community's diversity.

More recent trends reflect a view of Oak Park that places an emphasis on individual, as opposed to community, goals.[42] One skeptic, a district-level administrator, argued that the diversity commitment was fading: "They talk of it that way, but it tends to be thrown out like everyone accepts it and I think that, frankly . . . there has been a turnover of that attitude. I think more people are concerned more about their own child rather than someone else's children. I know when we have parent groups together, the people who are longtime residents are always talking about, 'Is it fair to other children?' The newer people to the community talk about, 'I want this for my child.'"[43]

One common perception was that the kind of person moving to Oak Park has changed. As the country's population was becoming more unequal and more conservative as the civil rights impulse faded, Oak Park was evolving in a similar direction. While earlier residents were actively committed to social diversity, more recent residents come to Oak Park for its amenities— including the schools—and its favorable property values. One community respondent put it this way: "On the social capital end, I think that when the real estate went in the direction where this was a great community to invest in because you bought a piece of property here and a couple of years later you could sell it for money, it changed the motivation of why people were moving to Oak Park. They would be moving to Oak Park because it was a great community, had all the stuff, but [they] weren't necessarily contributing to it other than paying their taxes."[44]

The notion of the Oak Park Way fostered a belief that Oak Park is unique. Respondents portrayed this as both positive and negative. For some, the Oak Park Way conveys a strong sense of pride in the community and its history, particularly as a leader during the 1960s and '70s in promoting integrated housing. For others, it reflects arrogance and often means that Oak Park has little to learn from those outside the community. One community respondent believed that, while there is a spirit of inclusion in Oak Park, there is little appreciation for diversity of thought; that is, "there is only one way and it's our way because we're special, we know how to do it, we're smart."[45]

Several respondents pointed out that some community structures that would attract blacks to Oak Park are not yet in place. For example, one noted, "There is not an African American church in the community."[46] This stands in sharp contrast to Chicago, which has a multitude of major black churches. In addition, minorities are underrepresented on appointed citizen boards and commissions.[47] For example, the 2010 village board of trustees included four white males (including the village president), one black male, and three white females.

PERSISTING RACIAL ISSUES IN THE SCHOOLS

The primary racial issue in the schools—in both the elementary and high school districts—has been defined as the achievement gap between black and white students. Closing this gap has been a central focus of federal policy as well in both the Goals 2000 law and NCLB. The dominant national educational reform movement since the 1980s has been based on the assumption that the schools are responsible for low student achievement and that appropriate policies, pressures, tests, and sanctions can produce equal outcomes. NCLB's central requirement was that all racial and ethnic groups of students be over the proficiency level by 2014—a goal that will clearly not be met, since racial gaps have not closed and school outcomes remain deeply linked to the race and socioeconomic status of families.[48]

NCLB and state reforms, however, produced massive data documenting inequalities in outcomes. In Oak Park, many acknowledge that the achievement gap has existed for years, but it was the disaggregated data required under NCLB, which revealed that the high school had failed to make required Adequate Yearly Progress (AYP) for all subgroups as required by NCLB, that clearly focused attention on this issue. According to one elementary district administrator, "When you publish the scores broken down by race and income and a few other things by subgroups, it gets a little bit harder to say everyone is at about the same place."[49]

This performance created a sense of urgency for the high school district to look more closely at the achievement gap. According to superintendent Attila Weninger, "The thing that drove the board [of education] to this sense of urgency about the achievement gap was because it was a very public set of numbers. Although in this community, people identified an achievement gap I think, ten, fifteen, twenty years ago. But this made it much more urgent because there were public reports."[50] While the reason the high school district has not made AYP varied by subgroup and subject from year to year, the achievement gap between white and minority students was persistent.

Because the high school has not made AYP under NCLB, the district has focused on differences in achievement among racial groups of students. In a letter to the high school board of education outlining a plan to address the achievement gap, Superintendent Weninger framed the gap as "minority students who enter OPRF HS [Oak Park-River Forest High School] academically achieve at a lesser rate than their Caucasian counterparts, and that gap grows through their high school years. We didn't start this achievement gap;

however, because we know it exists as students enter OPRF and continues, then we have an obligation to address it."[51]

The school's and community's awareness of the achievement gap at the high school level was documented as early as 1977 in an internal district report.[52] Over the next three decades, the district formed ad hoc committees, commissioned reports, and implemented a range of interventions to study and address the gap.[53] Many of these initiatives included focus groups or forums to solicit input from a variety of stakeholders. The current board is taking a similar approach. In 2009–10, it hosted a series of workshops on race and started a "Courageous Conversations" group to talk about personal experiences with race and racism.

The ability of the high school to serve *all* students has surfaced periodically as an issue. Many of those interviewed pointed out that the high school worked very well for some students, but not for all. One respondent described it this way: "It still runs the same way it did when I went there. I grew up here, moved away and came back, and it's set up very similarly. It's about three or four different schools within the school. I think it serves the very bright, very dedicated kind of student extremely well, and I think it generally fails the rest . . . Those kids that don't respond in class as well, they're doing the whole teenage thing, and until they get into deep trouble the teachers don't seem real interested in reaching out to them. There is no one there to really connect with them. It's a huge place."[54]

Another district-level respondent commented on the ability of the high school to address diversity within the black students: "We fail to recognize the diversity within the African American community itself . . . There is a divide between African American students whose parent have done very well economically and have positions of authority where they work . . . and then we have a set of African American students whose parents have not done as well economically in terms of position . . . [and] their own schooling. And we have not been successful in trying to address the needs of those students as much as we would like."[55]

Because most Oak Park residents are professionals, strong performance at school has been taken for granted, and to a large extent it still is. According to one administrator, the community tends to discount the NCLB classifications, as do many upper-status suburban communities where students meet the proficiency standards with little special effort.[56] But the disaggregation requirements of NCLB, coupled with new leadership at the district level, highlighted the achievement gap between black and white students. A new district administration came to Oak Park in 2005 from districts that had been using data for accountability purposes. So at the district level, there was an awareness of differences in performance among students that was not completely accepted by the community.

Data on the black-white achievement gap shows that between 1999 and 2009, the elementary district has made progress in narrowing the gap in mathematics in some grades. The largest gains have been in eighth grade, where the gap narrowed by 26 points between 1999 and 2009; the gap narrowed by 20 points in third grade. A different pattern emerges in fifth grade, where a 13-point black-white mathematics gap in 1999 had widened to a 25-point gap in 2009. Reading scores display similar patterns. At the high school level, there has been almost no change in the achievement gap in either mathematics or reading between 2001 and 2009. In reading, the gap has widened, particularly since 2005. These numbers reflect state trends in the black-white achievement gap, which suggest there may be issues with the tests that cut across communities. By identifying the primary racial issue as the underlying cause of the achievement gap, with few exceptions, the community has focused on racial groups of students—in this case, black students—who are not performing. It has not looked strongly at external factors that may contribute to the gap.

The dramatic public exposure of an achievement gap has not translated into a consensus on why the gap exists or what to do about it. To some, particularly blacks, it is viewed as a lack of responsiveness on the part of the schools to the needs of black students, particularly black males. Some see it as a lack of engagement on the part of the parents of these lower-achieving students. These parents are seen as not capable of or interested in helping their child succeed academically. Another prevalent belief is that much of the achievement gap can be attributed to people moving into Oak Park to attend the high school. River Forest's president described it this way: "They may be coming from the city (Chicago), they may be coming from districts that are different from an academic standpoint and they come in significantly behind their peers that have lived here their whole life."[57] A variant of this view is that there are significant numbers of nonresidents who "sneak" into the system from Chicago, primarily along the eastern border. Among those who attribute the gap to a subset of students, there is concern that resources will be diverted from the needs of "my child" to this other child who is not achieving and who may not be legitimately enrolled. Finally, there is the view that the achievement gap doesn't matter much because Oak Park has an elite school system and test scores cannot truly reflect the quality of the schools.

In 2003, a group of outside researchers and district leaders, the African American Achievement Study Team, conducted a comprehensive study of the high school, *The Learning Community Performance Gap*. For years the Oak Park NAACP and APPLE (African American Parents for Purposeful Leadership in Education) had been raising challenges to the high school leaders. The high school had created a number of interventions over the years, but the problems continued.[58] There had been efforts to retrain faculty in a teacher expectations program in the 1980s as well as well as cooperative learning strategies and the World of Difference program in the 1990s.[59] The district had joined the Minority Student Achievement Network when it was created in 1999 and been an active participant. Yet a survey showed that black students still felt less positively than whites about the school, that they were "less likely to seek tutoring," that they were in less-positive peer groups, and that they came from homes with far fewer resources.[60] Among a sample of black students, a substantial majority lived with single mothers.[61] The report used a variety of methods to explore the divisions and gaps within the school and found that the school's black students had to negotiate conflicting cultural pressures.[62] While white students' grades trended upward as they went through the school, black students' grades were flat. Less-successful black students tended "to 'act out' their African American identity in dreads, demeanor and speech" and "call attention to themselves in classroom and hallway situations" which were often seen as "disruptive and defiant of authority."[63] The study found that "one–third of the African American males in the Class of 2000–2001 were involved with the discipline system during their freshman year."[64] Some faculty members simply expected black students to perform worse.[65] Among high school seniors, there were 154 white students who had enrolled in twelve or more honors courses but only 6 blacks.[66] Obviously the racial differences were deep and damaging.

RESPONDING TO CHALLENGES IN OAK PARK

Both the community and the school districts discussed and investigated these issues and tended to adopt multiple programs to address them. There was considerable conflict, particularly at the high school level, when it comes to making institutional or systemic changes. Large high schools are notoriously difficult institutions to change because they are collections of subject matter specialists deeply connected with their own academic subject and decentralized into departments, more like colleges than elementary schools.[67]

Harvard professor John Diamond, former research director of the National Minority Student Achievement Network serving similar communities in several states, reports that both the problems confronting Oak Park and the kinds of solutions that are offered are characteristic of successful diverse suburban communities. Such communities, he notes, are eager to solve those problems and to operate demanding and excellent schools that provide the kind of academic intensity found in the best suburban schools. In a community with relatively affluent and highly educated parents, many of whom were professionals in educational institutions, there was both a commitment to the idea of equity and a very strong drive for education that would prepare their children for access to, and success in, competitive colleges. Since there are always limits on resources and priorities, there was a built-in tension between these commitments. Addressing the differences within the schools gave rise to many plans and programs but had disappointing results. There was community pushback against deeper changes some saw as taking from academically gifted children the accelerated education they needed to develop their talents fully. According to Diamond, these inherent cross-pressures and the perception of many parents that education was a zero-sum competitive game indicated "highly volatile communities around these kinds of changes." Residents, he said, tended to be "open to having the conversation but not open to changing the practices." On the other hand, critics sometimes ignored the fact that some of the roots of inequality were outside the school and would require collaboration from families and other community organizations if there were to be a comprehensive effort. So the school administrators faced the need to hold the confidence of the more affluent parents while trying to rebuild trust with minority families and create effective collaborations with other community institutions—no easy job. These cross-pressures, Diamond said, were probably related to conflicts and the repeated turnover of the superintendents in both districts.[68]

The community has also been involved in developing possible solutions. Two collaborations that provided programs aimed at specific student groups were mentioned frequently. There is a long-standing partnership between the Oak Park Township Youth Services program and the school districts. Both the elementary and high school districts contract with the Oak Park Township Youth Services to provide a variety of youth counseling, prevention, and intervention services that include programs that focus on prevention, intervention, and remediation. In other words, according to a village official, services for "before kids get in trouble, while they are in trouble, and after they have already gotten in trouble, we try to get them back on track."[69]

Another successful program is the Collaboration for Early Childhood Care and Education (CARE). CARE is a public-private partnership, with representatives from local jurisdictions—the village, park district, township, elementary and high school districts, and library—and Concordia University, Triton College, preschools, child care centers, and home providers.[70] This collaboration was initiated in 2001 over concern that opportunities for early childhood education were segregated by race and class or not available to low-income, primarily black preschool children. Race and class segregate early childhood care in Oak Park—there are many premier preschool programs for parents with means, but few for working or low-income families. Since these premier programs are half-day, they cater to parents who are not working or have childcare options for the remainder of the day. CARE provides a quality preschool program, among other services, for low-income families. As one interview respondent described it: "Our goal is to insure that every child arrives in kindergarten safe, healthy, eager to learn, ready to succeed."[71] In 2007, CARE secured funding from the two school districts to develop a strategic plan to expand its services and develop a well-coordinated early childhood system. More recently, the elementary district contracted with CARE to implement the state's universal preschool law for all three- and four-year olds.[72]

The Elementary District

Although Oak Park elementary schools are well funded compared with other districts in the state, the impact of resources on student achievement is hard to measure. Resources and related strategies have not been sufficient to overcome the achievement gap.

The elementary district strategic plan for 2009–10 outlined a number of initiatives and approaches designed to improve the achievement of all students.[73] These include differentiated instruction, heterogeneous grouping, increasing instructional time in core subjects, a focus on data to evaluate the effectiveness of academic programs, and increasing opportunities for student leadership, among other initiatives. The district's approach to instruction, according to an administrator, is to use various mechanisms, including flexible grouping and instructional differentiation, to meet the students where they are.[74] The district's strategic plan reflects research-based approaches to instruction that are beneficial to minority students without disadvantaging white or Asian students.

The emphasis on test scores fostered by NCLB has pushed the district to focus on the achievement gap. According to one administrator, "I have a feeling there were always gaps, but we've really started tracking that since about 2003."[75] The focus on the achievement gap has pushed the district in the direction of increased tracking, particularly in math. Officially, the district does not track, but there has been increased use of tracking in math in the middle schools. Since the 2008–09 school year, there have been two different math levels in the middle schools—grade-level math and accelerated math. The goal is to get more students through Algebra I by the end of eighth grade. There has also been a push from the parents of gifted students to provide more gifted services. The district's preference is to use differentiated instruction, where all students, including gifted students, receive appropriate instruction in the classroom. But in an effort to address these concerns, there are now academic pullout programs in reading, language arts, writing, and science. A district with ambitious parents of high-achieving students demanding a fast track to a good college and a significant group of students, often with less-powerful and insistent parents, needing special support to avoid academic problems has built-in tension, and the schools receive many sometimes inconsistent pressures and signals. There has also been a push by the district administration to use data and target students for interventions based on that data.

The High School District

Because the District 200 has not made AYP under NCLB, it has undertaken a number of initiatives to address disparities in achievement. These include improving the discipline system and counseling program, adopting focused academic programs in reading and math, fostering participation in cocurricular participation, and extending parent outreach, including hiring an outreach coordinator.[76]

Ideas for the cocurricular program came from a variety of sources. The Outreach Coordinator was superintendent Attlia Weninger's idea, as was developing four Pupil Support Services (PSS) teams (academic, curricular, cocurricular, and discipline). The teams were an attempt to address the divide between the counselors and the academic deans and initially met with resistance from the faculty. Pushing change, of course, risks disagreement, and when Weninger's contract was being debated, the faculty did not support renewing his contract.

Efforts to close the achievement gap were supported in principle but difficult in practice. Weninger noted: "I think there is a want on the part of everybody to solve the achievement gap. I think there is real disagreement about how to go about doing it, who's responsible for doing it, and the accountability measures for it." He conceded that there was faculty opposition, claiming that some "can't see the links because I think their world is so focused in the classroom when there is a much broader perspective."

The school implemented a wide range of academic programs. Reading/English efforts included a tutoring program (Learning Support Reading), a reading program to help special education students, and adopting a double English block that incorporates reading. In math, the school used a program call Agile Mind. The Success Scholar program provided extra help to students (primarily minority students) on the cusp of making it into the next academic achievement tier. The school looks at a variety of test scores and other indicators for all entering freshmen to identify students needing additional support. The school also has a summer program for students transitioning from grade 9 to grade 10 who need extra support and another program for entering grade 9 students (8 to 9 Connections). Superintendent Attila Weninger emphasized that these programs were interconnected to identify students needing help early and provide the supports they need, beginning in grade 9, to be successful.

Weninger reported that when he came to the district, he insisted that the board goals and superintendent goals be the same. But the conflict over the superintendent's contract and reform efforts illustrate the difficulty the community had in coming together around a common agenda. Renewal of Weninger's contract was a protracted and divisive issue. Contract negotiations broke down in October 2009 when the board voted three to four not to renew the contact. The board's three black members supported renewing the contract.[77] In November 2009, the board reversed itself and reopened contract negotiations, which led to the resignation of the board's president.[78] However, by December, contract negotiations ended when the board voted three to four to cut the superintendent's salary and Weninger submitted his resignation. In July 2010, Steven Tsutomu Isoye, a longtime science teacher at the Illinois Math and Science Academy who had been named Superintendent of the Year at another suburban district, was named the district's new superintendent.[79] The fact that there were still major issues to be addressed was apparent in 2011 when the district received unwanted national publicity over the disclosure that a student had been arrested for creating and distributing on Facebook a derogatory rating of the district's girls including racist remarks.[80]

CONTINUING CHALLENGES

The ongoing challenges in communities like Oak Park, John Diamond noted, include continuing efforts to find "people who recognize the challenges" as teachers and administrators, to further diversify the faculty and staff, and to continue the best of the existing efforts. The community needs to continue to collaborate with the Minority Student Achievement Network experiments in math curricula, to help develop better ways of clustering students within diverse classes based on broader concepts of intelligence and capacity, and to implement strong group-based bridges to college programs like AVID and the Puente Project, programs that create special classes for cohorts of minority students who might not otherwise get counseling and preparation for college. Outside the schools, there need to be broad-based community collaborations to deal with divisions and inequalities that emerged in the late elementary grades and were the roots of real problems in the high school.[81]

It is in places like Oak Park, where there are decades of experience with diversity and the schools offer vastly better opportunities than in resegregated communities, that there are still miles to go on the path to equality. Community leaders and citizens need to realize that these issues need the same kind of serious, sustained, and long-term effort that stopped resegregation four decades ago—efforts that will be needed, in all likelihood, until race is no longer so clearly linked to various forms of unequal experiences and resources in American society.

The community-oriented integrationist ethos that emerged in the 1960s and '70s is apparently being diminished by the rise of a more individualist focus. This reflects nationwide trends in politics and increasing competition for college. NCLB data has reinforced parents' concern about overall achievement levels and their own children but also reinforced concern in the black community about making diverse schools more equitable. In a sense, Oak Park's past may have hindered its ability to confront current issues facing the school district. The problems of avoiding resegregation and sustaining lasting residential and school integration are different than the current problems the schools confront in producing better race relations and closing the achievement gaps. Oak Park and similar communities across the country participating in the Minority Student Achievement Network have experienced continuing frustration along that front. It may well be that changes in social and economic policy reaching far beyond the schools and coming from higher levels of government are required to make substantial further progress. Until these gaps do close substantially, however, this will be an important and recurring challenge to the community's educators.

A part of the problem where solutions are somewhat less challenging and where progress would be visible and appreciated is increasing the diversity of the school districts' faculty and staff ranks. Recruiting a diverse faculty has been a challenge for the high school district: local administrators point to the limited pool of minority candidates combined with competition from other districts for these same potential teachers. There is, however, a very large pool of experienced and credentialed black teachers and administrators nearby in the Chicago Public Schools, home to the largest black community between the coasts. The high school district has adopted a range of strategies, including recruiting at a variety of colleges and universities, attending recruiting fairs, and collaborating with neighboring districts through the Northwest Personnel Administrators group.

The other issue is the district's internal recruitment process. Division heads are instrumental in the early part of the hiring process when potential candidates are identified. The district found that this process often resulted in a candidate pool that was not very diverse. The district began emphasizing its diversity hiring goals with faculty and making efforts to hire a qualified minority, particularly when there are multiple positions to fill.[82]

There are two large lessons for suburban educators in the Oak Park experience. The first is that educators can avoid some difficult and disruptive issues in the schools if there is an early, effective, and comprehensive attack on resegregation in housing. Oak Park schools have remained highly diverse and avoided serious resegregation for several decades without any significant mandatory busing or student reassignment because the neighborhoods are substantially desegregated and the location and districting of schools are designed to keep them that way. This means that educators and those who care about the schools have a strong incentive to support early community planning.

The second lesson is very different. It starts with taking nothing for granted. Communities that do solve the housing challenge and achieve lasting diversity must recognize that the challenge is not over. Though they do not produce the same level of possible community upheaval, the issues involved in making the schools fair and effective for all groups and fostering positive relationships among the community's young are complex. It is not enough to offer opportunities that are obviously far better than those in the nearby city—though those must be preserved—there must be a strong, skilled, and credible effort to make those opportunities equally available to all and to narrow the differences in educational outcomes. In successful diverse communities, these are a basic part of the job of educational leaders. They are continually challenged because even in this uncommonly successful community, deep racial differences in family resources often persist and students of color don't feel fully part of their schools. Those who confront today's frustrations should take heart from what was accomplished a generation ago and seek to create the same kind of comprehensive community focus on these challenges.

Conclusion

Going Forward

GARY ORFIELD

The suburbs will never be the same again. The idea that you could simply cross the city boundary and be in another world is long gone. Suburban communities are being buffeted by forces far outside their control, such as major streams of metropolitan and international migration. Suburbia is not one entity, it is many kinds of communities, some of which are untouched by change and others much worse off than their central cities. Many suburbs, once satirized as staid and homogeneous bedroom communities with rows of indistinguishable houses populated by people from exactly the same social strata, are now multicultural and home to immigrants from other nations. The day of a solid white middle-class suburbia is history, and some of the classic postwar suburbs that set the mold for a new suburban society are now deeply affected by the kind of poverty and resegregation that occurred long ago in the central city. There are still wealthy white communities with extraordinary resources and famous schools; there are newer lower-middle-class bedroom communities that recently drew many black and Latino families with the promise of low-cost housing and have been devastated by the foreclosure crisis—and have very poor school districts. Most Latinos, now the largest and most educationally disadvantaged minority group in the United States, are already living in suburbs, and as some urban areas are on the path to becoming majority white again, segregated black suburbs continue to spread.

INTEGRATION OR DIS-INTEGRATION?

Our new Main Street is in the midst of the suburbs, and our future will be decided there, as we become a society with no racial majority. The choice is between policies that will move these communities toward resegregation and those that foster and maintain integration. Resegregation by race, often the result of housing discrimination and community and government inaction is normally followed by resegregation by income and severe decline in educational opportunity and achievement. Stable integration, though requiring strenuous effort, produces very different and better educational, social, and economic futures for families and communities. Communities that succeed in producing lasting integration are successful, and their housing and schools are desired by all groups.

Given the massive failure of our cities to address the spread of residential segregation a half century ago, and the obvious continuing consequences, it is strange that there should be so little attention to the changes now. Black suburbanization began in earnest in some metropolitan areas in the 1970s, and there was a spate of research studies and policy battles about what to do, but Richard Nixon (from the suburbs of Los Angeles) torpedoed any significant response then, as did Ronald Reagan (of similar background) in the 1980s.[1] Members of the Department of Housing and Urban Development advocated taking initiative during both the Carter and the Clinton presidencies, to no avail. The two Bush administrations produced no initiatives in housing, urban policy, or civil rights; indeed, the federal role in civil rights was substantially reduced, resulting in major reversals in civil rights policy. To date, nothing of consequence has been done during the Obama administration. In a society with a black president elected from Hyde Park, Illinois—an island of integration in what is often classified as the nation's most segregated city (Chicago)—this is deeply disappointing.

Diverse suburbs are the frontier of American racial change, containing about one-third of the nation's population, and they often hold the balance of political power in national elections. They are central to the possibility of educational and occupational mobility for coming generations. They contain a great many solid homes and good schools, and have provided opportunity for generations of children. They are now the home of most black and Latino middle-class families and millions of white and Asian families who would like to remain in their communities and fear resegregation. And there is ample evidence of major resegregation, associated with educational decline, especially in our large metropolitan areas. Most of the responses, however, are limited and too late and often do not name or engage the real challenges. Local communities confronting these changes need and deserve help.

In the suburbs we have studied, there are many educators with some educational strategies they hope will stem the tide of resegregation. Educators realize that as student bodies diversify they need a different approach, and every school system we've studied is trying to do something. They often hope that what they are focusing their attention on anyway—raising test scores—will be the big answer. But that is not enough. We need a broader vision and more effective leadership.

The communities we studied in this book, and many others, have created small positive initiatives that could become part of the solution. They have experience that could help lead us to an awareness of scale and importance of the changes and the difficulty of addressing them. They are acting piece by piece, community by community, with little help and without a central vision or strategy. This is the foremost challenge for educators and community leaders and for state and national policy makers who have usually chosen, so far, to do nothing. In some cases, they take away potentially useful tools. Our highest courts have been particularly negative since 1990.

Adding up the experiences of the communities we studied, the findings of other research, and the various pieces of solutions, we can assemble a picture of what is needed and discuss how it could be done. This chapter does that and challenges the various institutions to play active roles in helping communities create and sustain successful integration. Segregation has never succeeded in producing equal schools or truly viable communities on any scale. In the context of American society, separate is unequal because of the imbalance of power and resources of many kinds across the racial lines and the deeply rooted attitudes that blame the victims of segregation for the inequalities they face. If we do not achieve integration where it is possible, we will be deepening the divisions in our society and undermining the future of many communities, just as the stakes are rising very dramatically. We now face the dual challenges of massive demographic transition and intense world competition, both of which demand that we educate all our people and prepare our youth to live and work successfully in extremely diverse communities.

CATCHING THE WAVE OF CHANGE EARLY

Racially changing suburbs and school systems are often trying to find a local educational solution to what is a more general problem with an origin in discriminatory housing markets. Local power in these circumstances is much more likely to be effective if it is used early and comprehensively before neighborhoods and schools take on a self-fulfilling prophecy of resegregation. But local concern often does not become serious until after racial transition is relatively advanced, when it may be too late for effective local action. By the time a community is 25 percent black or Latino, its elementary schools are likely to be about half nonwhite and changing rapidly because nonwhite families are younger and have more school-age children than established white residents. Such a community is seen as resegregating, not integrated, by many whites, and its housing market is likely to have a rising number of nonwhite home seekers and a rapidly declining number of whites. At that stage it may be very difficult to change things, though the transition could be slowed and made less disruptive.

The best time for a community to begin thinking about these issues is as early as possible, and that is particularly true for communities near other school districts where racial change is advanced. These changes do not stop at the boundaries of a school district and they do tend to affect contiguous districts. It is systems in such locations, not scattered outlying pockets of diversity, that are most susceptible to resegregation. To provide the most effective response, local educators and officials must begin to address the problems before the public is thinking about them. This is a real challenge. It would be much easier if there were a broader group of leaders working on the issues, or if people outside of local politics would proactively bring up the issue and help frame it positively by referencing successful strategies elsewhere.

Obviously, since the schools are only one part of this cycle, educators who want a different outcome need to partner with those shaping the housing market. Leaders of school districts and local suburban governments are usually not heroes or visionaries, and it is always much easier to avoid difficult and potentially explosive issues you really don't know how to handle. With no requirements for integration or support from outside institutions, things can be put off in favor of more easily understood issues and actions required by accountability systems. Superintendents know they will probably be somewhere else by the time the consequences of neglect become apparent. So the safest career strategy may be to do nothing. When someone shows courage and faces angry challenges or loses her job, it intimidates others. Yet many educational professionals care deeply about their schools and communities and feel a professional responsibility to not only the schools but the community, and some provide extraordinary leadership.

In a high-stakes accountability era, there is no significant accountability for integrating schools. States that had desegregation requirements have ended them, and federal court orders have been dropped in most districts. No external authority requires the school system address the problem, and no one offers any serious help about how to do it well. Although the law still forbids actions that intentionally increase segregation, such as providing an unneeded new school zoned for white residents, there is little enforcement.[2] There is very little professional training or attention on ways to deal with these issues and no targeted aid funds. Many educators and community leaders do not have a language to positively frame the issues. Often, the basic response is to hope for the best and talk positively about narrowing achievement gaps. If the scores go up, educators will often be considered a professional success even if race relations deteriorate, the community resegregates, and the middle-class families and the best teachers leave within a few years. Educators who understand the dynamics and have seen the long-term effects of resegregation by race and class, however, want to do something.

This book is not about blaming leaders for not doing something they were never asked to do and often do not know how to do. It is much more about describing the state of affairs on this issue across the country and measuring the local responses and strategies against what is known about the effects of resegregation and the hard statistics of demographic change in suburban communities and schools. We are bringing attention to the fact that, in most of our communities, leaders do not appear to recognize that specific actions must be taken to avoid resegregation, although many understand that something should be done to foster better racial attitudes and reduce the achievement gap. Almost all educational administrators are former teachers; they are not typically trained in demography, housing, race relations, or the dynamics of neighborhood change. The school board and other municipal officials are in much the same situation. The suburban media suffer from similar limits, covering elections, board meetings, press releases, and reports but not digging into potentially explosive issues no one is talking about in public. Many communities have resegregated without ever having a significant public discussion about what is happening and what could be done.

This does not mean that the educators and local leaders are not dedicated and well-meaning, and certainly not that they are racists. It means that if there are going to be more effective responses to the trend of resegregation, we need much better information about what is happening and what positive and effective things local officials and educators can do. These leaders need to understand the causes of, effects of, and alternatives to school resegregation. They need concepts and terms to frame a positive discussion. If the issue seems to be framed—as some whites privately frame it—that there are too many people of color moving in, it will be seen as clearly racist by families of color. If race-conscious remedies are implemented to assure integrated schools, there is a fear that some whites will charge antiwhite racism against their children and may organize legal or political challenges. It is a delicate and high-stakes business. Yet it needs to be acted on as early as possible if there are to be positive outcomes. To do that, leaders must produce a vision of an equitable and lasting integrated future that is credible and positive.

CREATING SUCCESSFUL STRATEGIES

Obviously it would be much better if the issues surrounding demographic shifts and resegregation of the suburbs were framed by leaders in higher levels of government and if those authorities were providing guidance, good research, legal standards, and technical support to help local leaders figure out what to do.[3] There were much more difficult and fundamental issues to deal with in ending centuries of segregation in Southern schools, change worked much better; there were clear policies and serious help to support districts in changing successfully.[4] There is little likelihood now that there will be judicial or congressional mandates for action in the suburbs. But suburbs face different and, in many ways, far less difficult challenges than those that were overcome in the South. The Southern changes required breaking up deeply institutionalized practices supported by a virtually unanimous white population for generations. The suburban challenge is not on that scale; the need is to find policies that change the flow of people in and out of communities and schools to achieve widely shared objectives. It is about changing the flows of people into and out of neighborhoods without coercion (except through vigorous punishment of lawbreakers in the housing industry), creating positive relationships between groups in neighborhoods and schools, and creating a shared positive vision about a community's future. If the effort works, the community flourishes and many of the policies become unnecessary.

Resegregation stops and the issues move from the community to the classrooms where they require other kinds of educational leadership and community support.

The problems the suburbs face are issues of racial sensitivity, lack of knowledge, and the necessity for early action and comprehensive planning. Communities need positive approaches to planning for successful integration, much better information about the mounting and eventually irreversible consequences of inaction, and support in designing the needed initiatives. Until there is more help, people who do have the vision and the courage to address this issue will be easy targets from demagogues claiming that they are engaging in unnecessary and destructive "social planning" and unfairly disrupting things, since civil rights opponents often deny that there is a problem and blame the messenger who says there is and that something must be done.[5]

It is easy to understand the fear of many local educators that they will be blamed or misunderstood if they raise issues of racial change. It is more difficult to understand and excuse the failure of higher levels of government, professional associations, journalists, and university researchers and administrators to provide leadership in bringing the challenges and possible solutions before the public outside of normal politics. Each of these institutions has a special capacity to do this and is not subject to the possible blowback of local politics, but they are often as silent as the local officials. The reality is that if no one clearly raises the issue in a timely and constructive way, nothing substantial is likely to be done.

Suspicion and distrust are common in complicated racial situations, particularly if there are not good communications and well-developed contacts and trust across racial and ethnic lines. It is very important to build understanding and networks within the education profession, in civil rights groups, in education, urban development, housing, and civil rights agencies, and in the press about the challenge and the possible solutions.

Finding and Facing the Facts

Changing birth statistics by race and ethnicity over the last decade are evidence of the change happening in a great many suburbs. The suburbs as a whole now reflect the growing diversity of the nation's population. Birth statistics and data on who is moving in and out of the community as well as rising suburban food stamp and school free lunch numbers show not only racial change but growing numbers of poor families in suburbs. Every large central city has a history of destructive racial transition and ghetto creation that did immense damage to the urban fabric a half century ago, and many of the families first came to suburbia as a result of that process. Now a simple projection of the trends in many suburbs often shows a continuing movement toward resegregation and impoverishment. If that happens, the community will no longer be able to hold on to the kinds of middle-class families that have lived there for generations, and many people will feel that they have to leave. Middle-class families looking for housing will turn elsewhere. Eventually such communities may be cut off from the flow of money that is essential to the maintenance of housing stock, local businesses, services, and the physical infrastructure of roads, parks, etc., that are so central to a community. Abandonment of or decline in strip malls and shopping centers make it all too apparent that many older suburbs are experiencing multiple dimensions of disinvestment.

The academic world needs to play a key role in the process of finding and facing facts. Every university has faculty who have the knowledge and the tools to show what is happening in terms of demographic change, to display those changes clearly on maps and charts, and to create projections to show what will happen if the current trends continue. Since universities are outside the political process and have credibility with the press, and since much of this information would simply be a presentation of indisputable facts about residents, birth and migration statistics, and enrollment, factual reports would offer an opportunity to turn the public spotlight on the issue and trigger press and public discussion that could lead to solutions.

In addition to presenting facts, researchers could suggest terms and concepts that would help frame the issues neutrally—or better yet, positively—rather than with loaded terms and threatening images. It is one thing to talk about "ghetto conditions" and "tipping points," and a completely different one to talk about what polls show to be a broad preference for some level of stable integration, including the success of some communities in creating conditions that have produced lasting racial diversity and positive views by all racial groups. Oak Park's record of maintaining school and neighborhood integration for more than four decades right across from Chicago's profoundly troubled and segregated West Side is a case in point.

The truth is that, as shown in Erica Frankenberg's research, there are thousands of schools with lasting integration.[6] And the overall black-white residential segregation level has declined (though it remains high) in many metropolitan areas.[7] Now is the time to think about the way to avoid resegregation and impoverishment and finding how to create a positive interracial climate that makes the community culturally rich and attractive to all, where no current or prospective residents are fearful of a future of total racial change and economic decline. In fact, stably integrated communities tend to flourish and have very healthy housing markets, facing more risks of excessive gentrification than of resegregation. If the issue could be framed as what it often is—a choice between the destructive process of resegregation and a far more successful outcome of lasting racial and economic diversity—the discussion would be more positive and the community more attractive.

In traveling to these communities and listening to their educational leaders, we have clearly seen that most lack a developed strategy to direct this choice and that many do not even have a vocabulary to describe or talk about the changes in public. In the absence of any kind of metropolitan policies or strategies for integration, the common practice has been to let resegregating communities decline and eventually depopulate and just build more new housing on the periphery even when there is no population growth, throwing away some neighborhoods and creating new ones without coping in any way with the mechanisms that drive these changes. Not only does this practice perpetuate the destructive patterns described above, it involves enormous waste and energy expenditure as open land is developed and sound infrastructure is abandoned and then duplicated elsewhere.

The goal of plans for lasting diversity and successful integration is to change the flows within the housing market and to maintain schools that are effectively integrated across the district and are welcoming to and effective with all groups of children. All communities must be constantly renewed as residents move away for a myriad of reasons—families split, children grow up and move away, people die, job markets change, etc. Even if no one flees a community, it can change radically in a very few years if whites stop moving in and there is heavy in-migration of nonwhite families wanting to improve their housing and educational situation. If white demand for housing and local schools disappears, the community rapidly resegregates. If nonwhite buyers are steered into the community by real estate and rental agents and whites are not or are advised to look elsewhere, it is a violation of fair housing law and the community rapidly resegregates. If the community shows signs of disinvestment, spreading crime and violence, and other signs of decay, the same thing is likely to happen. The key is to break and reverse the pattern at the earliest possible time and to create a positive belief about the future of the community—a set of expectations that make it attractive to all groups.

Especially in the early sensitive stages of racial change, the skill and equity with which the community's leaders and institutions respond is very important. Given the sensitivity and salience of racial and ethnic differences, it is extremely important that the institutions, especially the schools, handle each group with understanding and make certain that each feels supported and fairly represented in the educational process. The public commitment of leaders to a climate of equity, fairness, welcome, and respect sets a very important tone for the community. When educational leaders say nothing about the issues and fail to hire or invite in people who represent and understand the new populations, they are abdicating clear responsibilities. Conflicts inside the schools, if not effectively managed, can reinforce stereotypes and divisions that play out in the larger community.

Diversifying Public Agencies

One of the obvious problems in many school districts is that both administration and staff are dominated by older white educators with little or no experience in managing racial change, and they have few of the minority members they need to understand and to become meaningfully involved in any effective collaboration. Education, unlike other professional fields, happens to have a very large number of trained, certified, and experienced black and Latino professionals. Though the numbers do not reflect the proportion of nonwhite students, they are substantial, and experienced teachers and administrators of color often work within a few miles of suburban communities that have almost none. Many communities have no effective affirmative action programs, meaning that any minority professionals who consider working there have to consider joining institutions where they may feel like isolated tokens, marginalized outsiders among people who have lived and worked in the suburb throughout their careers. Such patterns are hard to break without a serious and sustained commitment. It is very difficult, as researchers and the courts recognized more than four decades ago, to have successfully integrated schools without well-integrated staff and leadership, and it is certainly difficult to launch a comprehensive integration strategy without an integrated team of leaders.[8]

The tacit assumption in some districts in recent decades has been that segregation need not be addressed because the Supreme Court was wrong in *Brown* and that we *can* have separate but equal schools if we have the right attitudes and accountability. Since separate but equal has never been achieved on any large scale, and since three decades of increasingly intense accountability has failed to close the racial achievement gap (which was clos-ing significantly during the civil rights era), it is very important to reexamine this assumption. We have implicitly (and sometimes explicitly) assumed that if we dismantle integration policies and let the market run free, things will fix themselves. There is no evidence that this has happened, in spite of rare but widely celebrated individual schools with high test scores. We have also assumed that with the passage of time prejudice and institutionalized dis-crimination will steadily decline and these issues will go away.

Educators, trying to respond to racial change, have embraced the idea of doing more of what they are already doing. Respondents in all the commu-nities we studied express a deep commitment to attacking the achievement gap, though they are still far short of that goal. These efforts are, of course, essential. In all communities, there has been some effort to provide more staff diversity, though staffs are often still far whiter than the communities, and local educators talk about training in race relations. It is, of course, hard to imagine any solution that would not include creating a genuinely diverse staff at all levels that can work successfully together. Much of the staff training we encountered seems well-meaning but is not research-based and is unlikely to seriously assist in the needed transformations to create equal and effective classrooms and schools with positive race relations. At worst, it is counterpro-ductive, with polarizing sessions about personal racism and training which embraces stereotypes about racial learning styles. This area needs much more systematic attention from government and the universities.

Need for New Collaborations

Some of the communities in this study have considered the racial and eth-nic impacts of their school site selections and boundary decisions, but others have simply let residential segregation spread, doing nothing or even letting whites exit diverse neighborhoods. Since school populations change faster than neighborhoods, doing nothing or facilitating resegregation means that the school system adds fuel to the fire of resegregation. It is very important to consider the best models and timing for making decisions of these kinds and the potential legal and social peril communities face when they chose actions that intensify segregation, such as drawing boundaries to protect and isolate remaining white areas.

We have seen very little awareness of more sophisticated methods of pursuing integrated schools available under current law. Some of the study's communities have reached out effectively to important external institutions, such as the chamber of commerce or housing agencies, for support but most have not. The reality is without effective relationships of these kinds, there is little chance of stopping negative change that is rooted in housing market steering and discrimination that often triggers economic decline and disinvestment. Some communities in our studies and elsewhere have made very effective use of federal magnet school funds, but the federal government has severely underfunded magnets as it has pushed for more charter schools, which tend to be highly segregated and lack key components such as free transportation that are essential to overcoming the effects of spreading residential segregation.

Except for a limited effort in one community, Osseo, there has been very little collaborative regional planning with other school districts. Though there are positive piecemeal efforts and good intentions, the net result is, in many ways, a disappointing story. Yet if all these pieces were put together in a comprehensive approach, if the priorities were recognized soon enough and assistance and support provided by national policy, much could be done. In some very important ways, the social trends are much more favorable to lasting diversity than they were in the civil rights era.

Although metropolitan areas have long been continuously sprawling out into very fragmented suburban communities, there are increasingly obvious costs as middle-class families are drawn into new segregated communities further away from the cities. Better-located older suburbs with healthy infrastructure are abandoned by white families, and then by middle-class families of color, as the destructive cycle continues. In the worst cases, gated communities proliferate within outer suburban municipalities—fragments within fragments—with walls and guards signifying the problems that have not been solved. We need a new vision and new forms of collaboration, an acceptance that we must learn to live together in stability in communities that are successfully diverse. As the expanding borders of minority communities sweep over sectors of suburbia, it is apparent that coping with the changes is often beyond the capacity of many individual communities unless they understand and deal with them at the early stages when those communities might be strong enough to produce different outcomes. Large sectors of historically white suburbia are threatened with change and resegregation by race and poverty, but in most communities no one is figuring out how to have a serious discussion about the issue, let alone formulating and winning support for a plan that could change the local dynamics.

When there is rapid housing change that resegregates schools and small school districts in a few years, the affected communities would have a far better chance for a stable, diverse future if there were regional collaborations that could help break the cycle and weaken the belief that families could escape change by moving to the next suburb. Regional magnet schools could, for example, make it much easier to continue to attract white and middle-class families to live in communities facing racial change by assuring long-term access to diverse and high-quality schools. If communities cannot learn to collaborate or be required to collaborate by higher levels of government, it could well be like what happened in the vast resegregation of the central cities from 1940 to the 1980s: most neighborhoods did nothing, feeling that they were not immediately affected, but one by one they were incorporated into spreading ghettos and barrios. Breaking this vicious cycle, which has now run far into many suburban rings, does not happen spontaneously, but takes a coherent, well-executed plan. There were a variety of efforts in federal policy encouraging such plans in both schools and housing in the 1960s and 1970s but very little of significance after the Reagan era began.[9]

Improving practices in the housing and planning sectors and local government leadership are critical to long-term success in creating conditions for lasting community integration. In successful communities, there tends to be pride and positive publicity about the robust diversity that welcomes all and recognizes and celebrates its diversity as a community asset. As school administrators see substantial racial change occurring in any of their elementary schools, they need to connect with municipal housing, planning, and civil rights officials. It is not enough to have a workshop on diversity or set up a committee on the achievement gap. There has to be a concerted plan to make certain that a pattern of racial steering and housing market discrimination does not develop, that the schools and the community avoid symptoms of decay, and that both are positively marketed to all potential buyers and renters. Community leaders need to create a strong and consistent positive message, be certain that community institutions' staffs are diverse, and positively communicate the story of their community and its schools. Any racial incidents that occur in the schools or the communities need to be forcefully and rapidly addressed so that confidence is built and rumors and fears abated. Nothing should be covered up, where it will fester. Leaders need credibility and trust, and no big social change is ever simple. If real problems are honestly confronted and solutions devised, confidence will grow. When local leaders cover up problems, rumors and fears can expand out of proportion.

Needed: Civil Rights Focus on the Suburbs

Suburban minority communities are often hurt by the lack of civil rights leadership in suburban settings and the lack of understanding of the meaning and effects of resegregation among minority communities. Civil rights organizations such as the NAACP, the Urban League, LULAC, and local Latino organizations, as well as national litigators such as the NAACP Legal Defense Fund and MALDEF, still focus largely on big cities, which continue to face severe civil rights challenges. However, most of the issues of increasing segregation are now in the suburbs, where suburban nonwhite communities need support to foster minority access to good schools. In most of the communities studied in this book, there is no concerted action of any sort to produce or sustain integration and no civil rights organizations demanding it. Where there have been modest efforts to integrate schools—for example, in several suburbs of Minneapolis—there have been fierce and ugly battles, in some cases stoked and supported by conservative legal action groups. On the other hand, the inner suburban community of St. Louis Park has quietly implemented school diversity initiatives by building community consensus. Suburban leaders taking action need strong support from civil rights organizations, and community leaders need to learn about positive experiences, not just the disputes that find their way into the newspapers.

One key reason, of course, for the civil rights focus on the city is that the city is one big consequential target for protest and action, and the suburbs are a confusing maze of small districts with nonwhite communities often of modest size in a given suburb. Middle-class nonwhite movers to suburbia are often in deep denial about the necessity of focusing on issues of race, as was apparent in the Georgia case study (chapter 8). They are living in what were often historically unattainable communities; they can buy homes and go to local schools; and they are often in relatively comfortable situations with a substantial group of middle-class neighbors of similar race and ethnicity as well as a good number of the whites and Asians who lived there before substantial racial change began. Why worry? Unhappily, however, this situation is often not stable and, by the time the transition becomes apparent, the housing market may well have already changed so much that sweeping racial and class changes are highly probable. The dramatic resegregation of major sectors of suburbia outside Washington, DC, Atlanta, Los Angeles, and Chicago are good examples of communities where change occurs without any effective local response. What is needed is civil rights organizations operating on a metropolitan scale and able to analyze change and develop strategies to protect diversity and opportunity in diverse communities and open up access to those that are still closed. This will require understanding and monitoring the data on racial change and its correlates.

The right kind of civil rights enforcement could determine the future of many suburban communities. Since racial steering of prospective home buyers is a major contributor to the trend of resegregation, carefully monitoring the market through regular audits using testers would be an important response. In addition, illegal discrimination needs to be vigorously prosecuted. Since there are severe penalties for housing discrimination but very few cases are ever prosecuted, active local enforcement would make an impact. Aggressive attacks on discrimination combined with a training program for realtors and rental agents can make a big difference in behavior in the housing market. Both public and nonprofit civil rights agencies, together with the suburban government, need to offer real estate and rental agents and those in the mortgage finance industry courses in how to assure equity in the housing market by showing buyers of all racial and ethnic backgrounds housing options in all kinds of neighborhoods in the community and other communities to offer them the broadest possible choices. Such training would also include providing potential buyers and renters with positive information about all the schools and communities, which each school would be encouraged to produce and the school district would make available online and in handouts. Real estate is a business of self-fulfilling prophecies. If rumors spread that a community is in decline, especially with racial overtones, that community can disappear from the white housing market. If, on the other hand, people believe it is a good investment with a stable future and that integration will last, it can produce a very different market and a different future.

Providing Essential Information: The Challenge to the Press and Universities

It is understandable, though deeply regrettable, that politicians and educators avoid the issue of racial change. It is a complex and sensitive issue, and most leaders have little understanding of the dynamics and no ability to talk about it in public in a positive way that can draw the support of both white and nonwhite groups and lead toward solutions. There is also the temptation for elected officials to seek power by playing on stereotypes and stoking fears of racial change or to denounce officials who support positive action to improve race relations.

When there is an issue that has great importance for the future of a community that is apparent to informed observers, but that no one is mentioning or addressing, a special responsibility devolves on the institutions whose mission it is to discover and report inconvenient truths—the press and the universities. Each has special status and enjoys special protection: the press has the power to create new issues, and the academy has the knowledge to systematically research them and relate them to what is known from research and experience elsewhere. These are needed where the political parties and those holding power often have an incentive to cover up problems. The role of the press was very important, for example, in the development of a regional solution in metropolitan Omaha, Nebraska, after a legislative initiative threatened to split up the city system in a way that would have severely intensified segregation.[10] It was a researcher whose frightening predictions mobilized the community in Oak Park to prove him wrong by successfully mobilizing for stable integration. Though they might be criticized for surfacing new issues, such initiatives could help the public understand and put pressure on the local leaders to do something to foster a better outcome. You cannot solve what you don't know or cover up.

Universities and foundations could provide a great service to suburban communities by offering expert training for civil rights staffs, local administrators, educational leaders, and the press. If there could be a quiet nonpolitical opportunity to learn from experts and from leaders in other communities who had devised positive strategies, there would be the possibility of a much better conversation and a broader range of possible approaches as well as a network to exchange information and create support from other communities.[11]

More Creative Approaches to Maintaining Diverse Schools

Since the Supreme Court forbade the use of race-conscious assignment of individual students in voluntary desegregation plans, many communities have the impression that nothing can be done to foster integration or that the only alternative is to use social class in the hopes that it will produce diversity. Given the fact that social-class desegregation often does not produce racial integration, and that it can even speed the exit of lower-income whites from interracial neighborhoods and thus accelerate resegregation, other alternatives are needed. The reality is that the Court has specifically authorized siting schools and drawing attendance boundaries to produce integration, which would often be sufficient in a suburb with a small minority population not adjacent to an expanding black or Latino community. Developing zoning and land use plans fostering affordable housing in middle-class areas is likely to be helpful. Additionally, school choice and magnet plans can legally consider any other variables such as language, neighborhood, test scores, etc., in intentionally integrating schools. In Berkeley, California, with the help of a software engineer, the school district analyzed the racial composition of hundreds of mini neighborhoods and built the data into the formula for selecting students in its choice program, maintaining a high level of diversity without assigning individual students on the basis of race or ethnicity. This approach was upheld by the courts.[12] Some of the strategies described above were among those held up as examples in the recently released guidance from the federal government about how to create diverse elementary and secondary schools.[13]

Regional Magnet and Student Exchange Policies

Many cities have highly regarded magnet schools offering special educational opportunities that cannot be offered in every school. In a city with twenty high schools, the district can offer all students the opportunity to attend a special program in health sciences or performing arts housed at one school. This cannot be done at a high level in a suburb with two or three high schools or even only one school. But suburbs can combine to offer similar opportunities on a regional basis. This has been done effectively in the suburbs of several Connecticut cities, for example, which created a number of very popular schools.[14] There is a substantial body of research showing favorable impacts of interdistrict transfer programs on students in metropolitan Boston, St. Louis, Hartford, and Milwaukee.[15]

Needless to say, if a racially diverse suburb offers access to excellent regional schools, it increases its attractiveness in the housing market in ways that could help create stability. There are also important positive possibilities in interdistrict transfer plans, which are already authorized in a number of states but could be employed much more effectively on behalf of diversity if they included policies favoring transfers increasing diversity.

Mergers and Metro School Districts

One of the central problems in dealing effectively with racial diversity is the very small scale of many suburban school districts. Some suburbs are only the size of a single urban neighborhood, making them especially vulnerable to relatively rapid resegregation. We know from many years of research that the most stable desegregation plans and the most progress on housing integration come in areas with countywide school systems that were completely desegregated under court orders.[16] This was because the large area of the plan avoided rapid resegregation, increased the stability of schooling for students in interracial neighborhoods, and eliminated any incentive there might have been for white residents to flee from one area to a more segregated one.[17] In those regionalized areas there was little evidence of real estate steering related to the race of the area. Those plans tended to replace the parochialism of residents caring only about their own immediate area with more of a sense of common responsibility for the larger community, and they enabled much more creation of specialized magnet options.

Given the enormous fragmentation of suburban governments in many metropolitan areas, the counties and state governments are also logical focal points for initiatives. In American law, municipalities and school districts are creatures of state government, and the states have broad authority to regulate or change them. Areas in which the school districts have been consolidated into countywide systems have fared much better in preventing sudden resegregation and achieving higher levels of integrated education and better educational outcomes.[18] For example, for many reasons, the state government in North Carolina for many years strongly pushed for the consolidation of schools into countywide districts across the state. This was one reason why, for decades, metropolitan Charlotte and Raleigh were among the nation's most desegregated areas, and the school districts continued to attract large numbers of new white families. Two major Tennessee counties in the Chattanooga and Knoxville areas also provide good examples of these benefits.[19] The striking difference in racial and class segregation between metropolitan Raleigh and Richmond or Atlanta, with their separate nearby suburbs, show how much more beneficial it is to take action in a much broader segment of the metropolitan population. At a time when it becomes increasingly costly to have a duplicate school administration every few miles in suburbia, when there are massive fiscal and administrative challenges and housing market collapse in some sectors, and when there is an urgent need for some coherent plan to deal with diversity and large-scale educational reform as well as the challenge from charter schools, such reorganizations should be considered to create a framework in which many problems can be addressed, including the important challenges of racial change.

FAVORABLE TRENDS AND NEW POSSIBILITIES

The educational reform movements of the 1960s called for a central focus on unequal education for minorities and the poor. In the civil rights era, the schools were seen as a central element in reconstructing a profoundly unequal society and a key to a more equal, equitable, and unprejudiced society, but they were also part of a much broader set of reforms which addressed poverty and civil rights. In the 1980s under President Reagan, priority was shifted to raising math and reading test scores, and inequality was explained not in terms of external inequalities but as a failure of government to insist on the appropriate standards and the fault of teachers and teacher organizations. This limited vision, which has failed to narrow test score gaps and distracted attention from many of the broader social and economic realities which shape schools, helps explain the very narrow responses we have seen in some of the communities studied.

The shift in priorities, explanations, and policies left racially changing communities and schools with virtually no support or guidance for dealing with resegregation. The theory that the market was beneficent and would solve social problems turned out to be highly improbable in schools, but it was ridiculous in housing where there were literally separate housing markets by race and ethnicity for large sections of metropolitan areas, and where markets had produced the spread of segregated communities ever since major black and Latino migration to the metro areas began.

The extreme emphasis on publishing and evaluating schools simply on the basis of test scores without considering either that test scores are more influenced by family background and peer groups than educational reforms tended to devalue many good schools and teachers who were dealing with more diverse student bodies, creating the inaccurate impression that such schools would damage the education of middle-class students. At its worst, the widespread use of test scores in marketing housing and communities, widely circulated on real estate websites, encouraged whites to move still further out and sped the resegregation of communities. Obviously, it would be much better to have measures of the gains achieved in schools rather than the average scores since parents are primarily concerned about what their children are likely to gain and most are unfamiliar with extensive research that shows that middle-class children are not harmed by diverse schools on test scores and that they gain in many other ways.

Although the changes in desegregation policy have been discouraging, there are some very positive demographic trends that suggest that stable integration may be considerably more feasible now than in the past. Karl and Alma Taeuber, the great pioneering students of residential patterns, suggested nearly a half century ago that the extreme segregation and instability of that period was related to a large and rapidly growing black population pressing against a handful of white areas where block-by-block resegregaiton took place and the beginning of racial change brought rapid and virtually inevitable segregation.[20] Today many metropolitan areas see no net black in-migration, the black birth rate and family size have plummeted, and black housing demand is spread out across a much larger area. The number of stable black-white diverse neighborhoods has been growing since 1980 in spite of the policy vacuum. Recent data from the Great Recession period shows a dramatic decline in both migration from Mexico and family size among Latino families, lowering the demographic pressure for resegregation.

Most cities did not turn from white to all black as predicted in the 1960s, in part because the civil rights revolution brought an end to racial and ethnic limits on immigration. This change eventually made Latinos the nation's largest minority and brought in a large Asian migration, which already has made Asians a substantially larger population than blacks in the West. There is less social distance between whites and the newer minority communities, and white attitudes toward contact with blacks have considerably improved. Many of our urban complexes are now multiracial. The obstacles to stable racial equilibrium are now significantly less formidable and acceptance of interracial neighborhoods has clearly improved.

If there had been good school desegregation policies, there is a much better chance they would have succeeded now in many settings. Unfortunately, there were not. Policies were abandoned just as they could have worked better and easier and with methods employing much more choice and much less coercion. This creates an important space for policy leadership.

A half century ago, the ideal of stably integrated urban neighborhoods was widely seen as a fantasy since few had ever existed in many metros. Today we have communities that have been stable and successful for a half century, and proof of the advantages they create is obvious. In terms of income and education of residents, jobs, availability of regular mortgage finance, and other outcomes, those communities have very different fates.[21] Hyde Park-Kenwood in Chicago, which became the home of the nation's first black president, is a very well-known example, well integrated residentially since the 1960s.

THE SCALE OF NEEDED CHANGE

The changes needed to halt and reverse suburban resegregation are complex and challenging, but they are feasible and can produce major long-term benefits. The costs—both financial and societal—of doing nothing are staggering. What we need for a comprehensive attack is a different system of school districts and student attendance boundaries, a more regional operation of school choice and magnet efforts with a goal of stable diversity and equity. The goal should be supported by planners, housing officials, and local governments and embraced by the key operators in the private housing market—the realtors, rental agents, mortgage finance institutions, and so on. Ideally, in the long run we should move toward consolidated governments and school districts that embrace much larger parts of metropolitan areas so that they are not so vulnerable to very local conditions, incidents, and fears and draw on a larger public for support. We need a situation where educators are part of a larger community rather than competing and strategizing within narrow and highly vulnerable boundaries. Right now, individual suburbs tend to ignore the issues until too late and to have no broader allies to help with better policies when their fates lie in the balance. These reforms would, of course, have benefits in many areas beyond integration, since they would create a much more powerful capacity for common and skillful approaches to basic challenges facing aging metropolitan areas.

Researchers have a special responsibility—and it isn't to conclude what is politically feasible now. We have many politicians who always think about that, and the political approaches to date have badly failed and sacrificed the future of many communities. Instead, researchers' obligation is to speak truth when there are difficult truths that must be faced. There are several special targets for needed research: (1) preparing local statistics and summaries of national data on what has happened to diverse communities without coherent plans for integration; (2) assessing and reporting local policies, if any; (3) preparing case studies of local communities and summaries of national studies of stably integrated suburban school systems; (4) examining the impact of different institutional structures such as school district size and metropolitan fragmentation on the level and duration of diversity; (5) helping school districts assess diversity training programs and providing summaries of research on methods for successful diverse schools; (6) auditing the local housing markets and developing information on racial steering; and (7) conducting research on local operation and effects of voucher-based housing subsidy programs and housing developed under the Low Income Housing Tax Credit.

There is an urgent need for a framework of national leadership and policy on these issues. If each suburb and its school district were part of a broader strategy with support and help from national and state leaders, local leaders would be much less reluctant to take action and have more tools at their disposal to create stable, diverse communities. We are convinced that were there an offer of funds and help from government or private institutions, many school districts would eagerly seek it. When the Obama administration in 2009 set aside a small bit of the emergency funds from the federal economic recovery program to help districts to work on integration plans, within a month, there were far more districts applying than could be funded.

The U.S. Departments of Education, Housing, and Justice should work together to create a framework for helping suburban communities to foster lasting integration. Congress should enact legislation making collaborative work on these issues eligible for expenditures under HUD and Education Department programs and should fund the expansion of regional magnet school funding. At the same time the Justice department should maintain active enforcement programs to both vigorously prosecute discrimination in the real estate markets and warn school districts against policies that site schools and redraw boundary lines to hold remaining white populations in racially changing suburban communities. Such policies are both illegal and ineffective since they affect only tiny enclaves and since they foster full resegregation and very unequal schooling on the other side of the attendance boundaries.

American suburbia has no plan to deal with America's diversity, nothing close to the scale needed to create widespread and stable integration and to block destructive resegregation of schools and communities. It is time to recognize and explain the costs, to bring together the partial solutions individual communities are pursuing, and to pursue more comprehensive positive policies that have worked in some of our communities. We have the chance to channel the great forces of demographic change toward a model of successful community life in a richly multiracial society or to remain on a path that has never worked. This choice should not be made from fear or from short-term political advantage. It will require serious leadership to produce better outcomes, but those leaders who take up the challenge would move their communities and their nation toward a far better future. Wishful thinking does not work. Courage, good information, and clear vision can save communities and help give whites and blacks, Latinos and Asians, and all our social groups healthy places where they feel welcome, where they can make commitments to a common future without fear, and where communities can provide good homes and good schools that will prepare young people for life in a multiracial society for generations to come.

Notes

Chapter 1

1. Gary Orfield and Erica Frankenberg, *The Last Have Become First: Rural and Small Town America Lead the Way on Desegregation* (Los Angeles: Civil Rights Project/Proyecto Derechos Civiles, UCLA, 2008).

2. Myron Orfield and Thomas F. Luce Jr., *Region: Planning the Future of the Twin Cities* (Minneapolis, MN: University of Minnesota Press, 2010).

3. William H. Frey, *Melting Pot Suburbs: A Census 2000 Study of Suburban Diversity* (Washington, DC: The Brookings Institution Press, 2001); John L. Logan, "Ethnic Diversity Grows, Neighborhood Integration Lags," in *Redefining Urban and Suburban America: Evidence from Census 2000,* vol. 1, ed. Bruce Katz and Robert E. Lang (Washington, DC: Brookings Institution Press, 2003), 235–256.

4. Orfield and Frankenberg, "The Last Have Become First."

5. Alan Berube and Elizabeth Kneebone, *Two Steps Back: City and Suburban Poverty Trend 1999–2005.* (Washington, DC: The Brookings Institution Center on Urban & Metropolitan Policy, 2006).

6. *Diversity:* John B. Diamond, "Still Separate and Unequal: Examining Race, Opportunity, and School Achievement in 'Integrated' Suburbs," *Journal of Negro Education, 75, no.3* (2006): 495–505; Gary Orfield and Chungmei Lee, *Historic Reversals, Accelerating Resegregation, and the Need for New Integration Strategies* (Los Angeles: The Civil Rights Project/ Proyecto Derechos Civiles, UCLA, 2007); *inner-ring suburbs:* William H. Frey, *Melting Pot Suburbs; teachers:* Erica Frankenberg with Genevieve Siegel-Hawley, *Are Teachers Prepared for Racially Changing Schools? Teachers Describe their Preparation, Resources, and Practices for Racially Diverse Schools* (Los Angeles: Civil Rights Project/Proyecto Derechos Civiles, UCLA, 2008); *limited resources:* Myron Orfield, *American Metropolitics: The New Suburban Reality* (Washington, DC: The Brookings Institution, 2002); *political institutions:* Carol Ascher and Edwina Branch-Smith, "Precarious Space: Majority Black Suburbs and their Public Schools," *Teachers College Record* 107, no. 9 (2005): 1956–1973; *infrastructure:* Mary W. Filardo, Jeffrey M. Vincent, Ping Sung, and Travis Stein, *Growth and Disparity: A Decade of U.S. Public School Construction* (Washington, DC: Building Educational Success Together, 2006); US General Accounting Office, *School Facilities: Condition of America's Schools*, Report to Congressional Requesters No. HEHS-95-61 (Washington, DC: U.S. GAO-HEHS, 1995).

7. Erica Frankenberg, "Exploring the Difference in Diverse Schools' Destinies: A Research Note," *Teachers College Record*, www.tcrecord.org/Content.asp?contentID=15929.

8. Gail Sunderman was part of the initial research team, along with the book editors, to conceptualize the project and successfully obtain funding for the study.

9. These were the largest twenty-five at the beginning of our study in 2009.

10. David Freund, *Colored Property: State Policy and White Racial Politics in Suburban America* (Chicago: University of Chicago Press, 2007). See also Brief amicus curiae of Housing Scholars and Research & Advocacy Organizations, *Parents Involved in Community Schools, Petitioner v. Seattle School District No. 1*, et al.; *Meredith v. Jefferson County Board of Education*, 551 U.S. (2006 October).

11. *Sheff v. O'Neill*, 238 Conn. 1, 687 A.2d 1267 (1996); Erica Frankenberg, "Splintering School Districts: Understanding the Link Between Segregation and Fragmentation," *Law and Social Inquiry* 34, no. 4 (2009) 869–909.

12. Chungmei Lee, *Racial Segregation and Educational Outcomes in Metropolitan Boston* (Cambridge, MA: The Civil Rights Project, 2004).

13. *Swann v. Charlotte-Mecklenburg Board of Education*, 402 U.S. 1 (1971).

14. Charles M. Lamb, *Housing Segregation in Suburban America Since 1960: Presidential and Judicial Politics* (New York: Cambridge University Press, 2005).

15. *Board of Education of Oklahoma City Public Schools v. Dowell*, 498 U.S. 237 (1991); *Missouri v. Jenkins*, 515 U.S. 70 (1995)

16. *Parents Involved in Community Schools v. Seattle School District No. 1*, 551 U.S. 701 (2007).

17. National Commission on Fair Housing and Equal Opportunity, *The Future of Fair Housing* (Washington, DC: National Fair Housing Alliance, 2008).

18. Omnibus Budget Reconciliation Act, 1981.

19. The 2009 federal grant competition for technical assistance for student assignment policies is one small exception.

20. Erica Frankenberg, Genevieve Siegel-Hawley, and Jia Wang, "Choice Without Equity: Charter School Segregation," *Education Policy Analysis Archives* 19, no.1 (2011), http://epaa.asu.edu/ojs/article/view/779.

21. Larry M. Bartels, *Unequal Democracy: The Political Economy of the New Guilded Age* (Princeton: Princeton Univ. Press, 2008); Thomas Frank, *The Wrecking Crew: How Conservatives Rule* (New York: Metropolitan Books, 2008).

22. Orfield, *American Metropolitics*.

23. Douglas S. Massey and Nancy A. Denton, *American Apartheid: Segregation and the Making of the Underclass* (Cambridge, MA: Harvard University Press, 1993).

24. Camille Z. Charles, "Can We Live Together? Racial Preferences and Neighborhood Outcomes." In *The Geography of Opportunity: Race and Housing Choice in Metropolitan America,* ed. Xavier d. S. Briggs (Washington, DC: Brookings Institution Press, 2005), 45–80.

25. Richard P. Taub, D. Garth Taylor, Jan D. D. Dunham, *Paths of Neighborhood Change* (Chicago: University of Chicago Press, 1984).

26. Ingrid Gould Ellen, *Sharing America's Neighborhoods: The Prospects for Stable Integration* (Cambridge, MA: Harvard University Press, 2000); Orfield and Luce, *Region*; Frankenberg, "Exploring the Difference in Diverse Schools' Destinies"; Erica Frankenberg, "School Segregation, Desegregation, and Integration: What Do These Terms Mean in a Post-*Parents In-*

volved in Community Schools, Racially Transitioning Society?" *Seattle Journal for Social Justice* 6, no. 2 (2008): 553–590.

27. Gary Orfield, "Ghettoization and Its Alternatives," in *The New Urban Reality*, ed. Paul E. Peterson (Washington, DC: Brookings Institution, 1985), 161–196; see also Rebecca Jacobsen, Erica Frankenberg, and Sarah Winchell Lenhoff, "Diverse Schools in a Democratic Society: New Ways of Understanding How School Demographics Affect Civic and Political Learning," *American Educational Research Journal* (in press).

28. Erica Frankenberg, "America's Diverse, Racially Changing Schools and their Teachers." (unpublished dissertation, Cambridge, MA: Harvard University).

29. Jennifer J. Holme, "Buying Homes, Buying Schools: School Choice and the Social Construction of School Quality," *Harvard Educational Review* 72, no. 2 (2002): 177–205.

30. Gregory D. Squires, *Urban Sprawl: Causes, Consequences, and Policy Responses* (Washington, DC: Urban Institute Press, 2002).

31. Thomas M. Shapiro, *The Hidden Cost of Being African American: How Wealth Perpetuates Inequality* (New York: Oxford University Press, 2004); David J. Harris and Nancy McArdle, *More Than Money: The Spatial Mismatch Between Where Homeowners of Color in Metro Boston Can Afford to Live and Where They Actually Reside* (Cambridge, MA: The Civil Rights Project, Harvard, 2004).

32. *Inaction:* Frankenberg, "Splintering School Districts"; *Supreme Court decisions:* See, for example, *Bradley v. School Board of Richmond*, 416 U.S. 696 (1974); *Milliken v. Bradley*.

33. Massey and Denton, *American Apartheid*.

34. Berube and Kneebone, *Two Steps Back*.

35. Alan Berube and William H. Frey, *A Decade of Mixed Blessings: Urban and Suburban Poverty in Census 2000* (Washington, DC: The Brookings Institution Center on Urban & Metropolitan Policy, 2002); Michael L. Owens and David J. Wright, "The Diversity of Majority-Black Neighborhoods," *Rockefeller Institute Bulletin* (Albany, NY: The Nelson A. Rockefeller Institute of Government, 1998); Amy Stuart Wells, "Why Boundaries Matter: A Study of Five Separate and Unequal Long Island School Districts" (New York: Long Island Index, 2009).

36. Orfield and Luce, *Region*.

37. Orfield, *American Metropolitics*.

38. Bruce Katz and Robert E. Lang, "Introduction," in *Redefining Urban and Suburban America: Evidence from Census 2000,* ed. Bruce Katz and Robert E. Lang (Washington, DC: Brookings Institution Press, 2003), 9.

39. William H. Lucy and David L. Phillips, "Suburbs: Patterns of Growth and Decline," in *Redefining Urban and Suburban America: Evidence from Census 2000,* ed. Bruce Katz and Robert E. Lang (Washington, DC: Brookings Institution Press, 2003), 117–136.

40. Kenya Covington, Lance Freeman, and Michael A. Stoll, *The Suburbanization of Housing Choice Voucher Recipients* (Washington, DC: Brookings Institution, 2011).

41. Brookings Institution, *State of Metropolitan America: On the Front Lines of Demographic Transformation* (Washington, DC: The Brookings Institution Metropolitan Policy Program, 2010).

42. Chad R. Farrell, "Bifurcation, Fragmentation or Integration? The Racial and Geographic Structure of Metropolitan Segregation, 1990–2000," *Urban Studies* 45 no. 3 (2008): 467–499.

43. Gregory R. Weiher, *The Fractured Metropolis: Political Fragmentation and Metropolitan Segregation* (Albany: State University of New York Press, 1991).

44. Whites are more represented in small-town and rural America.

45. This takes into account charter school enrollment, but not private schools.

46. Gary Orfield, *Reviving the Goal of an Integrated Society: A 21st Century Challenge* (Los Angeles: Civil Rights Project/Proyecto Derechos Civiles, UCLA, 2009).

47. Every metropolitan area except Cincinnati experienced a decline in the percentage of white students from 1990 to 1999 as well.

48. Joe T. Darden and Sameh M. Kamel, "Black Residential Segregation in Suburban Detroit: Empirical Testing of the Ecological Theory," *Review of Black Political Economy* 27, no. 3 (2000): 103–123; the number of suburban black students in Detroit nearly doubled during this period, when the city school board in Detroit was removed by the state.

49. When evaluating the change in poverty composition, this section only examines 1999–2006. About three-fourths of schools in these twenty-five metropolitan areas reported missing or no free lunch students in 1990.

50. Berube and Frey, *A Decade of Mixed Blessings*.

51. Elizabeth Kneebone and Emily Garr, *The Suburbanization of Poverty: Trends in Metropolitan America, 2000 to 2008* (Washington, DC: The Brookings Institution, 2010).

52. Only twenty-two of the metropolitan areas studied are included in the comparison of 1999 and 2006 poverty. One or more states in the suburban regions of Phoenix, Seattle, and Chicago did not report free or reduced lunch data in 1999–2000.

53. Orfield and Luce, *Region*.

54. *Parents Involved in Community Schools v. Seattle School District No. 1*, 551 U.S. 701 (2007); Russlyn Ali and Thomas E. Perez, *Department of Justice and Department of Education Joint Guidance on the Voluntary Use of Race* (Washington, DC: The United States Department of Justice, 2011).

55. Diamond, "Still Separate and Unequal"; John B. Diamond, Amanda E. Lewis, and Lamont Gordon, "Race, Culture, and Achievement Disparities in a Desegregated Suburb: Reconsidering the Oppositional Culture Explanation," *International Journal of Qualitative Studies in Education* 20, no. 6 (2007): 655–680; Adam Gamoran, "Social Factors in Education," in *Encyclopedia of Educational Research*, ed. Marvin C. Alkin (New York: Macmillan, 1992), 1222–1229; Christopher Jencks and Susan E. Mayer, "The Social Consequences of Growing up in a Poor Neighborhood," in *Inner-city Poverty in the United States*, ed. Laurence E. Lynn Jr. and Michael. G. H. McGeary (Washington, DC: National Academy Press, 1990), 111–186.

56. James E. Rosenbaum, Marilyn, J. Kulieke, and Leonard, S. Rubinowitz, "Low-Income Black Children in White Suburban Schools: A Study of School and Student Responses," *Journal of Negro Education* 56, no. 1 (1987): 35–43; Leonard S. Rubinowitz, *Crossing the Class and Color Lines: From Public Housing to White Suburbia* (Chicago: University of Chicago Press, 2000).

57. Robert L. Linn and Kevin G. Welner, *Race-Conscious Policies for Assigning Students to Schools: Social Science Research and the Supreme Court Cases* (Washington, DC: National Academy of Education, 2007).

58. Clarence Stone, *Changing Urban Education* (Lawrence, KS: University Press of Kansas, 1998).

59. Gordon W. Allport, *The Nature of Prejudice* (New York: Perseus Book Publishing, 1954); Thomas F. Pettigrew and Linda L. Tropp, "A Meta-Analytic Test of Intergroup Contact Theory," *Journal of Personality and Social Psychology* 90, no. 5 (2006): 751–783; Erica Frankenberg and Gary Orfield, *Lessons in Integration: Realizing the Promise of Racial Diversity in American Schools* (Charlottesville, VA: The University of Virginia Press, 2007).

60. Frankenberg and Siegel-Hawley, "Are Teachers Prepared for Racially Changing Schools?"; Albert O. Hirschman, *Exit, Voice, and Loyalty* (Cambridge, MA: Harvard University Press, 1970).

61. This was also likely to provide some regional variation, since countywide districts are mostly located in the South and the surrounding Border region.

62. Gary Orfield, "The Growth of Segregation," in *Dismantling Desegregation*, ed. Gary Orfield and Susan E. Eaton (New York: The New Press, 1996), 53–72; Gary Orfield and Chungmei Lee, *Why Segregation Matters: Poverty and Educational Inequality* (Cambridge, MA: The Civil Rights Project, Harvard University, 2005).

63. Jeffrey R. Henig, Richard C. Hula, Marion Orr, Desiree S. Pedescleauz, *The Color of School Reform: Race, Politics, and the Challenge Of Urban Education* (Princeton, NJ: Princeton University Press, 1999); John Portz, Lana Stein, and Robin R. Jones, *City Schools and City Politics: Institutions and Leadership in Pittsburgh, Boston, and St. Louis* (Lawrence, KS: University Press of Kansas, 1999).

Chapter 2

Thanks to Jared Sanchez and John Kucsera for their data assistance.

1. Chad R. Farrell, "Bifurcation, Fragmentation or Integration? The Racial and Geographic Structure of U.S. Metropolitan Segregation, 1990–2000," *Urban Studies* 45 no. 3 (2008): 467–499.

2. Myron Orfield, *American Metropolitics: The New Suburban Reality* (Washington, DC: The Brookings Institution, 2002).

3. Emily Badger, "The Most Powerful Constituency in the 2012 Campaign: The Suburbs," (January 13, 2011 at www.theatlanticcities.com/politics/2012/01/most-powerful-constituency-2012-campaign-suburbs/930/).

4. The dataset uses the 2003 Office of Management and Budget's definition of metropolitan statistical areas (MSAs).

5. Three states did not report data by race/ethnicity in 1990–91; the earliest available data is used instead. For Virginia (Washington, DC, metropolitan area), we used 1992–93 data; Georgia (Atlanta) 1993–94; and Missouri (St. Louis) 1991–92. Poverty data was much less reliable in 1990–91, and is not examined here for that year. The following substitutions were made where free lunch or free and reduced-price lunch counts weren't available in NCES Common Core of Data, 1999–2000: Arizona (Phoenix metropolitan area), 2003–04; Illinois (part of the Chicago metropolitan area), 2001–02; and Washington (Seattle metropolitan area), 2001–02.

6. Douglas S. Massey and Nancy A. Denton, "The Dimensions of Residential Segregation" *Social Forces* 67, no. 2 (1998): 281–315; Douglas S. Massey and Nancy A. Denton, *American Apartheid: Segregation and the Making of the Underclass* (Cambridge, MA: Harvard Univer-

sity Press, 1993); Gary Orfield, *Public School Desegregation in the United States 1968–1980* (Washington, DC: Joint Center for Political Studies, 1983).

7. Because of their unique nature, charter schools, which in some states are separate local educational agencies, are excluded from the analyses in this chapter.

8. The decline of white student enrollment across all public school students during this period was 4.2 percentage points.

9. Although they are 9.4 percent of suburban districts, just 3.7 percent of students attend them, suggesting they are small districts.

10. The average increase for districts in low-income percentage was 3.9 percentage points; median increase was 2.3.

11. This section only pertains to twenty-four of the MSAs. Miami only has one suburban district, which makes it impossible to calculate district-level dissimilarity. Such analysis cannot account for any segregation existing within suburban districts, which might be relatively unimportant in small districts and more widespread in suburban districts with more schools.

12. The results described here are those analyzed without the inclusion of districts that contained only charter schools. However, a separate analysis including charter and noncharter districts found that dissimilarity rates were equal to or higher than rates for the corresponding racial pair in each metropolitan area without charter schools, except in Pittsburgh.

13. Orfield, *American Metropolitics.*

14. Gregory R. Weiher, *The Fractured Metropolis: Political Fragmentation and Metropolitan Segregation* (Albany: State University of New York Press, 1991).

15. Orfield, *American Metropolitics.*

16. Ibid.

17. Erica Frankenberg, "Exploring the Difference in Diverse Schools' Destinies: A Research Note," *Teachers College Record*, www.tcrecord.org/Content.asp?ContentID=15929.

Chapter 3

1. The name of the district and all schools are pseudonyms. Some geographic characteristics of the district, as well as features of the area (i.e. highway names) have been altered to protect the identity of the district.

2. National Center for Education Statistics (NCES), "Characteristics of the 100 Largest Public Elementary and Secondary School Districts in the United States" (NCES document no. 2011-301; Washington, DC: U.S. Government Printing Office, 2011).

3. Richard Valencia challenges the term *at risk*, claiming it is a deficit oriented term that places the blame for academic achievement gaps on low-income and students of color and their families. Valencia puts forward an anti-deficit view that recognizes that systemic and structural mechanisms within schools "thwart optimal learning."See Richard R. Valencia, *Dismantling Contemporary Deficit Thinking: Educational Thought and Practice* (New York: Taylor and Francis, 2010), 135–138.

4. Peter Dreier, John Mollenkopf, and Todd Swanstrom, *Place Matters: Metropolitics for the 21st Century* (Wichita, KS: University of Kansas Press, 2004), 59–60; Myron Orfield, *American Metropolitics* (Washington, DC: Urban Institute Press, 2002), 2–3.

5. Bureau of the Census, *Statistical Abstract of the United States: 2012 (131st Edition)* Washington, DC: Bureau of the Census, 2011, www.census.gov/compendia/statab, accessed December 9, 2011.

6. Orfield, *American Metropolitics.*

7. Ibid.

8. Interview with school principal, February 10, 2010.

9. Sean F. Reardon and Kendra Bischoff, *Growth in the Residential Segregation of Families by Income: 1970–2009* (New York: Russell Sage Foundation, 2011), 2–3.

10. Interview with district administrator, January 20, 2010.

11. Interview with district administrator, February 26, 2010.

12. Interview with school principal, March 12, 2010.

13. Interview with school principal, February 8, 2010.

14. Diana Lawrence-Brown, "Differentiated Instruction: Inclusive Strategies for Standards-based Learning that Benefit the Whole Class," *American Secondary Education* 47, no. 3 (2004): 34–62.

15. Interview with school principal, March 12, 2010.

16. Interview with school principal, February 8, 2010.

17. Interview with district administrator, February 26, 2010.

18. Interview with school principal, February 19, 2010.

19. Interview with school principal, February 8, 2010.

20. Kathryn Bell McKenzie and James J. Scheurich, "Equity Traps: A Construct for Departments of Educational Administration," *Educational Administration Quarterly* 40, no. 5 (2004): 601–632.

21. Interview with school principal, February 8, 2010.

22. Interview with school board member, February 7, 2010.

23. Interview with district administrator, January 26, 2010.

24. Interview with school PTA president, March 12, 2010.

25. Interview with school principal, February 19, 2010.

26. Interview with school principal, February 19, 2010.

27. Interview with district administrator, January 26, 2010.

28. Interview with district administrator, January 26, 2010.

29. Geneva Gay, *Culturally Responsive Teaching: Theory, Research, and Practice* (New York: Teachers College Press, 2000); Tyrone C. Howard, *Why Race and Culture Matter in Schools: Closing the Achievement Gap in America's Classrooms* (New York: Teachers College Press, 2010), 67–90.

30. Interview with district administrator, January 26, 2010.

31. Interview with district administrator, March 26, 2010.

32. Interview with teacher, March 12, 2010.

33. Interview with teacher, March 5, 2010.

34. Interview with district administrator, March 26, 2010.

35. Ibid.

36. Ruby K. Payne, *A Framework for Understanding Poverty* (Highlands, TX: aha! Process, 2005).

37. Randy Bomer, Joel E. Dworin, Laura May, and Peggy Semingson, "Miseducating Teachers About the Poor: A Critical Analysis of Ruby Payne's Claims About Poverty," *Teachers College Record* 110, no. 12 (2008): 2497–2531.

38. Interview with school principal, February 26, 2010.

39. Camille Wilson Cooper, "Performing Cultural Work in Demographically Changing Schools: Implications for Expanding Transformative Leadership Frameworks," *Educational Administration Quarterly* 45, no. 5 (2009): 694–724.

40. George Sugai and Robert R. Horner, "A Promising Approach for Expanding and Sustaining School-Wide Positive Behavior Support," *School Psychology Review* 35, no. 2 (2006): 245–259.

41. Interview with school principal, February 10, 2010.

42. Kent McIntosh, Kevin J. Filter, Joanna L. Bennett, Charlotte Ryan, and George Sugai, "Principles of Sustainable Prevention: Designing Scale-up of School-wide Positive Behavior Support to Promote Durable Systems," *Psychology in the Schools* 47, no. 1 (2010), 5–21.

43. Interview with school counselor, March 5, 2010.

44. AVID Decades of College Dreams, "About Page," www.avid.org/about.html.

45. Interview with school principal, February 15, 2010.

46. Interview with school district administrator, March 26, 2010.

47. Interview with school district administrator, January 26, 2010.

48. Interview with school board member, March 26, 2010.

49. Interview with school principal, February 19, 2010.

50. See Andrea E. Evans, "Changing Faces: Suburban School Responses to Demographic Change," *Education and Urban Society* 39, no. 3 (2007): 315–348; Andrea E. Evans, "School Leaders and Their Sensemaking About Race and Demographic Change," *Educational Administration Quarterly* 43, no. 2 (2007): 159–188.

Chapter 4

The author gratefully acknowledges the research assistance of Carrie LeVan and Stacey Greene.

1. All interviews were conducted in confidentiality, and the names of interviewees are withheld by mutual agreement. Pseudonyms are used for the names of district, schools, and geographic locations in this chapter.

2. DataQuest is developed and maintained by the California Department of Education (CDE). This online research tool provides statistical reports about California's schools and school districts. It contains a wide variety of information, including school performance indicators; student and staff demographics; expulsion, suspension, and truancy information; and a variety of test results; www.cde.ca.gov/ds/sd/cb/dataquest.asp.

3. Rob Kling, Spencer C. Olin, and Mark Poster, *Postsuburban California: The Transformation of Orange County Since World War II* (Berkeley, CA: University of California Press, 1991).

4. Lisa McGirr, *Suburban Warriors: The Origins of the New American Right* (Princeton, NJ: Princeton University Press, 2002).

5. Orange County Archives, www.ocarchives.com, accessed 11/30/12.

6. McGirr, *Suburban Warriors*.

7. Ibid.

8. This measure also required a two-thirds vote for legislative revenue increases and made any local government tax increase subject to a two-thirds approval of the local voters. See William H. Oakland, "Proposition 13—Genesis and Consequences," *Economic Review* [publication of the Federal Reserve Bank of San Francisco] (Winter 1979): 7–24.

9. U.S. Census Bureau's 2009 Public Education Finances Report (May 2011), www.census. gov/govs/school/. Also see W.A. Fischel, "How Serrano Caused Proposition 13," *Journal of Law and Politics* 12 (1996): 607–636; and George Lipsitz, "The Possessive Investment in Whiteness: Racialized Social Democracy and the 'White' Problem in American Studies," *American Quarterly* 47, no. 3 (September 1995): 369–387.

10. On Feb. 18, 1946, federal court judge Paul J. McCormick ruled that segregated schools violated the 14th Amendment. The decision was upheld by the Ninth U.S. Circuit Court of Appeals in 1947, making California the first state to desegregate schools. On June 14, 1947, California Governor and later Chief Justice of the Supreme Court Earl Warren signed the Anderson Bill repealing the remaining school segregation statutes in the California Education Code, including those allowing for segregation of "children of Chinese, Japanese or Mongolian parentage." *Mendez v. Westminster* 161 U.S. 774 (1947) was later cited in the historic 1954 *Brown v. Board of Education of Topeka* 347 U.S. 483 (1954) case that ended legal segregation nationally, for which Chief Justice Warren wrote the unanimous decision holding "separate but equal" schools to be unconstitutional under the Fourteenth Amendment's Equal Protection Clause.

11. David S. Ettinger, "The Quest to Desegregate Los Angeles Schools," *Los Angeles Lawyer* 26, no. 1 (2003):1–14.

12. *Crawford v. Board of Education of Los Angeles* 458 U.S. 527 (1982). The case began in August 1963, when the American Civil Liberties Union (ACLU) sued the Los Angeles City Board of Education on behalf of a group of minority students seeking to desegregate two high schools. See Gary Orfield and Susan E. Eaton, *Dismantling Desegregation: The Quiet Reversal of Brown v. Board of Education* (New York: The New Press, 1996).

13. Adai Tefera, Erica Frankenberg, Genevieve Siegel-Hawley, and Gina Chirichigno, *Integrating Suburban Schools: How to Benefit from Growing Diversity and Avoid Segregation*" (Los Angeles: The Civil Rights Project/Proyecto Derechos Civiles, UCLA, 2011).

14. Patricia C. Gándara and Gabriel Baca, "NCLB and California's English Language Learners: The Perfect Storm," *Language Policy*, no. 7 (2008): 201–216; also see Laura McCloskey, Nathan Pellegrin, Karen Thompson, and Kenji Hakuta, *Proposition 227 in California: A Long-Term Appraisal of Its Impact on Language Minority Student Achievement*" (Los Angeles: The Civil Rights Project/Proyecto Derechos Civiles, UCLA, 2008).

15. Mark Baldassare, *When Government Fails: The Orange County Bankruptcy* (Los Angeles: University of California Press, 1998).

16. Orange County Department of Education Internal Business Services Report, January 23, 2008, www.ocde.us/Business/Documents/Guidance-and-Advisories/20080123_ 2008-09%20District%20Advisory%20Governor%27s%20January%202008%20Budget%20 Proposal.pdf.

17. Richard Fry, *The Rapid Growth and Changing Complexion of Suburban Public Schools* (Washington, DC: Pew Research Report Center, 2009).

18. Ibid.

19. Gary Orfield, Genevieve Siegel-Hawley, and John Kucsera, *Divided We Fail: Segregation and Inequality in the Southland's Schools* (Los Angeles: The Civil Rights Project/Proyecto Derechos Civiles, UCLA, 2011).

20. Ibid.

21. Ibid.

22. Ibid.

23. Interview with Allenson High School (AHS) principal, May 21, 2010. All quotes from this principal are derived from this interview.

24. Interview with district superintendent, March 17, 2010. All quotes from the district superintendent are derived from this interview.

25. Interview with district administrator, April 6, 2010. All quotes from this district administrator are derived from this interview.

26. Interview with Langston Elementary teacher, June 8, 2010. All quotes from this Langston Elementary teacher are derived from this interview.

27. Interview with Langston Elementary principal, May 21, 2010. All quotes from this principal are derived from this interview.

28. Discounted prices apply for annual and semester one-way bus services.

29. According to district records, a small number of students have elected to participate in the Public School choice (transfer) program: in 2007–08, 9 students out of 2,667 eligible; 2008–09, 10 students out of 2,150 eligible; 2000–10, 2 students out of 2,079 eligible; and 2010–11, 5 students out of 2,760 eligible.

30. In 2006, an Orange County Superior Court rejected an anti-integration lawsuit in its entirety which would have prohibited another district, Capistrano Unified, ability to consider race to avoid segregation in its schools policy when drawing school attendance boundaries, ruling that such actions were constitutional under Prop 209 (ACLU News Release 2006 https://www.aclu-sc.org/releases/view/102024). However, the 2007 landmark U.S. Supreme Court decision (*Parents Involved in Community Schools v. Seattle School District No. 1* together with *Meredith v. Jefferson County Board of Education*) struck down some types of race-conscious voluntary desegregation in public schools. In a narrow 5-4 ruling the Supreme Court rejected the use of race as a criterion for assigning students for different schools. See *Preserving Integration Options for Latino Children: A Manual for Educators, Civil Rights Leaders, and the Community* (Los Angeles: MALDEF and The Civil Rights Project/Proyecto Derechos Civiles, UCLA, 2008), www.maldef.org/assets/pdf/6.1.3_Integration.Options. Manual.pdf.

31. More research is under way to examine the implications and aftermath of the school boundaries debate, interdistrict transfer policies, and any efforts on behalf of parent groups to promote voluntary desegregation.

32. There are also three alternative or independent high schools in the district.

33. Interview with an assistant district superintendent, March 17, 2010. All quotes from this assistant district superintendent are derived from this interview.

34. Students are identified for GATE programs beginning in the third grade and are placed in fourth grade. In fourth grade, they can attend one of three elementary magnet schools

that have classes specifically set for GATE students, with both an accelerated and enriched curriculum. If parents do not want their children to travel to the GATE magnet school but to instead stay within their home school, the district offers GATE "cluster programs," where the administration will cluster those kids in their home school for part of their day for academic instruction at their ability level. These students are mixed in with a heterogeneous group of non-GATE kids rather than attending a GATE school where they are with fellow GATE kids throughout the day.

35. Kate Menken, "NCLB and English Language Learners: Challenges and Consequences," *Theory Into Practice* 49, no. 2 (2010): 121–128; also see James S. Kim and Gail L. Sunderman, "Measuring Academic Proficiency Under the No Child Left Behind Act: Implications for Educational Equity." *Educational Researcher* 34, no. 8 (2005): 3–13.

36. Patricia C. Gándara and Megan Hopkins, *Forbidden Language: English Learners and Restrictive Language Policies, Multicultural Education Series* (New York: Teachers College Press, 2010); Patricia C. Gándara "Learning English in California: Guideposts for the Nation," in *The New Immigration: An Interdisciplinary Reader*, edited by Carola Suarez-Orozco, Marcelo M. Suarez-Orozco, and Desiree Baolian Gin-Hilliard (New York: Routledge Press, 2005).

37. Ibid.

38. The state's accountability program is based on closing the gap between the school's API score and the target of 800 by 5 percent per year. NCLB is based on meeting an established target of 100 percent of students' scores at "proficient" or "advanced" on the California Standards Tests or CAHSEE in English/language arts and math by 2014.

39. Some of these programs include School Readiness, Even Start, Project INSPIRE parent education, and the Community-Based English Tutoring (CBET) program.

40. A new state board of education system of reporting was approved in 2009–10. This system includes splitting the cohort into those students enrolled in US schools for less than five years, and those enrolled for five years or more. District data shows that Azalea Unified English language learners classified as ELL for fewer than five years exceed their AMAO target. However, those classified as ELL more than five years did not meet their AMAO target. District officials suggest that this cohort of long-term ELLs will be their focus in the coming year.

41. Interview with ELL program coordinator, March 29, 2010. All quotes from this ELL program coordinator are derived from this interview.

42. Tefera et al., *Integrating Suburban Schools*, 17.

Chapter 5

1. At their requests, respondents in this chapter were given pseudonyms.

2. City of Waltham Official website, www.city.waltham.ma.us (accessed October 2, 2011).

3. "Best Places to Live 2010," *Money*, http://money.cnn.com/magazines/moneymag/bplive/2010/maps/state/MA.html.

4. For reasons of consistency, this case study uses three-year U.S. Census estimates. Thus, population figures will differ somewhat from this 2009 estimate.

5. U.S. Bureau of the Census, http://quickfacts.census.gov/qfd/states/25/2572600.html.

6. U.S. Bureau of the Census, http://quickfacts.census.gov/qfd/states/25/2572600.html.

7. In 2009, the percentage of people in poverty, based on 2009 estimates, were: Newton, 5.6 percent; Watertown, 6.8 percent; and Belmont, 3.7 percent. In 2000 (2009 data unavailable), the poverty rate for individuals in Lincoln was just .8 percent; in Weston, it was 2.9 percent. U.S. Bureau of the Census.

8. "DHCD Community Profiles," www.mass.gov/?pageID=ehedterminal&L=4&L0= Home&L1=Economic+Analysis&L2=Executive+Office+of+Housing+and+Economic+ Development&L3=Department+of+Housing+and+Community+Development&sid=Ehed& b=terminalcontent&f=dhcd_profiles_profiles&csid=Ehed (accessed October 2, 2011).

9. http://actionma.org/wp-content/uploads/2011/01/State-Assisted-Housing_in_ Massachusetts.pdf.

10. U.S. Bureau of the Census, http://quickfacts.census.gov/qfd/states/25/2572600.html.

11. Ibid.

12. Massachusetts Department of Housing and Community Development, "Chapter 40B Subsidized Housing Inventory (SHI)," www.mass.gov/hed/docs/dhcd/hd/shi/shiinventory.pdf.

13. Information in this section is drawn largely from Charles Nelson, Kristen Peterson, and Thomas Murphy, *Waltham, Past and Present and its Industries* (Waltham, MA: Self-published, 1988); "History of Waltham," www.waltham-community.org/history.html.

14. Andy Sum, Dana Ansel, Ishwar Khatiwada, Paulo Tobar, Johan Uvin, Frimpomaa Ampaw, and Greg Leirson, *The Changing Face of Massachusetts* (Boston: Mass Inc., 2005).

15. Stephanie Siek, "Haitian-Americans Resurrect a French-Language Church," *Boston Globe*, November 27, 2005.

16. In 1990, 3,239 Latinos lived in Waltham, making up 5 percent of the city's population. By 2008, about 6,538 Latinos lived in Waltham, with the overall share at 11 percent. In 2008, according to U.S. Census Bureau estimates, 15,194 Waltham residents—about 25 percent of the city's total population—were foreign born. A substantial share—42 percent—of the city's foreign-born population entered the United States after 2000.

17. In 1990, according to the U.S. Census, 1,778 black people lived in Waltham. At that time, blacks made up 3 percent of the city's population. By 2008, according to U.S. Census estimates, 3,364 blacks lived in Waltham. One research report, using 2000 data, estimates that about 40 percent of Waltham's black residents are of Haitian descent, www.census.gov/ prod/cen1990/cp1/cp-1-23.pdf.

18. In 1990, according to the U.S. Census, 52,885 white people lived in Waltham. By 2008, according to U.S. Census estimates, this population had shrunk to 45,969, declining from 91 to 77 percent.

19. In 1990, according to the U.S. Census, 3,288 people or 5.6 percent of the city's population was poor. By 2008, 11.7 percent or 6,971 of the city's residents were poor. Further, about 60 percent of Waltham's households that were headed by single women with children younger than five years old, were poor.

20. From 1990 to 2010, the student population in Waltham dropped from 5,344 to 4,763, a decline of 10.6 percent; see "School and District Profiles," http://profiles.doe.mass.edu/ search/search.aspx?leftNavId=11238 (accessed October 2, 2011). For example, since 1995, in Weston, enrollment was up 35 percent; Lexington, 22 percent; Newton, 5 percent; Belmont, 21 percent. Watertown's enrollment declined by 2 percent.

21. In 1990, Waltham enrolled 625 Latino students. In 2010, the district enrolled 1,350 Latino students with that share more than doubling to 28.3 percent. The number of black students increased from about 283 students in 1990 to 442 students in 2010, an increase of about 56 percent. The share of the black population is about 9 percent of the city's students. While there is no data to confirm this yet, there was a strong perception among teachers and principals that the Haitian population increased during the most recent school year (2009–10), following the devastating earthquake there in 2010.

22. Waltham Schools' Demographic Trends. On file with author.

23. http://profiles.doe.mass.edu/profiles/student.aspx?orgcode=03080000&orgtypecode=5&leftNavId=305&.

24. In 1990, Waltham enrolled 4,162 white students. In 2010, the district enrolled 2,551 white students, a decline of 38.7 percent. In 2010, white students accounted for 53.6 percent of the district's enrollment. White enrollment is declining in the early grades too. In the first grade in 2000–01 school year, about 64 percent of students were white. By 2007–08, 52 percent of the city's first-graders were white.

25. By the 2007–08 school year, about 30 percent of the city's first-graders were Latino. This share is only slightly higher than the district's overall share of Latino students in 2007 (27.6).

26. Massachusetts Department of Elementary and Secondary Education, http://profiles.doe.mass.edu/profiles/student.aspx?orgcode=00350000&orgtypecode=5&leftNavId=305&, (accessed October 2, 2011).

27. Interview with city government official, July 13, 2010.

28. Interview with author, July 10, 2010.

29. Interview with author, August 8, 2010.

30. Interview August 19, 2010. All quotations are derived from this interview.

31. "Student Data," School and District Profiles," http://profiles.doe.mass.edu/profiles/student.aspx?orgcode=03080065&orgtypecode=6&leftNavId=300& (accessed October 2, 2011).

32. Interview with author, June 24, 2010. All quotations are derived from this interview.

33. "Student Data," School and District Profiles.

34. Interview, June 2, 2010.

35. Interview, July 8, 2010.

36. Interview, June 2, 2010. All quotations are derived from this interview.

37. Interview with school board member, June 4, 2010.

38. Massachusetts is one of three states where restrictive language policies were put in place following a referendum. Prior to the passage of this law, Spanish-speaking ELLs in Waltham were typically enrolled in transitional bilingual education programs in which a child took English classes but was taught content subjects in Spanish. Typically, after three years, a child transitioned into classes taught in English. ELLs who spoke a language other than Spanish (i.e., French Creole) would learn English as a separate subject and take their other subjects in English, often with assistance from a teacher certified to teach ESL.

39. Massachusetts Department of Education, www.doe.mass.edu/ell/chapter71A_faq.pdf (accessed October 2, 2011).

40. State of Massachusetts, General Laws, Chapter 71, Section 37C.

41. "School Profiles," Massachusetts Department of Elementary and Secondary Education, profiles.doe.mass.edu/profiles/student.aspx?orgcode=03080032&orgtypecode=6& (accessed October 2, 2011). The share of Black and Latino students at other elementary schools in the city: 40.8 percent; 49.5 percent; 32.2 percent; and 33.9 percent.
42. Interview, September 3, 2010.
43. Interview, August 10, 2010.
44. Interview, July 18, 2010. All quotations are derived from this interview.
45. "Student Data," School and District Profiles.
46. Ibid.
47. Interview, September 10, 2010.
48. Interview, August 4, 2010.

Chapter 6

The editors are grateful to Jennifer Ayscue for her help in adapting this chapter from the original Osseo case study.

1. Throughout the chapter, the school district and public officials are referred to by their real names. All other names of participants and individual schools used in this chapter are pseudonyms.
2. Myron Orfield and Thomas F. Luce Jr., *Region: Planning the Future of the Twin Cities* (Minneapolis, MN: University of Minnesota Press, 2010), 100–112.
3. Dr. Kim Riesgraf, "ISD 279—Osseo Area Schools Enrollment Trends," report to the School Board, December 15, 2009, 9–10.
4. Ibid.
5. Lin Myszkowski (director, District 279 Osseo Area Schools Board of Education), in discussion with the author, February 2010.
6. Steve Lampi (mayor, Brooklyn Park), in discussion with the author, March 2010. All quotes from Steve Lampi are derived from this interview.
7. Michelle Fisher (district-level staff member, Osseo Area Schools), in discussion with the author, March 2010. All quotes from Michelle Fisher are derived from this interview.
8. Keith Johnson (founder and executive director, community organization), in discussion with the author, March 2010. All quotes from Keith Johnson are derived from this interview.
9. Chris Richardson (former superintendent, Osseo Area Schools), in discussion with the author, February 2010. All quotes from Chris Richardson are derived from this interview.
10. Greg Howard (district-level staff member, Osseo Area Schools), in discussion with the author, February 2010. All quotes from Greg Howard are derived from this interview.
11. Kate Maguire (assistant superintendent, Osseo Area Schools), in discussion with the author, February 2010. All quotes from Kate Maguire are derived from this interview.
12. See Edward G. Goetz, *Clearing the Way: Deconcentrating the Poor in Urban America.* (Washington, DC: The Urban Institute Press, 2003), 102–104.
13. Mark Steffenson (mayor, Maple Grove), in discussion with the author, April 2010. All quotes from Mark Steffenson are derived from this interview.
14. John Williams (leader, parent group), in discussion with the author, March 2010. All quotes from John Williams are derived from this interview.
15. Berryhill and Shady Grove are both pseudonyms.

16. Letter from Joshua P. Thompson (attorney, Pacific Legal Foundation) to superintendent Susan Hintz and the members of the school board, February 22, 2008 (on file with author). The letter stated that "it is our understanding that . . . certain school and magnet closures will take place based primarily, if not exclusively, on the desire to racially balance the district." Claiming that if true, this "would be in violation of federal and Minnesota law," Thompson urged the "School Board to carefully consider the legal implications of any decisionmaking based on race and ethnicity."

17. Memorandum from Families Involved In Neighborhood Schools to Judith M. Eaton Lamp, Ed.D., Minnesota Board of School Administrators, July 24, 2008, p. 6, http://fiins.district279united.com/fiins/complaint/.

18. Susan Hintz (superintendent, Osseo Area Public Schools), in discussion with the author, February 8, 2010. All quotes from Susan Hintz are derived from this interview.

19. Jessica Thomas (principal, Berryhill Elementary), in discussion with the author, April 2010. All quotes from Jessica Thomas are derived from this interview.

20. Wendy Erlien, "Northwest Family Services Center Project Moves Forward in Brooklyn Center," *Sun Newspapers*, May 20, 2010, available at www.mnsun.com/articles/2010/05/23/news/fw/fw20familyservices.prt.

21. For a detailed description of the racial transition trends in the suburban school districts of the Twin Cities metropolitan area, see Myron Orfield, Baris Gumus-Dawes, Thomas F. Luce Jr., and Geneva Finn, "Neighborhood and School Segregation in the Twin Cities Region," in Orfield and Luce, *Region*, 85–174.

22. Principal and assistant principal, Pineville Elementary, in discussion with the author, March 2010. All quotes from Pineville administrators are derived from this interview.

23. Principal, vice principal, teacher, and student learning advocate, Oakwood High School, in discussion with the author, March 2010. All quotes from Oakwood High School administrators and staff are derived from this interview.

24. Margaret C. Hobday, Geneva Finn, and Myron Orfield, "A Missed Opportunity: Minnesota's Failed Experiment with Choice-Based Integration," *William Mitchell Law Review* 35, no. 3 (2009): 936–976.

25. Ibid.

26. Ibid.

27. Ibid.

28. Letter from Cindy Lavarato (assistant commissioner) to Chris Richardson (superintendent of Osseo Area Schools), February 4, 2000.

29. For a list of all the programs offered by the NWSISD, see *Northwest Suburban Integration School District Desegregation Plan, 2008–2012*, available at www.nws.k12.mn.us/about_us/documents/08-12DesegPlanFinal- web.pdf (accessed 3/29/10).

30. Jackie Harris (district-level staff member, NWSISD), in discussion with the author, October 2009.

31. Data provided by Jackie Harris.

32. Richard Melvin (assistant superintendent, Osseo Area Public Schools), in discussion with the author, May 2010. All quotes from Richard Melvin are derived from this interview.

33. Minnesota Department of Education Data Center, https://education.state.mn.us/MDEAnalytics/Data.jsp.

Chapter 7

1. To maintain confidentiality, the name of the district, as well as the names of all people and schools, have been replaced with pseudonyms.

2. Myron Orfield, *American Metropolitics: The New Suburban Reality* (Washington, DC: The Brookings Institution, 2002).

3. An external actor involved in migrant advocacy explained that about 90 percent of migrant laborers in Florida are Mexican American. There are Asian migrant laborers largely working in fish farms. In addition, there are migrants from the Caribbean, etc. She saw very few white or black laborers. Most farms are corporate or owned by white growers; a few migrant Mexican Americans have acquired land and became growers as well.

4. U.S. Census Bureau, 2000 Census.

5. U.S. Census Bureau, State and County 2010 QuickFacts.

6. The Department of Labor statistics show the labor force increased from 1 million to 1.3 million in the metropolitan area from 1990 to 2010.

7. Haya El Nasser, "For Florida, 'End of an Era' of Population Growth," *USA Today*, September 1, 2009.

8. Federal Housing and Finance Agency, *Report to Congress* (Washington, DC: FHFA, 2009), 10, 11.

9. Steve Zurier, "Battle Lines Drawn, Florida HBA Claims That the City of Tallahassee's Affordable Housing Law Is Unconstitutional," *Builder*, May 1, 2006. Mattson, 12. See also David L. Powell, "Growth Management: Florida's Past as Prologue for the Future," *Florida State University Law Review* 28 (2000): 519–543.

10. NCES Common Core of Data.

11. Deenesh Sohoni and Salvatore Saporito, "Mapping School Segregation: Using GIS to Explore Racial Segregation Between Schools and Their Corresponding Catchment Areas," *American Journal of Education* 115, no. 4 (2009): 569–600; Salvatore Saporito and Deenesh Sohoni, "Mapping Educational Inequality: Concentrations of Poverty Among Poor and Minority Students in Public Schools," *Social Forces* 85, no. 3 (2007): 1227–1253.

12. Bob Tuttle (district-level administrator), in interview with second and third author, November 2009.

13. Ethnic Enrollment Trend by School, District Schools, Beach County, 2004–2011

14. The Civil Rights Project/*Proyecto Derechos Civiles, Resources on Major Court Decisions*, http://civilrightsproject.ucla.edu/legal-developments/court-decisions.

15. Robert Tate (district-level administrator), in interview with second and third author, November 2009. All quotes from Robert Tate are derived from this interview.

16. Bob Tuttle (district-level administrator), in interview with second author, November 2009.

17. AVID Organization website: www.avid.org/sta_avidelective.html

18. College Board, "Florida Partnership Data Highlights," http://media.collegeboard.com/floridapartnership/pdf/Florida_Partnership_Ten_Year_Highlights.pdf

19. Maxwell Reilly (principal), in interview with second and third author, June 2010. All quotes from Max Reilly are derived from this interview.

20. Steve Davis (teacher), in interview with second author, May 2010. All quotes from Steve Davis are derived from this interview.

21. Bruce Cartwright (community member), in interview with second author, May 2010.

22. Electronic communication, College Board.

23. Frances Noel (ESL teacher), in interview with second author, June 2010. All quotes from Frances Noel are derived from this interview.

24. Donna Star (principal), in interview with second and third author, May 2010. All quotes from Donna Star are derived from this interview.

25. Julia Baxter (teacher), in interview with second and third author, June 2010.

26. Florida Department of Education, Class Size Reduction, www.fldoe.org/classsize/.

27. For example, if a school had a student enrollment maximum of 1,200 students, it would have previously been considered overcrowded at 1,440 students, whereas now the same school is considered overcrowded at 1,140 students.

28. Bob Tuttle (district-level administrator), in interview with second and third author, November 2009.

29. Julia Baxter (teacher), in interview with second and third author, June 2010.

30. Leslie Jensen (principal), in interview with second and third author, June 2010

31. Frank McCourt (district-level administrator), in interview with second and third author, June 2010.

32. James Kim and Gail Sunderman, *Does NCLB Provide Good Choices for Students in Low-Performing Schools?* (Cambridge, MA: The Civil Rights Project at Harvard University, 2004).

33. Sonia Alvarez (director of metropolitan area nonprofit), in interview with second and third author, November 2009.

34. For example, Erica Frankenberg, *Improving and Expanding Project Choice* (Washington, DC: Poverty Race and Research Action Council, 2007).

35. Lolita Colón (teacher), in interview with second author, June 2010.

Chapter 8

1. Gary Orfield and Erica Frankenberg, *The Last Have Become First: Rural and Small Town America Lead the Way on Desegregation* (Los Angeles: The Civil Rights Project/*Proyecto Derechos Civiles*, UCLA, 2008), 8.

2. *Swann v. Charlotte-Mecklenburg Board of Education*, 402 U.S. 1 (1971).

3. The county name has been changed and all names of interviewees removed.

4. Drawn from Atlanta Regional Planning Commission, "Demographic Profiles," accessed from www.atlantaregional.com on December 13, 2011.

5. Shaila Dewan, "A Racial Divide Is Bridged by Recession."

6. Ibid.

7. Erica Frankenberg and Chungmei Lee, *Race in American Public Schools: Rapidly Resegregating School Districts* (Cambridge: The Civil Rights Project at Harvard University, 2002), 6.

8. Interview with county Chamber of Commerce president, November 12, 2009.

9. William Frey, *The New Migration: Black Americans' Return to the South, 1965–2000* (Washington, DC: Brookings Institution Center on Metropolitan and Urban Policy, 2004).

10. Drawn from Atlanta Regional Planning Commission, "Demographic Profiles," www.atlantaregional.com.

11. Interview with real estate agent, January 27, 2010.

12. Interview with chair of Chamber of Commerce's cultural diversity committee, December 3, 2009. Research in other metropolitan areas has found racial differences in access to neighborhoods, beyond class. See D. J. Harris and N. McArdle, *More Than Money: The Spatial Mismatch Between Where Homeowners of Color in Metro Boston Can Afford to Live and Where They Actually Reside* (Cambridge, MA: Harvard Civil Rights Project, January 2004).

13. Dewan, "A Racial Divide Is Bridged by Recession."

14. Two of the three schools where we conducted interviews—one elementary and one high school—fit this profile of being racially balanced. In 2009–10, the year of our study, the composition of the elementary school was 41 percent black; 40 percent white; 7 percent Latino; 6 percent Asian; and 6 percent other. The composition of the high school was 54 percent black; 30 percent white; 7 percent Latino; 4 percent Asian-American/Pacific Islander; 4 percent interracial; and 1 percent other.

15. Interview with elementary school assistant principal, March 19, 2010.

16. Interview with former assistant superintendent for administrative services, November 20, 2009.

17. Interview with former superintendent, December 5, 2009.

18. Ibid.

19. Ibid.

20. Interview with school board member, December 15, 2009.

21. Interview with former superintendent, December 5, 2009.

22. Interview with assistant superintendent for curriculum and instruction, November 12, 2009.

23. Interview with former assistant superintendent for administrative services, November 20, 2009.

24. Interview with superintendent, November 12, 2009.

25. Interview with assistant superintendent for curriculum and instruction, November 12, 2009.

26. Ibid.

27. Ibid.

28. Interview with former assistant superintendent for administrative services, November 20, 2009.

29. Ibid.

30. Interview with assistant superintendent for administrative service, November 20, 2009.

31. Interview with school board member, December 15, 2009.

32. Interview with assistant superintendent for human resources, November 20, 2009.

33. Ibid.

34. Interview with assistant superintendent for curriculum and instruction, November 12, 2009.

35. Interview with elementary literacy instruction lead teacher, March 4, 2010.

36. Interview with elementary principal and assistant principal, February 2, 2010.

37. Interview with county school system's director of professional learning, March 31, 2010.

38. Ibid.

39. Interview with elementary school principal, February 2, 2010.

40. Interview with high school principal, February 19, 2010.

41. Interview with high school English department chair, April 2, 2010

42. Interview with high school guidance counselor, March 4, 2010.

43. Interview with superintendent, November 12, 2009.

44. Interview with chair of Chamber of Commerce's cultural diversity committee, December 3, 2009.

45. Interview with director of Connect Sewall, May 26, 2010.

46. Interview with assistant superintendent for curriculum and instruction, November 12, 2009.

47. Interview with chair of Chamber of Commerce's cultural diversity committee, December 3, 2009.

48. Interview with chair of Chamber of Commerce's education committee, December 3, 2009.

49. Ibid.

50. The quote is taken from a national newspaper in 2009, citation withheld to preserve confidentiality.

51. Jeffrey Henig, Richard Hula, Marion Orr, and Desiree Pedescleaux, *The Color of School Reform: Race, Politics, and the Challenge of Urban Education* (Princeton, NJ: Princeton University Press, 1999), 161.

Chapter 9

All interviews in Oak Park were conducted by Gail Sunderman as part of the original research project. We are deeply grateful for her important work on these interviews.

1. The school district and public officials are referred to by their real names. All other names of participants used in this chapter are pseudonyms.

2. Sam Bass Warner, *Streetcar Suburbs, The Process of Growth in Boston, 1870-1900* (Cambridge, MA: Harvard University Press, 1962).

3. U.S. Census Bureau, American Factfinder, "Profile of General Population and Housing Characteristics, 2010," at Census.gov.

4. Jane Jacobs, *The Death and Life of Great American Cities* (New York, NY: Random House, l961).

5. Martin Luther King Jr., *Where Do We Go from Here: Chaos or Community?* (New York: Harper and Row, 1967).

6. James R. Ralph, Jr., *Northern Protest: Martin Luther King, Jr. Chicago, and the Civil Rights Movement* (Cambridge, MA: Harvard University Press, 1993), 101.

7. Pierre de Vise, "Chicago's Widening Color Gap," *Integrated Education*, November–December (1971): 37–42, 45.

8. Pierre deVise, *Predicting Pediatric and Geriatric Population Needs of New Life Cycle Communities: The Case of Oak Park, Illinois* (Chicago, IL: Chicago Regional Hospital Study, 1968); Pierre deVise, "Housing Discrimination in the Chicago Metropolitan Area," *De Paul Law Review* 32, no. 2 (1985): 492–513.

9. Kathryn Divine, *Housing Integration: Municipal Strategies* (master's thesis in public administration, University of Illinois, Urbana, 1981), 26.

10. Ibid., 27.

11. Ibid.

12. Deborah Haines, *Black Homeowners in Transition Areas* (Chicago: Chicago Urban League, 1981), 170. (The Chicago Urban League's research department was nationally famous among civil rights organizations.)

13. Ibid., 172.

14. Haines, *Black Homeowners in Transition Areas*, 173.

15. "Arson Fails at Home of Negro Scientist," *New York Times*, November 23, 1950.

16. Juliet Saltman, *A Fragile Movement: The Struggle for Neighborhood Stabilization* (New York: Greenwood Press, 1990), 305.

17. Ibid.

18. Ibid., 305–307.

19. Gregory D. Squires, Larry Bennett, Kathleen McCourt, and Philip Nyden, *Chicago: Race, Class and the Response to Urban Decline* (Philadelphia: Temple University Press, 1987), 119.

20. W. Denis Keating, *The Suburban Racial Dilemma: Housing and Neighborhoods* (Philadelphia: Temple University Press, 1994), 213.

21. Richard P. Taub, Jan D. D. Dunham, D. Garth Taylor, *Paths of Neighborhood Change: Race and Crime in Urban America* (Chicago: University of Chicago Press, 1984).

22. Gary Orfield, "Ghettoization and Its Alternatives," in *The New Urban Reality*, ed. Paul E. Peterson (Washington, DC: Brookings Institution).

23. Carole Goodwin, *The Oak Park Strategy: Community Control of Racial Change,* (Chicago: University of Chicago Press, 1979).

24. Saltman, *A Fragile Movement*, 306.

25. Goodwin, *The Oak Park Strategy*.

26. Village of Oak Park, I. *Analysis of Impediments to Fair Housing Choice*, January 2010).

27. Village of Oak Park, I. *Analysis of Impediments to Fair Housing Choice: Draft for Public Review*, October 2009.

28. Ibid.

29. Ibid., 25–26.

30. Village of Oak Park, I., *Analysis of Impediments to Fair Housing Choice*, January 2010.

31. Sabrina Tavernise, "Poor Dropping Further Behind Rich in School," *New York Times*, February 10, 2010.

32. Village of Oak Park, I., *Analysis of Impediments to Fair Housing Choice*, January 2010.

33. Ibid. The rates are contained in a figure; exact percentages for all groups and years are not given.

34. The 2010 Village Board of Trustees included four white males (including the village president), one black male, and three white females.

35. The National Citizen Survey, "Village of Oak Park, IL 2011," pp. 1–6.

36. *Oak Park-River Forest Patch*, "District 97 Referendum Passes," April 5, 2011, www.oakpark.patch.com.

37. Bob Spatz, in discussion with Gail Sunderman, November 2009. All quotes from Spatz are derived from this interview.

38. Keith Belonte (pseudonym), in discussion with Gail Sunderman, November 2009.

39. Gary Orfield, *Dropouts in America* (Cambridge, MA: Harvard Education Press, 2004).

40. Belonte, discussion with Sunderman, November 2009.

41. Tom Polite (pseudonym), in discussion with Gail Sunderman, June 2010.

42. Peter Demerath, *Producing Success: The Culture of Personal Advancement in an American High School* (Chicago: The University of Chicago Press, 2009).

43. Belonte, discussion withSunderman, November 2009.

44. Polite, discussion with Sunderman, June 2010.

45. Deborah King (pseudonym), in discussion with Gail Sunderman, June 2010.

46. Peter Thompson (pseudonym), in discussion with Gail Sunderman, November 2009.

47. Village of Oak Park, I., *Anaylsis of Impediments to Fair Housing Choice*, January 2010).

48. Gail Sunderman, ed., *Holding NCLB Accountable: Achieving Accountability, Equity, and School Reform* (Thousand Oaks, CA: Corwin Press, 2008); Richard Rothstein, *Class and Schools: Using Social, Economic and Educational Reform to Close the Black-White Achievement Gap* (New York: Teachers College Press, 2004).

49. Spatz, interview.

50. Attila Weninger, in discussion with Gail Sunderman, November 2009.

51. Attila Weninger, letter to high school board of education, October 22, 2007.

52. African American Achievement Study Team, *The Learning Community Performance Gap: Oak Park and River Forest High School*, report to Oak Park and River Forest High School District 200, Oak Park, IL, 2003.

53. For example, see M. J. Hollis, *Final Report: Building a More Hospitable Learning Community: A Community Wide Dialogue of Oak Park and River Forest High School District 200* (Oak Park, IL: Oak Park and River Forest High School District 200, 1998); Oak Park and River Forest High School, *Report of the African-American Achievement Committee* (Oak Park, IL, 1991); African American Achievement Study Team, *The Learning Community Performance Gap*, 2003.

54. Samantha Rosenberg (pseudonym), in discussion with Gail Sunderman, June 2010.

55. Thompson, discussion with Sunderman, November 2009.

56. Belonte, discussion with Sunderman, November 2009.

57. John Rigas, in discussion with Gail Sunderman, June 2010.

58. African American Achievement Study Team, *The Learning Community Performance Gap*, 19.

59. Ibid., 22.

60. Ibid., 25.

61. Ibid., 54.

62. Ibid., 10.

63. Ibid., 11.

64. Ibid., 66.

65. Ibid., 17.

66. Ibid., 39.

67. Leslie Santee Siskin, *The Subjects in Question: Departmental Organization and the High School* (New York: Teachers College Press, 1995); Leslie Santee Siskin, *Realms of Knowledge: Academic Departments in Secondary Schools* (London and New York: The Falmer Press, 1994); Leslie Santee Siskin, "Achievement and Attainment: The Comprehensive High School and the Problem of Reform," in *Crucial Issues in California Education*, ed. E. Burr et al. (Berkeley, CA: PACE, 2006).

68. John Diamond, in discussion with the author, February 2012.

69. Polite, discussion with Sunderman, June 2010.

70. Collaboration for Early Childhood Care & Education, 2009.

71. Rosenberg (pseudonym), in discussion with Sunderman, June 2010.

72. Ibid.

73. Oak Park Elementary Schools, *Strategic Plan*, November 2009.

74. Belonte, discussion with Sunderman, November 2009.

75. Ibid.

76. Weninger, discussion with Sunderman, November 2009.

77. Terry Dean, "Why Weninger Chose Retirement: Split OPRF Board Saw Superintendent as Strong Leader or as Polarizing Force," *Wednesday Journal*, November 24, 2009.

78. Terry Dean, "OPRF Finds 4th Vote to Keep Weninger: Hard Feelings over How Discussion of One-Year Extension Surfaced," *Wednesday Journal*, December 6, 2009.

79. OakPark-RiverForestPatch, www.oakpark.path.com/local_facts.

80. Jim Jaworski and Vikki Ortiz Healy, "Oak Park Student Circulates List Degrading Female Students, Girls, Parents Band Together to Press for Strong Disciplinary Action," *Chicago Tribune*, January 17, 2011.

81. Diamond, discussion, February 2012.

82. Thompson, discussion with Sunderman, November 2009.

Conclusion

1. Charles M. Lamb, *Housing Segregation in Suburban America Since 1960: Presidential and Judicial Politics* (New York: Cambridge University Press, 2005).

2. *Keyes v. Denver School District No. 1*, 413 U.S. 189 (1973).

3. A step in the right direction is the release of guidance by the federal government in December 2011 affirming the value of diversity in K–12 schools, and explaining what is legally permissible to accomplish diverse schools.

4. Gary Orfield, "Why It Worked in Dixie: Southern School Desegregation and Its Implications for the North," in *Race and Schooling in the City*, ed. Adam Yarmolinsky, Lance Liebman, and Corrine Schelling (Cambridge, MA: Harvard University Press, 1981), 24–44.

5. Kelly Smith, "Eden Prairie School Boundary Changes Divide Parents," *Minneapolis Star Tribune*, October 12, 2010.

6. Erica Frankenberg, "Exploring the Difference in Diverse Schools' Destinies: A Research Note," *Teachers College Record*, www.tcrecord.org/Content.asp?ContentID=15929; Erica Frankenberg, "School Segregation, Desegregation, and Integration: What Do These Terms Mean in a Post-*Parents Involved in Community Schools*, Racially Transitioning Society?" *Seattle Journal for Social Justice* 6, no. 2 (2008): 553–590.

7. Reynolds Farley, "The Waning of American Apartheid?" *Contexts* 10, no. 3 (2011): 36–43.

8. *Green v. County School Board of New Kent County*, 391 U.S. 430 (1968).

9. Lamb, *Housing Segregation in Suburban America Since 1960*; Gary Orfield, *Toward a Strategy for Urban Integration* (New York: Ford Foundation, 1981).

10. Jennifer J. Holme, Sarah L. Diem, and Katherine C. Mansfield, "Using Regional Coalitions to Reduce Socioeconomic Isolation: The Creation of the Nebraska Learning Community Agreement," in *Integrating Schools in a Changing Society: New Policies and Legal Options*

for a Multiracial Generation, ed. Erica Frankenberg and Elizabeth DeBray (Chapel Hill, NC: UNC Press, 2011), 151–166.

11. University think tanks like the Civil Rights Project or educational organizations such as the National School Boards Association could facilitate such conversations. Since its founding, the Civil Rights Project has held similar types of convenings for university presidents around affirmative action.

12. Lisa Chavez and Erica Frankenberg, *Integration Defended: Berkeley Unified's Strategy to School Diversity* (Berkeley, CA: Chief Justice Earl Warren Institute on Race, Ethnicity and Diversity, 2009).

13. Russlyn Ali and Thomas E. Perez, *Department of Justice and Department of Education Joint Guidance on the Voluntary Use of Race* (Washington, DC: The United States Departments of Justice and Education, 2011).

14. Casey D. Cobb, Robert Bifulco, and Courtney Bell, *Evaluation Of Connecticut's Inter-district Magnet Schools* (The Center for Education Policy Analysis, University of Connecticut report to Connecticut State Department of Education, January 2009).

15. Amy Stuart Wells, Miya Warner, and Courtney Grzesikowski, "The Story of Meaningful School Choice: Lessons from Interdistrict Transfer Plans," in G. Orfield and E. Frankenberg, *Educational Delusions: Why Choice Can Deepen Inequality and How to Make It Fair* (Berkeley, CA: University of California Press, forthcoming).

16. Charles T. Clotfelter, *After Brown: The Rise and Retreat of School Desegregation* (Princeton, NJ: Princeton University Press, 2004).

17. Diana Pearce, "Breaking Down the Barriers: New Evidence on Impact of Metropolitan School Desegregation on Housing Patterns" (Washington, DC: National Institute for Education, 1980)

18. Gerald Grant, *Hope and Despair in the American City: Why There Are No Bad Schools in Raleigh* (Cambridge, MA: Harvard University Press, 2009).

19. Genevieve Siegel-Hawley, *City Lines, County Lines, Color Lines: An Analysis of School and Housing Segregation in Four Southern Metropolitan Areas, 1990–2010* (unpublished doctoral dissertation, University of California, Los Angeles, 2011).

20. Karl E. Taeuber and Alma F. Taeuber, *Negroes in Cities: Residential Segregation and Neighborhood Change* (New York: Atheneum, 1969), 101.

21. Gary Orfield, "Ghettoization and Its Alternatives," in *The New Urban Reality*, ed. Paul E. Peterson (Washington, DC: Brookings Institution, 1985) 161–196.

Acknowledgments

This book reports the findings from a collaborative, national research project, and as such, there are many people to thank. First, we are grateful to the Spencer Foundation for supporting this research. Our conclusions are our own, not those of the Foundation. Gail Sunderman played a leading role in developing the concept and the proposal for the project. We are grateful to the University of Minnesota's Institute on Race and Poverty and its director, Myron Orfield, for hosting the key planning session among the participants in the summer of 2009.

This book relied on the willingness of researchers from around the country and several academic disciplines to contribute case studies of suburban communities facing racial change. They include: Elizabeth DeBray, Ain Grooms, Jennifer Jellison Holme, Anjalé Welton, Sarah Diem, Susan Eaton, Lorrie Frasure Yokely, Gail Sunderman, Barbara Shircliffe, Jennifer Morley, Baris Gumus-Dawes, Thomas Luce, and Myron Orfield. They were very stimulating colleagues and did a great deal with limited resources. At UCLA, we relied on the excellent administrative support of Laurie Russman. We also appreciate the research assistance of Jennifer Ayscue, Gil Cujcuj, John Kucsera, Daniel Liou, Jared Sanchez, and Cecelia Xia at UCLA; Kathryn Wiley at CU-Boulder; and Tiffanie Lewis and Hilario Lomeli at Penn State. Jennifer Ayscue was very helpful in the preparation of this book manuscript, and particularly helpful in revising the suburban Minneapolis case study. Numerous colleagues gave us feedback throughout the development of the project and manuscript, and we thank Genevieve Siegel-Hawley for her valuable feedback. Carolyn Peelle also provided editorial assistance as she has on a number of Civil Rights Project books and reports.

This research was possible only through the cooperation and candor of educators, local officials, and others interviewed or providing data and research materials from the suburban communities we studied across the United States. The leaders of these districts had the courage to accept an independent study of a sensitive subject in their communities and school districts, making it possible to illuminate issues and dilemmas affecting large numbers of communities across the United States. We thank them.

About the Editors

Erica Frankenberg is an assistant professor in the Department of Education Policy Studies at the Pennsylvania State University. Her research interests focus on racial desegregation and inequality in K–12 schools, and the connections between school segregation and other metropolitan policies. Prior to joining the Penn State faculty, she was the Research and Policy Director for the Initiative on School Integration at the Civil Rights Project/Proyecto Derechos Civiles at UCLA. She received her doctorate in educational policy at the Harvard University Graduate School of Education.

Gary Orfield is a professor of education, law, political science, and urban planning at the University of California, Los Angeles. His research interests are in the study of civil rights, education policy, urban policy, and minority opportunity. He was cofounder and director of the Harvard Civil Rights Project, and now serves as codirector of the Civil Rights Project/Proyecto Derechos Civiles at UCLA. He received his PhD from the University of Chicago.

About the Contributors

Elizabeth DeBray is an associate professor in the Department of Lifelong Education, Administration, and Policy in the College of Education, University of Georgia. She received her EdD in administration, planning, and social policy from the Harvard Graduate School of Education in 2001. Her major interests are the implementation and effects of federal and state elementary and secondary school policies, and the politics of education at the federal level.

Sarah Diem is an assistant professor of educational leadership and policy analysis at the University of Missouri. Her research focuses on the social and cultural contexts of education, paying particular attention to how the politics and implementation of educational policy affect diversity outcomes.

Susan Eaton is Research Director at the Charles Hamilton Houston Institute for Race and Justice at Harvard Law School. Her scholarly and research interests center around the causes and cures for unequal opportunities for racial, ethnic, and linguistic minorities in the United States. She is particularly concerned about the challenges of schooling and childrearing in high-poverty, urban neighborhoods.

Lorrie Frasure-Yokley is an assistant professor of political science at the University of California, Los Angeles. Her research interests include racial and ethnic politics, state and local governance, and the political economy of metropolitan areas. Her book project in progress examines international and domestic migration to American suburbs and the responsiveness of state and local institutions to the political and policy concerns of immigrant and ethnic minority groups.

Ain Grooms is a third-year doctoral student in the Educational Administration and Policy program at the University of Georgia. Her research interests include school choice, the achievement gap, and equity and adequacy. She received her MEd in organizational leadership from Vanderbilt University and her BA in educational studies from Emory University.

Baris Gumus-Dawes is a senior researcher at the Metropolitan Council, having previously worked for the Institute of Race and Poverty. She has served as a policy analyst for the Minnesota Housing Partnership and worked with Ameregis, Inc. as a research associate. She holds a PhD in sociology from Yale University as well as a master's degree in economics from the University of Cambridge.

Jennifer Jellison Holme is an assistant professor of educational policy and planning in the Department of Educational Administration at the University of Texas at Austin. Her research focuses on the politics and implementation of educational policy, with a particular focus on the relationship among school reform, equity, and diversity in schools.

Thomas Luce, Research Director of the Institute on Race and Poverty, has a thirty-year record of research on economic development and fiscal issues in American metropolitan areas. Most recently, he coauthored *Region: Planning the Future of the Twin Cities*, a book on development and planning issues in the Minneapolis-St. Paul metropolitan area. He received his BA from Swarthmore College, has an MS from the University of London, and a PhD in public policy from the University of Pennsylvania.

Jennifer Morley is a sociologist of education who focuses on various issues including school choice, multicultural education/cultural competence, and urban educational constructs. She is also a practitioner, working in the Magnet Schools and Programs office of a large Florida school district, where she oversees new grant-funded programs. She has a BA in psychology, a dual MA in secondary education and interdisciplinary social sciences, and a PhD in curriculum and instruction from University South Florida.

Myron Orfield is the Executive Director of the Institute on Race & Poverty at the University of Minnesota Law School, a nonresident senior fellow at the

Brookings Institution in Washington, DC, and an affiliate faculty member at the Hubert H. Humphrey Institute of Public Affairs. He teaches and writes in the fields of civil rights, state and local government, state and local finance, land use, questions of regional governance, and the legislative process.

Barbara Shircliffe is an associate professor of social foundations of education at the University of South Florida. As a historian of education, her research interests include history of education; school policy; school desegregation; school community relations; and effects of class, race, and gender in structuring policy and outcomes.

Anjalé Welton is an assistant professor at the University of Illinois at Urbana-Champaign. Her research examines the educational opportunity structures of low-income students of color and social justice leadership, with the aim of preparing educators to teach and lead in an increasingly diverse society.

Kathryn Wiley is a doctoral student in the School of Education at the University of Colorado, Boulder. She is interested in examining racial and economic segregation in schools and the stratification of student educational opportunities.

Index